BETT

Some Press Opinions

TIMES EDUCATIONAL SUPPLEMENT : ' It will help the appren-
tice to letters, but the master man will consult it with
profit. Mr Vallins knows the secret of communicating
his own absorbing interest in the subject ; and he lards the
lean earth of syntax so well that while many will keep this
book by the inkpot many, too, will have it by the bed.'

ECONOMIST: 'Mr Vallins avoids the pedantic and the
pernickety; he preserves the graces and an admirable sense
of proportion; at the same time he is always—in the best
senses of the adjective—practical. No learner need
hesitate to follow the excellent advice set forth so clearly.'

JOHN O' LONDON'S WEEKLY: 'Mr Vallins is that very rare
bird—a born teacher who is not a pedant . . . For those
who want an exciting adventure among the tangled ways
of usage, *Better English* could hardly be bettered.'

By the same author in Pan Books

GOOD ENGLISH
THE BEST ENGLISH

CONDITIONS OF SALE

This book shall not, by way of trade or otherwise, be lent, re-sold, hired out or otherwise circulated without the publisher's prior consent in any form of binding or cover other than that in which it is published and without a similar condition including this condition being imposed on the subsequent purchaser. The book is published at a net price, and is supplied subject to the Publishers Association Standard Conditions of Sale registered under the Restrictive Trade Practices Act, 1956.

BETTER ENGLISH

G. H. VALLINS

THIS BOOK IS THE PROPERTY OF
Wanstead High School
REDBRIDGE EDUCATION COMMITTEE
NIGHTINGALE
SECONDARY SCHOOL
ELMCROFT AVENUE
WANSTEAD, E.11
702

Date	Form	Name and Initial

PAN BOOKS LTD : LONDON

First published 1953 by Pan Books Ltd.,
33 Tothill Street, London, S.W.1.

ISBN 0 330 13039 0

2nd Printing (revised) 1953
3rd Printing (revised) 1955
4th Printing 1957
5th Printing 1958
6th Printing 1959
7th Printing 1961
8th Printing 1962
9th Printing 1963
10th Printing 1966
11th Printing 1972

Copyright 1953 by George Henry Vallins

Dedicated to
the memory of my friend
and fellow-worker in many enterprises
HENRY ARTHUR TREBLE
who helped and encouraged me at the
beginning of this work but did not live
to see its ending.

Printed in Great Britain by
Cox & Wyman Ltd., London, Reading and Fakenham

CONTENTS

NOTE TO THE SECOND EDITION

In this edition a number of corrections and a few additions have been made. I am grateful to reviewers and correspondents who have pointed out errors and omissions ; in particular, to Studienrat Eitzen of Hamburg, who put me right on several matters of detail and suggested many additional entries in the Index, the most important of which I have now included, and to Mr G. V. Carey, the author of that excellent book *Mind the Stop*, who gently and courteously chided me on certain points of punctuation. I may add that certain omissions were deliberate, the words or constructions concerned having already been dealt with in my previous book *Good English: How to write It*.

G. H. V.

NOTE TO THE THIRD EDITION

I have to thank several readers for pointing out misprints and errors in the earlier editions. In this edition all the misprints have (I hope) been corrected, and I have tried to put right what my generous critics have, with justice, found to be wrong. I cannot do better than repeat my final remark in the Note to the Fourth Edition of *Good English*, that ' their kindly interest has encouraged and their erudition has challenged me '.

G. H. V.

PRELUDE

IN my former book on language, *Good English: How to Write It*,[1] I stated certain principles that govern the writing of the language, and illustrated them with examples of English, mainly bad, from some half-dozen magazines and newspapers. This book follows the same plan. It is in fact a sequel to *Good English*, and it has the disadvantage, or the advantage, of all sequels, that it can be fully understood only by those who have read its predecessor. Quite often it harks back to *Good English*, to which indeed I have often made detailed references. Certain principles of grammar or matters of usage have been restated, emphasised, elaborated, or even modified. But in the main it leaves the world of accidence and syntax for that of idiom, figure, the logical expression of thought, the niceties of language. *Good English* dealt with the elements of writing, and by precept and example put the reader on his guard against basic error. This book discusses important trifles that are in reality not trifles at all, and urges a perfect correspondence, within the limits of language, between thought and its expression. It keeps continually under fire the unsound sentence which is apparently sound, and does not avoid subtle distinctions where subtle distinctions are necessary. That is why it is called *Better English*.

But, as in all books on the writing of English, the problem of usage arises. One or two critics and correspondents have chided me for avoiding the issue in *Good English*, for sitting on the fence between grammar and usage, for failing to pronounce upon this and that. I can quite understand why. We are all proud of the democratic freedom of our language, and secretly regret that it is not an autocracy. But we are not usually aware that our regret arises from the fact that at one comparatively short period there was a kind of autocracy—not absolute or

[1] See p. 2.

authoritative—in English. That period begins with Cobbett, about 1800—strictly, perhaps, a little before; and
ends during the first quarter of this century. It ends,
that is, as far as the pundits, the grammarians, the self-
appointed guardians of the language are concerned; but
for most of us it has not ended even now. For that
autocracy, as I have called it, was strongest in the first
fifty years of compulsory education (1870-1920). The
grammar taught in schools had to have its rights and
wrongs, like arithmetic. And that tradition remains to
this day. Nor is it to be wondered at. After all, the formal
rules of grammar can be taught, but not the indefinable
spirit that underlies usage. What is more, we remember
them, as much to the schoolmaster's surprise as our own.
Indeed, some of them have already developed into super-
stitions.

So when in *The King's English* (1906) the two Fowlers
made a new approach to ' grammar ', and H. W. Fowler
finally popularised the term *usage* in the title of his great
book (1926), we were caught, like the early Christians in
the Pauline churches, between the law and the spirit.
And that is where we are still. On the one side is the
belief, fostered and developed through school and school
examinations, that certain constructions are wrong—' bad
grammar ', as the phrase was—and on the other the undoubted fact that eminent journalists, learned writers, and
great literary men quite frequently use them. It is for
this very reason that most of us are interested in points
and problems of language today. What seemed sure is
no longer sure. We are bewildered. Nesfield was a hard
task-master; but at least we knew where we were with
him. Usage as interpreted by Fowler, whilst polishing off
(a little too brusquely sometimes) a few old bogeys like
the split infinitive, only raised problems hitherto unsus-
pected and doubts that almost prevented us from ever
again putting pen to paper. We were in the new democracy
of usage, the custom of the practised and practising writer,
and behold! it seemed more autocratic, more hedged about
with laws and penalties, than the old autocracy of the
schoolmaster.

And so, in a sense, it is. I revere Fowler only this side

of idolatry. But I have this against him. Too often he
wrote not of modern usage but of what he considered
should be modern usage. So well did he write (though, as
Somerset Maugham says, he had no car for prose), and
with such authority, that he became in spite of himself a
dictator. *Modern English Usage* is a kind of paradox; it
seeks to give rigidity to what is essentially flexible, and
provides a tested and accurate standard for what (rather
oddly) is better measured with a rough working rule.
Some of his own sentences are so carefully (I had almost
written ' meticulously ') fashioned according to his own
pronouncements that they hardly read like English at all.

The general result of all this is that, in spite of the
change of emphasis from grammar to usage, there is still a
gap between precept and practice. And this is partly
because there is a kind of hang-over from that carefully
formulated system to which I have already referred, and
usage is incongruously forced into the straight-jacket of
grammar. To give a simple example. The loosely related
participle phrase was common in the eighteenth century
even in such ' correct ' writers as Addison and Swift.
Then it was outlawed by the pundits, and writers on
language have, for the most part, followed them, as I have
myself both in *Good English* and in this book. But to
judge from the examples on pp. 58-60 from contemporary
magazines all published within a period of at most three
weeks, the usage persists. And it would seem that if
usage is really the criterion of good English, then the loose
participle is by no means to be condemned. The same
argument holds for certain other constructions that have a
similar long and tolerably honourable ancestry.

There is, however, a fallacy in it. After all, the fact
remains that syntax has been tightened up during the last
hundred and fifty years. We cannot ignore Cobbett,
Nesfield, and Fowler, who at different times and in their
own different ways formulated certain ' laws ' that should
govern the writing of English. They were often dogmatic,
sometimes wrong, now and then cranky; and the first two
set up a good many Aunt Sallies that Fowler and later
writers have rather perversely knocked down. But for
good or evil they unofficially standardised the language.

They made a grammatical system and Fowler called it usage. There is no putting the clock back. Modern usage cannot escape the learned attentions of those who, in a phrase of Pepys, reduce it to an alphabet.

So in this book, as in *Good English*, I have accepted, sometimes with reservations and usually with tolerance, the established conventions of syntax. In the matter of idiom I have been more severe, holding that established idiom is (with spelling) the most surely fixed element in the language. I do not forget of course that certain idioms die out and others are born; but I have contended that a living idiom is not to be tampered with. For that reason the section on ' mixed idiom ' in *Good English*[1] is here elaborated, with many more examples, as being of particular importance.

I have tried to keep an open mind on the question of new idioms and new words, or old words with new meanings. Whenever I read Sir Alan Herbert's amusing and often prejudiced *What a Word!* and his later articles on the same subject in *Punch*, I wonder what all the fuss is about. During the seventeen years or so since that book was written many of the words he condemns have been accepted and others have dropped out, in the natural progress of language. This is where usage is most democratic, and therefore most impatient of the autocrat; and in time it usually has its revenge on him. I have used the word ' prejudiced ' of Sir Alan; it applies equally to most people. Often our prejudice arises because a word is what Shakespeare called ' overworn '. I have one against *integrated*, which I aired in *Good English* (p. 198); and I had much ado to prevent myself from airing another in this book, against the word *awareness*. But I refrained, remembering that— luckily for the language—our prejudices tend to cancel out; and an individual word is finally accepted or rejected by a kind of popular intuition. True, men who speak with a certain authority have some influence. Fowler frightened a whole generation off *meticulous* and Sir Ernest Gowers may, perhaps, reconcile the next generation to *teenager*. But in the main, like Gallio of old, we care for none of these things.

[1] pp. 153-67.

Above all, I have usually welcomed a new word that expresses in itself what could otherwise be expressed only in a phrase. Thus *editorialise* (p. 197) seems to me an admirable way of saying ' make editorial comments upon'. The genius of the language for ellipsis and telescoping (p. 36) is not to be thwarted by our own arbitrary likes and dislikes. *Teenager* itself happens to be one of my dislikes; but as it fulfils this condition of verbal brevity I would not raise my voice against it. Neither am I overmuch concerned about the etymological or phonetic construction of words. Here, as in other ways, the wind bloweth where it listeth. There are so many hybrids among established words that I see no reason whatever for excluding a new one if on other counts it passes muster. A rich vocabulary has its embarrassments, but these are to be preferred to the embarrassments of poverty.

The doubts that have arisen in these modern days about the meaning of such words as *democracy*, *liberty*, *freedom*, *welfare* and *peace* have brought to the fore the comparatively new art or science of semantics. Into this realm of linguistic analysis I have rarely entered. This is only another way of saying that my concern has been with function rather than with meaning. Of *welfare* in the phrase ' the welfare State ' I should content myself by saying that it is a noun-adjective. What it means I leave to the semanticists, if the word may be allowed. Truth to tell when I read Mr William Empson, for example, on the use of a single word or image in Shakespeare, I am bewildered and incredulous and frightened. I also feel a little sorry for Shakespeare.

As in *Good English*, I have taken my examples mainly from ' literary ' newspapers and magazines. This time, acting upon a hint in a review of *Good English*, I have given their names. These examples were gathered in a period of weeks, not years. There is no significance in the fact that one or two magazines are more frequently represented than the others. They happen to be the ones I regularly read—that is all. If any of the others had been fortunate (or unfortunate) enough to be among my ' regulars ', they would no doubt have been as generously represented. In our use of language we are all sinners, prone to carelessness and error. This book merely seeks to reveal our sins and exhort us to repentance. It will, I know, have its own mistakes, which the reader will detect and to which, ironically, I may myself be blind.

Throughout the book I have sought the reader's co-operation and asked his opinion. And towards the end (pp. 187-203) I have even gone so far as to set him an examination paper. I hope this will not frighten him. In answering it myself (pp. 204-20) I have taken the opportunity of dealing with some points that could not conveniently be dealt with in the text.

Better English has profited from many just and erudite criticisms of *Good English* by reviewers and correspondents in England and overseas. For these and to them I am sincerely grateful. Now and then they made me wince, sometimes they provoked me to disagreement, and always they compelled me to think again. I learned much from them—and not least (I trust) the grace of humility. Finally, to Mr George Kamm, to whose encouragement and help *Good English* owed much, this book owes even more.

In one or two particulars I have departed from my practice in *Good English*. Except in quotations, where of course I have followed the original, I have omitted the point (.) when the last letter of a complete word is included in a contraction, and have made a clean sweep of points from groups of initials representing titles, etc.; for example, I have written *Mr* not *Mr.* and *BBC* not *B.B.C.* But I have kept the points after initials in personal names, after initials representing the points of the compass, and in conventional contractions like *p.* for *page* and *i.e.* for *id est*, ' that is '.[1]

The chief contractions used are as follows:

COD	Concise Oxford Dictionary
SOED	Shorter Oxford English Dictionary
RCR	Rules for Compositors and Readers at the Oxford Press
DT	Daily Telegraph
JL	John o' London's Weekly
L	The Listener
MG	Manchester Guardian
NS	New Statesman
O	Observer

[1] See *Good English*, pp. 126-8.

RT	Radio Times
S	Spectator
T	The Times
TES	Times Educational Supplement
TLS	Times Literary Supplement
TT	Time and Tide

Here and there the origin of a quotation is not given. This means nothing more than that the original cutting was carelessly or inadequately marked.

Words or compounds (like *as well as*) commented upon in the text are italicised, and groups of words are enclosed in single quotation marks. Double quotation marks are used only for literary illustrative quotations.

CHAPTER I

'IN NUMBER AND PERSON'

> Verbs, of which there must be one at least, expressed or under-stood, in every sentence, must *agree* in *person* and in *number* with the nouns or pronouns, which are the *nominatives* of the sentence; that is to say, the verbs must be of the same person and same number as the nominatives are. Verbs frequently change their forms and endings to make them-selves *agree* with their *nominatives*. How necessary is it then, to know what is, and what is not, a nominative in a sentence!—COBBETT: *A Grammar of the English Language*

COBBETT, as always, is refreshingly dogmatic; he never fails to call a spade a spade. "How necessary is it to know what is, and what is not, a nominative in a sentence!" —and sometimes how difficult to determine its number and person! It is in fact remarkable how often we have to ask ourselves such questions as 'Is the subject singular or plural?', 'Have I actually joined the two nouns, or are they still grammatically separate?', 'How does the verb agree with two pronouns of different person?'. In brief, the simple agreement outlined by Cobbett is not so simple as it looks. This the examples given below will sufficiently illustrate; and it is hoped that the comments will at once reprove the careless and help the careful writer.

Collective Puzzles

> A wide series of views of the English scene, of architec-ture, historic events, transportation and industry, of celebrities and sporting subjects, can be seen in *The Times* Picture Library, and are available for reproduc-tion.—*T*

True, the noun *series* has the same form in the plural as in the singular, and itself looks like a plural; but the indefinite article here seems to stress the singular. How-ever, the plural verb can be explained if not quite forgiven, especially as attraction (see below) has also been at work.

And row upon row of delicate green now breaks the
monotony of the carefully prepared beds.—*S*

Even Cobbett would be hard put to it to determine exactly
what he calls his 'nominative' in this sentence. It is
best explained as a collective hyphenated expression (*row-
upon-row*), in which each separate row is thought of in
turn, not the whole number of rows at once and together.
The verb is, therefore, correctly singular; indeed, a plural
verb would destroy the useful and effective idiom. So
also with *after*: 'Ship after ship *sails* [not *sail*] by'. But
see p. 206.

> One or more gas-rings, hot plates or portable electric
> ovens are not by themselves enough to be called a cooking
> stove or range.—Census Paper, 1951

This piece of telescoping (see p. 42 ff.) results in an expression that is more concise than logical. Again we have to
resort to imaginary hyphenation and assume that *one-or-
more* is a kind of collective adjective idiomatically qualifying
a plural noun: the *one* is entirely lost in the *more*. Rather
oddly, the parallel expression *more than one* is singular—
'More than one man *has* [not *have*] been dismissed'.

' Here is . . . '

(*a*) Here is a university town, students and professors, and
gaily unhappy wives, and lovers, and the outlying
farmers.—*O*

(*b*) Here is no prophet, no moralist, no great genius entertainer, no stylist even.—*TT*

"There is pansies, that's for thoughts", said Shakespeare;
and the formula 'There/Here is' often tends to be independent of the subject that follows it. The singular (*is*)
steadfastly remains, even when the subject is a long list
($a + b + c + d$ . . .), and some of the items in it are
themselves plural, as in sentence (*a*) above. Within limits,
the reader may use his discretion; but here are one or two
suggestions:

(i) The singular (*is*, *'s*) has become idiomatic in certain
types of expression before a simple plural, as in the
Shakespeare quotation above. We say 'There's

peaches for tea ', ' There's ten minute to go '. But the usage is colloquial; in formal writing the plural is recommended.

(ii) If the subject is multiple, the singular (*is*, *'s*) is permissible if each item of the subject is singular; in other words, the force of attraction has its way. The plural tends to be a trifle stilted; but the fastidious writer will probably prefer it. If some of the items are plural, the plural verb (*are*) is preferable where the first item is singular (thus, sentence (*a*) would begin ' Here *are* a . . . '), and necessary where the first item is plural. But this applies only to sentences in which the subject is truly multiple.

(iii) Note that in sentence (*b*) the subject is not multiple but alternative (no prophet *or* moralist *or* entertainer *or* stylist), and the verb, since each item is singular, must itself be singular; ' here *are* ' would be wrong. Or we may think of the sentence as an ellipsis (see p. 51) for ' Here is a man who is no prophet, moralist etc.'

Attraction

Four simple examples are quoted without any comment except that this error (" a matter ", says Fowler, " of carelessness and inexperience only ") seems to be becoming more common. The subject in each sentence is italicised; the verb is printed in small capitals, and its attracter is in black type:

> The *passion* for maps, for the study of geography, and for the organization of **voyages** of discovery or trading **trips** ARE largely Elizabethan in origin.—*JL*
>
> The *worth* of its **contents** ARE sufficiently well known.
>
> There are occasions when the *validity* of Fleet Street's **complaints** about the newsprint shortage ARE more acceptable than others.—*NS*
>
> However, even if *New Writing* must share in the common guilt of intellectuals for our present distresses, its vital *achievement* in the pre-war and war **years** STAND unquestioned.—*NS*

There is one idiom in which attraction legitimatises, as it were, an otherwise false agreement. We say ' A quarter of it *is* ' but ' A quarter of them *are* ', the verb being attracted into the number of the noun or pronoun governed by the *of*. So with fractions that are themselves apparently plural (*two-thirds*, *three-quarters*). In the following sentence the verb should be singular (*is*):

> About two-thirds of the site are laid out in a delightful series of terraces and flower-beds, shops and beer gardens, lakes and pavilions.—*NS*

Difficult Distributives

The force of attraction (see above) is strong when we use distributive subjects (*each*, *either*, *neither* of us/them); the pronoun in the partitive[1] phrase attracts the verb and any subsequent related pronouns into its own number and person—' Each of us *are* entitled to *our* ', for ' Each of us *is* entitled to *his* '.[2] Sometimes the writer tries to make the best of both worlds:

> " We are funny characters," proclaims each of these personages by their appearance and their gestures, from the missionary who opens the play right through to the American captain.—*NS*

In this, as in other matters of ' grammar ', inconsistency is unpardonable: ' each *proclaims* . . . *his* ' observes the letter of the law; ' each *proclaim* . . . *their* ' is condoned, if not entirely accepted, by modern usage; but the confused construction in the above sentence is a careless illiteracy.

One or two idiomatic constructions are worth noting:

> Let us grant that Mr. Roger Livesey and Miss Ursula Jeans are neither of them ideally cast.—*NS*

The subject is double, and the verb (*are cast*) correctly plural. It is difficult to define the function of the phrase ' neither of them '; at any rate, it has no grammatical relationship with the verb. We might call it, perhaps, a parenthetic emphasis: ' are (neither of them) ideally cast '. Or the phrase may be in apposition: ' They (neither of them) are . . .'

[1] A convenient term for the '*of* + noun ' phrase in which one thing or person is represented as being part of a group. The construction is usually called in grammar books ' partitive genitive '.

[2] Or *her*: this question is fully discussed in *Good English*, p. 76.

> Every character and each development of the plot are
> subordinated to its message.—*NS*

The subject is apparently double and therefore plural;
but the distributive adjectives *every*, *each*, suggest that
each half of the subject shall be taken separately.   Idiom,
therefore, demands *is* where ' grammar ' would demand *are*.
The emphasis is on the singularity, as if the epithet *single*
were qualifying each noun.   So in this sentence:

> Each man, woman, and especially one small boy, fit into
> life, the closely integrated life of a provincial town, as
> freely and spontaneously as birds gather in a tree.—*JL*

Here three singular nouns are in turn subject, and the
verb should be idiomatically *fits*.   The omission of the
each before *woman* is merely a careless error.

This ' parenthetic emphasis ' is seen also in the following
sentence, where the writer, having stated his subject,
immediately amends it for effect with the help of the
adverb *indeed*: that is, although the two halves of the
subject are joined by *and*, the subject is not really double.
The writer recognises the parenthetic construction by
enclosing his amended subject in commas (see p. 132); he
could equally and perhaps more effectively have used dashes.
The verb is correctly singular:

> But nineteenth-century French poetry, and indeed the
> whole of French poetry from the seventeenth century
> onwards, was possibly a greater influence than any other
> for Pound and Eliot in his earlier verses.—*NS*

The use of *as well as* for *and* often implies a similar kind
of parenthesis.   Thus in the following sentence the subject
may be regarded as ' kind of disillusion ', and the two
(plural) nouns introduced by *as well as* as a ' parenthetic '
subject.   The verb would then, of course, be singular
(*comes*):

> It is a bit of an evasion to quote typical instead of
> successful poems, but his kind of disillusion as well as
> his technical gifts and limitations come across well in
> the title piece.—*NS*

It must be remembered, however, that *as well as* is a
conjunction, unlike *with* in the construction ' The Duke,

with his two daughters, walks to church ', which, by the way, means something rather different from ' The Duke walks to church with his two daughters '.

Ellipsis

For the general treatment of ellipsis see pp. 51–4. In the following three sentences bracketing has caused a problem of agreement:

> The poetic and the prophetic genius are, in this sense of the word poetry, indistinguishable.—*NS*

It is better here to open the bracket, $(a + b)c > ac + bc$, especially as the complementary adjective *indistinguishable* implies a plural (see p. 49): ' The poetic genius and the prophetic genius *are* indistinguishable '.

> It is in moments like this that Mr. Spender, rather than his victims, seems to be the Golden Ass.—*NS*

The elliptical construction is idiomatic here. We ' understand ' the verb (plural) after ' rather than '; ' rather than do his victims ' observes the letter but not the spirit of the law. But in the following sentence it is wiser to express the verb for each half of the subject, even at the expense of a trifling awkwardness:

> Few writers have the gift of producing such work consistently; two of those in Mr. Wyce's list, or at least one of them, has it.—*NS*

Say—' two of those in Mr Wyce's list have it, or at least one of them has '.

Antecedent and Relative Pronoun

" When it [the relative pronoun] is subject of its own clause it agrees in number and person with its antecedent, the agreement being visible not in the actual pronoun form but in the verb associated with it."[1] But antecedents are not always simple and straightforward; and in this section a few typical problems are dealt with. In all the quoted sentences the antecedents are printed in small capitals and the verbs in italics so that the disagreement may be easily visible.

[1] *Good English*, p. 81.

Fanny Burney, although she catches domestic conversation very brilliantly, and is one of the most entertaining WRITERS-DOWN of dialogue who *has* ever lived, falters with the great.—*JL*

This error is of the common, simple type illustrated in *Good English*; the writer is too careless to recognise his antecedent, which is *writers-down*, not *one*. It is an example of attraction in reverse. In the three following sentences, however, ordinary attraction has been at work:

(*a*) Less happy, to my taste, is the fourth member, Meadows, who in the Cain and Abel dream is God himself, and in the others is some close emissary, with that TOUCH of the rustic about his speech which an urban civilisation romantically imagines *bring* one closer to the Deity.—*NS*

(*b*) The distinction of his case is that he does not indulge in the usual recriminations and has avoided in his book any of that SELF-ADVERTISING and SELF-RIGHTEOUSNESS which *has* characterised so many converts from Communism.—*NS*

(*c*) This writing for an overcultivated audience or none at all results in A SELF-CONSCIOUSNESS and SENSE OF STRAIN that *comes* out in the verse and the construction, and *helps* to make the plays unstageable.—*NS*

It is arguable that in sentences (*b*) and (*c*) the subject is not double (therefore, plural) but composite, two nouns linked together by a qualifying adjective (*that*, *a*) in a single unit [$a(x + y)$ not $ax + ay$]. If so, the verbs (*has*, *comes*, *helps*) have not been attracted into the singular by the second and clearly singular half of the respective subjects but may be allowably and idiomatically singular in their own right.

In the following sentence the writer has tried to make the best of both worlds. He begins by taking his antecedent as *laws* and making the verb of the relative clause plural; then, apparently, changes his mind, takes *mass* as the antecedent, and accordingly makes the verb singular. So, reducing the construction to its lowest terms, we have ' " mass of laws " which *make* or *sends* '. It is possible, however, that the verb (*sends*) was so far removed from its antecedent that it felt the pull of the undeniable singular *alcohol*:

He deplores the " mass of LAWS " which *make* people criminals through ignorance or, as in the case of drugs and, previously, alcohol, *sends* them to the underworld because forbidden pleasures are sweet.—*TLS*

The question of ' parallel ' subjects, which is discussed on p. 22, sometimes arises in connection with the ante-cedent-relative relationships. Thus, two parallel nouns of different number may be antecedents to the relative pronoun:

> Even Miss Rosamund Lehmann's brilliant " Red-Haired Miss Daintreys " is subdued to avoid those wonderful FLASHES of violence, that great SENSE of climax that *make* " The Ballad and the Source ", in my view, one of the few novels of the last twenty years with the " affect " of the great English nineteenth-century novels.—*NS*

Here is the problem set out diagramatically:

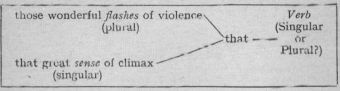

If the parallelism is to be kept, there is no answer: the verb cannot at one and the same time be singular and plural. But to think of the subject as double (flashes *and* sense) for the sake of the grammatical agreement is to weaken, and indeed destroy, the intended effect of the sentence. There is something to be said for letting attrac-tion do its work; then in this sentence the verb should agree with the *second* of the two parallel nouns, which is singular: ' that great sense of climax that *makes* '.

A kind of misplaced zeal has misled the writer of the following sentence. His subject is certainly multiple $(a + b + c)$ and therefore plural, but only the third and last item (c) in this subject (*design*) is antecedent to the relative clause. His verb therefore should be *seems*, not *seem*. The main verb (*keep*) is of course correctly plural:

THIS BOOK IS THE PROPERTY
Wanstead High School

Liveliness of mind and inventiveness of imagination and a DESIGN that *seem* to suit him particularly well keep the play alive for its whole length (about ninety minutes). —*NS*

Finally, in this sentence the parenthetic effect of *as well as* (see p. 18) causes a problem of agreement which the reader is invited to solve for himself; I have reserved my own solution and comment for p. 184.

He is always able to freshen the argument with some striking examples of the MUDDLES as well as of the INSPIRATION which *have gone* to the making of English in its long passage from " Beowulf " to " Finnegan's Wake ". [1]—*O*

Parallelism

Rather akin to the alternative subject is the subject which consists of parallel nouns: ' The *courage*, the *coolness*, the *daring* of the hero was/were remarkable '. Singular or plural? *Was* or *were*? Here are four examples:

(a) The ATMOSPHERE, the TENSION, *are* sustained remarkably well, and the reader is impressed with a sense of the conflict of irreconcilable forces.—*JL*

(b) Boswell's very LACK of foundation, his LACK of judgment, *are* seen merely as the price he pays for the marvellous fluidity, transparency and curiosity of his nature.—*NS*

(c) Mr. Spender's TRUTH to himself, his REFUSAL to argue away, hide or reject the value of the mystery of private motive, *is* of fundamental importance to humanists.—*NS*

(d) The DRUDGERY of research, the ENERGY needed to boil down one's notes into a consecutive and readable narrative, *are* apt to overwhelm the biographer with discouragement and to make him feel that he has expended his labour on no more than a handful of dust.—*O*

The plurals have it by three to one. Yet if the parallelism is being stressed for reiterative effect (as it seems to be in each of these sentences, especially (b), where the same noun, *lack*, is repeated) the singular would seem to be more

[1] For this punctuation see p. 132. Note that there is no apostrophe in the actual title of the book.

appropriate. Sentence (c) is, in fact, stylistically preferable to the others. But there is a bread-and-butter argument for the plural. If, in spite of the parallelism, the subject is considered double or multiple the plural is, of course, correct; and the number (singular or plural) of the separate nouns in the subject does not matter. But if, as in an ordinary alternative subject, the nouns are taken separately, the verb must agree with each one in turn, but cannot where they are of different number. In the four sentences quoted no such difficulty arises, since each subject consists of singular nouns only; and the writer might legitimately (and more effectively) have written *is* for *are*.

' What' as Subject

What is the number of *what*? Fowler has a long and rather pedantic article on this question, which may be summed up as follows:

(i) Where *what* is ostensibly and deliberately singular, special care must be taken that its verb is not attracted into the plural by a plural complement. We should write ' What is required *is* [not *are*] houses at rents that the people can pay '.

Certainly in this way, and only in this way, is grammar satisfied; but idiom is usually offended by a clash in number between subject and complement;[1] and the best remedy is to reconstruct the sentence in some such way as ' What is required is the erection (or provision) of houses etc.'[2]—that is, to equate subject and complement in number.

(ii) Where *what* can be resolved into ' plural noun + which ', the plural noun actually appearing in the comple-ment, *what* is plural: ' for what *were* doubtless good and sufficient reasons ', where *what* = ' reasons that '. If the plural noun does not actually appear in the complement, then the reader has to decide for himself whether the *what* is represented by singular + *which* or plural + *which*.

---

[1] *Good English*, p. 18.

[2] It may be justly objected that such reconstruction changes, however slightly, the meaning of the sentence. It does; so does any reconstruction of any sentence—we have to accept the fact.

The reader is invited to exercise his power of choice in the following sentences:

> What stand out in Miss Coburn's volume are not, perhaps, the discursive psychological sections, nor [1] the philosophising, but some exquisite pieces of natural observation.—*O*

> But those who loved their Münchhausen will be glad to be told how the stories came to be written and what were the career and character of the individual by whom they were composed.—*O*

Fowler has so bemused me that I defer my answer. It will be found on p. 184. The moral of it all is—avoid the construction where possible.

[1] Double negative. See p. 60.

CHAPTER II

BEGINNING AND ENDING

There is no consonancy in the sequel.
—*Twelfth Night*

" BETTER is the end of a thing," says Ecclesiastes, or the Preacher, " than the beginning thereof." It may be so. The point is—to use a strange and solitary English word—a moot one. On the whole, the classical parallel, *Finis coronat opus*, " The end crowns the work ", is more easily acceptable. Of a sentence we may use a variant of the dictum—as, " The end is the test " or " It is easier to begin than to end ", or " The proof of the sentence is in the ending ". For sentences, by the time they wind somehow to the full-stop, have an odd way, like Gonzalo's commonwealth, of forgetting their beginning. What the first clause promises the last often does not perform.

It is not difficult to understand why. In ordinary informal speech, we express our thoughts casually, even inconsequently, without much regard to the construction or pattern of our sentences. Gestures, pauses, changes of intonation serve us for syntax and idiom; and for that very reason the spoken language is not subject to some, at least, of the laws and principles that govern the written language. When in writing a sentence we cause the end to conflict syntactically with the beginning, we are allowing ourselves a looseness and freedom legitimate only in speech. Shakespeare knew it:

Rather proclaim it, Westmoreland, through my host,
That he which hath no stomach to this fight,
Let him depart.

The speaker (King Henry V) gets to the word *fight* without syntactical mishap, but then with a dramatic and effective gesture changes his construction altogether; the subject of his noun clause (*he*) is left high and dry without a predicate. Westmoreland's proclamation would, in direct paraphrase, run something like this: " Any man who lacks the courage for this battle may go home ". Subject and predicate are here correctly related, but at the expense of the dramatic vividness which is possible in loose colloquial syntax.

For when we put pen to paper we have to subject ourselves to the discipline of thought: to ' see ' the sentence *whole* in our mind before we even begin to write, or (less satisfactorily) to fashion and shape it after we have roughed it out in writing. The pattern of the sentence is not a mere fiction of the grammarian; it is determined by usage. If as writers we ignore it, we imperil the communication of thought between ourselves and the reader. To put it more particularly, we fall into obscurity, prolixity, faulty syntax, and some other errors that belong to the commerce of language.[1]

This-that-and-the-other

The enumerative ' this-that-and-the-other ' sentence is most liable to this type of constructional fault. Here are a few examples:

> How does the magic [of Hudson] work? First, there is the style. Secondly, Hudson was a master of the art of telling a story. In the third place, his books are imbued with an interest in humanity.—*TT*

We note, first, that the writer quite unnecessarily divides what should be one sentence into three, and, second, that though he takes the trouble to number his three points, he does not stick to a single system of enumeration. It is as if an examiner numbered the first three consecutive questions of an examination paper 1, (i), and (*a*). But that is merely symptomatic of a deeper trouble —a failure to maintain the shape of the sentence. He begins in one way, continues in another, and ends in yet another. Here is a simple reconstruction:

> There is, first, the style; second, the art of telling a story; and, third, an interest in humanity.

[1] It ought to be said, however, that the loose constructions of speech are often introduced for effect into the written language, even when it is not, as in drama or the dialogue of a novel, reproducing the written word.

It is difficult to see, even then, how either the writer's own threefold pronouncement or my reconstruction of it answers his original question. He meant, no doubt, ' What are the ingredients of Hudson's magic? '. At any rate, that is the question implied in the answer.

> When Victoria came to the throne the Royal Family was unpopular, hard up and did not move among the best families. When she died it was beloved, rich and allied with all the leading houses in Europe, taking primacy among them. Edward VII was brother-in-law of the Kings of Denmark and Greece and of the Empress of Russia. He was uncle of the German Emperor, father-in-law of the King of Norway and uncle of the Queen of Spain and the Queen of Rumania.

In the first sentence the enumeration should depend on the verbs (' the Royal Family [i] *was* unpopular and hard up, and [ii] *did not move* . . ') or on the adjectives (' . . . was [i] *unpopular*, [ii] *hard up*, and [iii] *outside the pale* of the best families '). The writer in avoiding the repetition of *and* fell between two stools. In the second sentence the enumeration is sound. But it is a pity that the august relationships of Edward VII and the particulars of his avuncularity could not be more deftly catalogued: ' . . . of Russia, uncle of the German Emperor, the Queen of Spain and the Queen of Rumania, and father-in-law of the King of Norway '.

> It can be put down to serious defects of character: the desire for power, money, the quick fame of the publicist, and to an egotism too suddenly enlarged.—*NS*

This sentence owes its muddled enumeration and apparent ambiguity to an omitted *and* and an intrusive *to*. The writer has not properly grouped his items. Only two serious defects are mentioned, not four as we imagine at first sight. Add *and* after *money*, and delete *to* before ' an egotism '. The defects are: (*i*) the *desire* for $a + b + c$, and (ii) an *egotism*.

> He was a visionary with more genius than balance, passing through a long series of conflicting loyalties, to melodrama and romantic costume roles (his " Spanish Boot " parts), to a fussy kind of naturalism and to

> poetic fantasy, to mysticism, Hinduism, Yogi, and to interminable and often confused theorising on the nature of dramatic art.—*O*

The writer of this sentence is even more troubled and troublesome with his *and*s and *to*s. But he has only to group his items sensibly by (i) substituting a comma for *and* after *naturalism* and (ii) substituting *and* for a comma after *Hinduism*.

> It contains Lucien's life in the garrison at Nancy, his love affair with Madame Chasbellar, and ends with the grotesque episode which broke the affair and sent Lucien galloping back heartbroken to his mother in Paris.—*NS*

The writer apparently intended at least three objects of the verb *contains*, since there is no conjunction (*and*) linking the second to the first. But the reader looks in vain for the third. Either *and* must replace the comma after *Nancy* or the words ' ends with ' must be omitted, the phrase beginning ' and the grotesque—— ' doing duty as the third object; that is, the construction is either ' It contains *a* and *b*, and ends . . . ' or ' It contains *a*, *b*, and *c* '.

> But they have not yet paid sufficient attention to the question of maintenance, nor appreciated that some of the serial features now on the air should be revised, others developed, a few—such as " Kaleidoscope," " In the News " and " The Course of Justice "—left exactly as they are, while one or two ought never to have been let out at all.—*O*

In this sentence the last clause breaks the pattern. The writer is faced with the real difficulty that he requires a change of tense (*should have been* instead of *should be*) and he chooses this way out of it. But there is a better way—to use the auxiliary in each dependent clause, so bringing the first three into line with the last one, where owing to the change of tense the auxiliary cannot be avoided (' some should be revised—others should be developed—a few should be left—and one or two should never have been ').

It is interesting to note that the writers of the preceding five sentences have all fallen from grace, in different ways, because they hesitated at the repetition of *and*. The first four, having ventured upon an enumeration, tried to manage with one *and* where two were necessary; the fourth fled to the substitute, *while*. Certainly *and* is a word to be used as sparingly as possible, but not so sparingly that the construction, and therefore the meaning, of the sentence is imperilled. Nor is *while* a legitimate equivalent. What an unnecessary and otiose *while* can do to the shape of a sentence and to its economy is illustrated in the next two examples:

> Even the non-Carthusian will enjoy these accounts of the vagaries of masters and boys, the former including Mallory, who disappeared on Everest, while among the latter we find Vaughan-Williams, Baden-Powell, Forbes Robertson, Cyril Maude, Lord Ismay and Lord Beveridge.—*JT*
>
> It is true that certain other accusations could be levelled at the editors and at some of the poets represented in the first series; Mr. Jack Lindsay, for instance, will probably be blamed for not being obscure enough, while other readers may be shocked to find Mr. Barker using words which would make an ivory tower blush. —*NS*

Each writer should stick to his original construction and, like a good golfer, follow through:

> ' the former including Mallory, and the latter Vaughan-Williams,[1] Baden-Powell etc.'
>
> ' could be levelled at the editors and some of the poets, at Mr. Jack Lindsay, for instance, for not being obscure enough, and at Mr. Barker for using words which would make an ivory tower blush.'

In the next sentence, since the *while* is not a mere connective but implies antithesis, its use is justifiable. All the same, it has betrayed the writer into upsetting the balance (see p. 34) he apparently intended, and into undue verbosity:

> The only difference between propaganda under a dictatorship and propaganda under a Liberal Government is that in the first it is centralized and uniform,

[1] I have followed the original in inserting the hyphen; but no hyphen should be there.

> while in the second latitude is given to individuals, or groups, to generate their own propaganda and get it across if they can.—*TT*

He had only to think of an appropriate antonym for *centralized* and *uniform*. Here is a suggestion: ' while in the second it is *localised*[1] and *individual* '.

> He has failed to provide a battle cry for the Labour movement while on the other hand he has destroyed the reputation for soundness which he enjoyed with the floating voter.—*NS*

In this sentence the *while*, fortified by the phrase ' on the other hand ', implies an antithesis that is not actually there. The writer is stating two related but not contrasted facts; his neatest construction would be ' has not only failed to provide but has also destroyed '.

> Among other[2] contributors to a varied number are Mr. Geoffrey Gorer, who discusses the concept of national character; Mrs. Margaret Knight, who writes on the theoretical implications of telepathy arising from the pioneer investigations of Dr. Rhine, of Duke University; and a survey of the fundamentals of aircraft flight by Mr. H. Pearson.—*TLS*

The writer promises us the names of some contributors, gives us two, forgets his promise, and for the third contributor's name substitutes a brief description of his theme. His sentence should end: ' and Mr H. Pearson, who makes a survey . . . '. Strange that having deliberately set a pattern for his sentence he so carelessly destroyed it at the end.

> But Miss Wedgwood has in good measure that gift so valuable in the outline history: that of summing up, in a single felicitous phrase or image, the essence of a writer and his achievement. Thus we have Vaughan's " visions of Heaven innocent and bright as a Fra Angelico painting "; the " compelling, dark and difficult eloquence " of Donne's Sermons; or her lively evocations of the teeming, tumbling vitality of Jonson's or of Pepys's world.—*O*

[1] Except in quotations the ending *-ise* (not *-ize*) is used throughout the book, as in *Good English*.

[2] For this idiom see p. 67.

The writer promises us examples of the ' single felicitous phrase or image ' that sums up ' the essence of a writer and his achievement '. But after giving us a couple, he forgets what he set out to do, and we are left wondering in what felicitous phrase or image Miss Wedgwood summed up the tumbling vitality of Jonson's or Pepys's world. He fobs us off instead with a misleading semi-colon, an illogical *or*, and a casual reference of his own to ' her lively evocations '.

> I should like to mention (besides the main performances of Michael Gough and Rachel Kempson) Geoffrey Dunn's Mayfair exquisite, Yvonne Mitchell's adolescent girl and Robert Harris as the civilised, ungenial husband.—*NS*

The pattern of the enumeration is broken at the third item, which should read ' Robert Harris's civilised, ungenial husband '.

> Within the space of 180 pages, she manages to convey most vividly the insatiable curiosity of that restless, argumentative age; and the diversity of a literature which could encompass Pepys and Evelyn, Congreve, and coney-catching pamphlets with the Authorised Version, Milton and the sermons of Lancelot Andrewes.—*O*

For this reviewer any mixed medley of names (or items) will serve as object of *encompasses*—an expansive and (it must be admitted) undiscriminating verb. But it is not clear whether he is speaking of authors or of works, and his punctuation has made an extraordinary jumble of both. If the names (Pepys, etc.) stand not for the writers but for their works, then the sentence, except for the odd association of the Authorised Version *with* coney-catching pamphlets, will pass muster. But all ambiguity would be removed and a more reasonable order achieved if the items were arranged in some such way as this: ' could encompass the works of Pepys, Evelyn, Congreve and Milton, the sermons of Lancelot Andrewes, coney-catching pamphlets, and the Authorised Version '.

> The fact that Belgium exists today as an independent country; that Greece was not restricted to the Morea but started with the Arta-Volo line; that the Ottoman Empire was not partitioned between France and Russia;

> that the latter was brought into the concert of Europe
> and the former restrained; that liberalism became a
> constructive and not merely a revolutionary impulse;
> that our prestige in the world became greater than ever
> since 1815; that the Eastern Question did not provoke a
> crisis for fourteen further years: all these achievements
> were due to Palmerston's knowledge, industry, sense of
> timing, and fortitude.—*O*

Here the writer piles up seven noun clauses beginning
with *that* in apposition to his subject *fact*: ' the fact (i) that
Belgium . . . (ii) that Greece . . . (iii) that the Ottoman
Empire . . . etc. '. But by the time he has reached the end
of this breathless and breath-taking enumeration, and has
inserted a meaningless colon he has quite forgotten how
he began. His subject (*fact*) is left in mid-air without
a predicate, and a new subject (' all these achievements ')
takes its place. Syntactically, all he could properly do
was to substitute a more appropriate stop (say, a dash)
for the colon, and repeat his original subject: ' . . . further
years—this fact was due '.

If he wants to use ' these achievements ' as subject, he
must recast the whole sentence, remembering, by the way,
that not all the seven enumerated matters of fact are, in
fact, achievements.

> Few poets of Stevenson's magnitude, and not many
> greater, could hope for a more industrious, sensible and
> informative editor, who wears her scholarship with an
> expert lightness and displays his jewels (though they are
> not of the first water) more temptingly than, to take only
> one instance, has ever been done for Burns.—*TLS*

This sentence is sound down to the very last clause,
where the writer suddenly changes from active to passive.[1]
The proper active ending would run something like this:
' than any editor has ever displayed those of Burns '.

> This anthology is an enlargement of that idea, for the
> two collectors have been concerned rather to emphasise
> the records of the scene and the events, rather than
> poetic attitudes and literary musings, relating to the
> River, which every Cockney must spell with a capital
> letter.—*S*

[1] See *Good English*, p. 70.

This writer is merely—and unpardonably—careless. He promises a comparison of infinitives: ' rather to emphasise than to . . . '. But he forgets this, and actually gives us a comparison of nouns: ' records rather than poetic attitudes '. So his formula is ' rather to emphasise *a* rather than *b* '. His use of commas after *musings* and *river* is equally careless. Correct: ' . . . concerned to emphasise the scene and the events rather than poetic attitudes and literary musings relating to the River which every Cockney . . . '.

Balance of Thought

In the following examples the balance of the thought is upset by a change of construction:

> It was, partly, a period seen through a temperament, a personal impression of an age. —NS

The writer has attempted what may be called an ' appositional climax '; that is, he intended the key noun in his final phrase to be in apposition to the key noun (*period*) in the simple sentence. But unfortunately he forgot his good intention, and placed in apposition two unlike things, a *period* and an *impression*. ' It was a period . . .' he begins, with a flourish, and the reader rightly expects in the reiterative phrase a ' synonym ' to *period*. The writer could have maintained the balance in two ways. In each reconstruction the nouns in apposition are italicised:

(a) It was, partly, a *period* seen through a temperament, an *age* visualised as a personal impression.

(b) It was the *picture* of a period seen through a temperament, a personal *impression* of an age.

> It will be the condition of Western survival for the foreseeable future, just as (though the analogy is fallacious) the Roman Empire depended on maintaining for centuries a stable frontier against the barbarians.—O

The writer uses an ' equals ' sign (*just as*) but does not properly finish his equation; the ' condition ' formula must appear on both sides, even if the sentence becomes a little clumsy: ' . . . just as it was the condition of the survival of the Roman Empire that it maintained . . . '.

The equation breaks down in much the same way in the

T—B

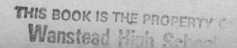
THIS BOOK IS THE PROPERTY OF
Wanstead High School

following sentence; correctly stated it would be ' Just as Great Britain has done . . . so she has (I believe) better opportunities '. ' I believe ' should be in parenthesis, not a main verb:

> Just as Great Britain has done more than any other country during the last five years to mark out new lines of social and economic advance, so I believe that she has better opportunities than any country to lay the foundations of an educated mass democracy.—*O*

Balance and Style

The next two sentences are not open to criticism on points of meaning or construction. They conform to usage, and they express adequately the thought of the writers. But each writer, having promised a certain symmetry in his sentence, either unconsciously or deliberately renders it unsymmetrical. He is an offender not against syntax but against style:

> For the former her adoration was ecstatic and therefore blind; her admiration for the latter, although equally devoted, was less uncritical.—*O*

Unless the writer was deliberately attempting the stylistic effect called *chiasmus* (Greek = ' cross-fashion '), he should have satisfied the reader by giving him what he expects after the semi-colon—' for the latter her admiration . . . ', the phrase being truly parallel, instead of not very effectively crossed. This is not to say chiasmus is never justified; but here it is not as effective as the natural parallel construction.

> On her part it was a fervent and deeply affectionate admiration for his genius and moral qualities: and he, in all simplicity, was ' glad to have someone to whom he could say anything.'—*O*

This writer far more than the writer of the previous sentence promises a symmetrically balanced construction: first by the use of the phrase ' on her part ' and second by the use of the colon, the punctuation mark of balance.[1] The reader rightly expects the second half of the sentence

[1] See *Good English*, p. 109.

to begin ' and on his '. Nor would it have been difficult for the writer to satisfy him; he could have done it in this way: ' and on his a simple delight in having " someone to whom he could say anything " '. Nothing is sacrificed, not even the quotation, and the general ' shape ' of the sentence is certainly improved.

Mental Fog

And here, to end the section, is a short passage in which faulty balance is the result of confused thought on the part of the writer:

> The widely quoted remark about teaching children not to have confidence in the press which was made by the editor of this journal was *not* inaccurately reported It was, on the contrary, the deliberate conclusion of one bit of a sustained argument, and, as such, justifiable.—NS

He unfurls, as it were, his flag of antithesis (' on the contrary '), and then runs away from it. There is only one possible ending to his sentence once he has used that phrase—' It was, on the contrary, accurately reported '—and even that is not worth the flourish, since it is not a real antithesis at all, merely saying the same thing over again. No doubt all he meant to say was ' The remark was not reckless and unjust; on the contrary, it was deliberate and just '. But a mental fog gathered round him, and he lost his way.

CHAPTER III

ECONOMY, TRUE AND FALSE

No doubt, if in one word, without violating idiom, I can
express what others have done in more, and yet be as fully and
easily understood, I have manifestly made an improvement.
—COLERIDGE: *Table Talk*

THE good writer will express his thought in the most
concise, and therefore the briefest, way possible. This does
not mean that he will always write in short simple words,
or strain after a sturdy Saxon vocabulary. Far from it.
He will realise, if he is sensible, that he has all the resources
of the language to draw upon. Our classical vocabulary,
for example, enables us to express in one word what can be
said in native English only in a phrase or in a clause:
imperceptible for ' unable to be seen or perceived ', *orthodox*
for ' according to accepted teaching ', *telephone* for ' an
instrument for conveying sound from afar '. These are
simple examples, but they are representative. Because
the classical languages (Latin and Greek) are themselves
concise in vocabulary and syntax, conciseness of expression
in English depends partly upon the considered use of
classical derivatives. It is well to remember this always:
to avoid a Latin word merely because it is Latin and long
is to be both foolish and false to the genius of the language.

We achieve economy in the structure of the sentence in
three main ways: (i) by ' bracketing '—that is, expressing
only once a part of the sentence which has a common
relationship with two (or more) other parts; (ii) by ' telescoping '—that is, concentrating into (usually) one word
the sense that would normally be expressed in a phrase;
and (iii) by ellipsis—that is, omitting or ' understanding '
certain words or units in the sentence.

(i) ' BRACKETING '

The simple principle of ' bracketing ' may be illustrated

like this. We normally combine the two sentences ' Jack
went up the hill ' and ' Jill went up the hill ' in one sentence
' Jack and Jill went up the hill '. That is, we bracket the
two subjects and express the predicate, the common
factor (call it x), once only; our sentence is of the pattern
$(a + b)x$. It is obvious that we can make various simple
types of sentence patterns in this way. We may have,
for example two verbs with a common subject and/or[1] a
common object; two objects or two complements with a
common verb.[2] The bracketing is normally easy and
straightforward; we do it without thinking, as part of the
natural custom of language—a fundamental idiom of
syntax.

But we have only to turn to the section on agreement
(pp. 14–24) to realise that complications may arise. The
subject may consist of two (or more) parts which are not
necessarily added together; and our bracketing may have
repercussions elsewhere in the sentence, mainly in the form
of the verb. The varied examples given in that section
illustrate the point sufficiently: there is no need to add to
them here.

Difficulties arise sometimes (but not so frequently) in
other sentence patterns. More especially, we tend to
bracket in constructions where bracketing is not syntactically possible. Here is an example:

> Neither the company nor he had, nor would, in any way
> edit or expurgate the report.—T

We have bracketed like this—' (had + would) edit or

---

[1] See p. 54.

[2] Sometimes an idiom or a figure of speech develops. Thus, we
may have a ' common ' verb with two nouns (as direct objects or in
prepositional phrases) to only one of which it is actually appropriate.
Fowler gives two examples from literature—Shakespeare's "*Kill*
the boys and the luggage*" and Pope's " See Pan with flocks, with
fruits Pomona *crowned* " (' *plunder* the luggage', 'with flocks
surrounded '). This figure is called *zeugma* (Greek = ' yoking ').
In a more deliberate figure called *syllepsis* the common verb has
two shades of meaning, and gives to the sentence an air of incongruity. It is generally used for humorous effect—by Dickens, for
example—but it sometimes appears in solemn and august contexts:
Mr Wellwood *took* the oath and his seat as Ulster Unionist
member for Londonderry in the room of Sir Ronald Ross.—T

expurgate '; but the infinitives *edit* and *expurgate* cannot be common to both auxiliaries (' had *edited/expurgated* ').

Here is a sentence where the error is more subtle:

> However, even he would, no doubt, admit that how far we can and ought still to tighten our belts and sacrifice the present for the future are questions of degree, and that different views may reasonably be taken.—*TLS*

The auxiliary *can* is followed by the infinitive without *to*: ' (*can* and *ought*) to tighten ' is bad bracketing. Substitute *are able* for *can*.

This simple type of false economy often arises when we try to bracket two adjectives of different degree, positive and comparative:

> Mr. Hunt must know this as well or better than I do, and yet he has elected to do it.—*NS*

We must open out—' as well *as* or better *than* '. There cannot be a conjunction common to both positive and comparative. So also with prepositions:

> Local Authorities have no knowledge or interest in Education, except as it affects the rates.

Knowledge and *interest* cannot be related (through bracketing) with the common preposition *in*: ' knowledge *of* or interest *in* '.

Prepositional Verbs

More especially, because here the error may be less obvious, we have to be careful of bracketed verbs intended to have a common object. Clearly, if both (or all) the verbs are transitive there is no difficulty: " I hate and detest that animal called man " (Swift). But the verbs are not always so simple: following prepositions have to be reckoned with, and the bracketing has to be arranged or modified accordingly. Here are two examples:

> He had a divining faculty, by which he detected where that individuality lay, and he growled, grumbled at,

praised and corrected his initiates until they were firmly established in that self-knowledge without which no artist can become truly himself and truly a professional worker.—*O*

There are two possible corrections: (i) ' growled *at*, grumbled *at* '; (ii) with a simple piece of internal bracketing, a bracket within a bracket, ' growled and grumbled at '. So the whole construction is:

PREPOSITIONAL VERBS	SIMPLE TRANSITIVES	OBJECT
growled *at*, grumbled *at* *or* growled and grumbled *at*	praised and corrected	his initiates

The best way to describe his method is to quote a passage, words spoken by the woman who has been in love, and still loves, the now successful sitter.—*JL*

Correct: ' who has been in love *with*, and still loves, the now successful sitter '. A phrasal prepositional verb (' be in love with ') is coupled with a simple transitive. For the punctuation in this type of bracketing see p. 135.

Syntactical bracketing is, indeed, like mathematical bracketing: we have to relate correctly the common term to the separate terms, to make sure that $(a + b)c$ does really represent $ac + bc$. Questions of number may arise, as we have seen on pp. 14–24; and sometimes even questions of case. The point to remember here is that the effect of the word outside the bracket (verb, preposition) is to make objects of the nouns or pronouns inside: ' let (you and *me*) ', ' between (you and *me*) '.[1] But see also p. 173.

---

[1] *Between* suggests also the ' *between* $(a + b)$ ' formula (*Good English*, pp. 78, 97). In the following sentence the writer has been betrayed into false bracketing:

Mr Auden does not disappoint in this respect and his book is full of arresting asides which point the sharp difference between the criticism of a poet and of a professional critic.—*TLS*

The fact that his two terms are related to a common element (*criticism*) has tempted him into bringing this element outside the bracket, so that *between* is, in effect, governing a singular. Correct: ' *between* the criticism of a poet *and* the criticism (or *that*) of a professional critic '.

Bracketing with Correlatives

The difficulties and dangers of bracketing with correlatives are also dealt with in *Good English* (pp. 62 ff.), and again in Chapter I of this book in connection with subject and verb agreement. Here are a few sentences as a reminder and a warning:

> Four American professors of English have dealt with successive periods, and to dip into the book at any point and come either upon an author who is well known or one unfamiliar to the reader is to realise the knowledge, the freshness and the lucidity of the treatment.—*JL*

Here we have the familiar error in ' bracketing ' with *either—or*. Each of the correlatives should be followed by the same pattern or type of expression: ' either *upon* an author or *upon* one . . . '.

> First, any organised community must establish a principle of ownership, for it may neither lay down a scale of rights and duties nor a system of justice until it has cast the balance between the *meum* and *tuum*.—*NS*

The verb should be brought outside the brackets: ' lay down (neither a scale . . . nor a system) '—unless two parallel verbs are intended: ' neither lay down a scale . . . nor propound a system '.

- (a) Neither in the nationalised industries nor in the trade unions nor in the Co-operative movement has it given its own stalwarts anything challengingly constructive to do.—*NS*
- (b) Neither in the docks, the engineering works or the coal mines is there any real sense that there is a call for men to give of their best.—*NS*
- (c) With considerable courage he proclaimed the belief that his sexual deviation was neither an illness, an aberration, nor a crime.—*NS*

The correct correlatives are *either—or* and *neither—nor*, Strictly speaking we should not add another *or* or *nor*. since *either* and *neither* imply two, and two only. If it is necessary to express three (or more) alternatives[1] the positive correlative construction is better abandoned—

[1] See p. 65.

that is, *either* should be dropped. With *neither* the situation is a little different, since except as a simple negative, usually as the first word of a sentence or clause, *nor* cannot exist without its partner *neither*. If the *neither—nor—nor* construction is to be avoided, therefore, the negative must be transferred elsewhere in such sentences as those quoted above: ' in industries, unions, and movement it has not given ', ' in docks, works and mines there is no real sense ', ' his sexual deviation was not an illness, an aberration or a crime '. But here is a case where to do a great right we should be allowed to do a little wrong, and *neither* may have its extra *nor* either expressed or, as in sentence (*c*), unexpressed. The *or* in sentence (*b*) is an illiteracy.

There is a tendency to be lenient towards small aberrations in the position of *not only . . . but also*;[1] but the following sentence, in which the writer seems quite conscious of the danger and yet fails to avoid it, will not pass muster:

> The land that had always been silent and undisturbed began not only to be minutely stirred by small burrowings and by the growth of plants, but was marked by the impress of feet, even though between the footprints went the groove of a scaly tail.—JACQUETTA HAWKES: *A Land* (quoted in *O*)

There are two possibilities: ' began not only to be stirred but (to be) marked ' and ' not only began . . . but was '. The omission of *also* is permissible in modern usage, though it often encourages the faulty bracketing by disguising the balanced correlative. It is interesting to note that a reviewer of the book from which this quotation and that on p. 58 are taken said of the two sentences, " They are written in a style that appears to me both excellent and rare ".

Zeal Unrewarded

It is remarkable how some writers, having decided to bracket, forget their good intentions and in an excess of zeal retain the very words they could have dispensed with, or even add extra ones. There is an example in a sentence quoted on p. 27, where, having kept the preposition *to*

[1] See *Good English*, pp. 65ff.

outside the bracket, the writer pops it in again before the end.

But the chief temptation is to wreck the simple *whether —or* construction with an intrusive *whether*: ' *whether—or —whether* '.[1] The error is so common that a few examples are given here to point the moral. Words that could and should be omitted are italicised:

> Whether succeeding poets adopted his prayer in licensed imitation, and continued to do so till this became a covenient convention, or *whether they* sincerely believed in a benignant deity who determined the poetic faculty in the favoured is a question.—*TLS*

> And it is hard to know whether they were seriously abashed by his refusal or *whether they* were just showing him that they always had one more throw in the battle of wits.—*NS*

> I cannot presume to judge whether such apocalyptic outbursts are compatible with Mr. Merton's present vocation or *whether they* are provoked by images of the past recollected in tranquillity.—*NS*

> My mind goes back to a visit to the United States in 1942, when I recall writing that the future of America and the world depended on whether the U.S. would use her surplus to feed and develop backward countries, or *whether* the Republican imperialist forces would win the day.—*NS*

> Lucas's other major argument in this volume turns upon whether literature has an ethical content or *whether it* is written for pleasure alone. It is an old question of whether art is for art's sake, or *whether*, to use Mr. Lucas's own language, *it* is " influence-value ".—*JL*

The last writer not only stumbles twice over *whether—or* but also permits himself to misuse ' question of '.[2]

(ii) TELESCOPING

As has been hinted in the introduction to this section (p. 36), telescoping, the concentrating in a single word of the sense of a whole phrase or clause, is inherent in our vocabulary. The subject is a fascinating one, but it is

[1] See *Good English*, pp. 63-4.   [2] See p. 63.

concerned with the history and growth of the language rather than with problems of modern usage; so it is outside the scope of this book. But one or two manifestations of the process that belong to idiom and even syntax are considered here.

1. The Attributive Noun

This neat and concise usage is so much a part of the language that it does not normally, in the words of Matthew Arnold, " abide our question "; ' house agent ', ' bicycle tyre ', ' Borough Council ', ' library book ', ' cricket pitch '—examples are legion. Each noun-adjective is a telescoped adjective phrase; it represents a convenient piece of linguistic shorthand. One or two points, however, are worth noting:

(a) An attributive noun may represent in different contexts different telescoped phrases: ' a library book ' (' from or in a library '), ' a library ticket ' (' for use in borrowing library books '), ' a library edition ' (' suitable or fit for a library '). We are not normally conscious of these shades of meaning, but they are nevertheless interesting and significant.

(b) Out of this noun-noun association have arisen many of our familiar compounds. But when two nouns really coalesce to become one (armchair, cupboard, bookcase, schoolboy), when they are linked by a hyphen (lawn-mower, plate-rack, pen-holder, book-mark), and when they remain separate are questions that in the present state of usage are past the wit of man to answer.

There is a further note on the peculiar ways of the hyphen on p. 145ff.

(c) Purists, who seem oddly insensitive to the genius of the language, sometimes object to the attributive noun when there is available what they regard as a ' synonymous ' real adjective. To give a very simple example, they would have us talk of an urban, a rural scene, instead of a town, a country scene. They fail to recognise that the language is richer for having two modes of expression which either mean different things or distinguish fine shades of meaning: we say ' sea fisheries ' but ' marine parade ', our ' island home ' but ' an insular outlook ', ' a flower show ' but ' a

floral display ', ' a *day* trip ' but ' the sun's *diurnal* course '.
And as I have pointed out elsewhere,[1] ' an *England* team '
has not exactly the same meaning as ' an *English* team '.
Odd things happen sometimes. In the following sentence
the writer forgot, or perhaps preferred to forget, that there
is a convenient English noun + noun compound *song-bird*:

> This suggested the broadcasting of other *avian* songsters,
> and in the 1930s[2] programmes such as *The Chorus of
> Birds* began to appear.—*RT*

Sometimes, so strange are the ways of words, a new adjective
arises to compete with a well-established attributive noun.
It is a sign of development in both life and language that we
now speak of *global* [3] as well as of *world* war.

(*d*) Attributive nouns have a habit of piling up before
the noun they qualify, often in official titles. Thus
' Croydon Borough Education Committee ' is shorthand for
' The Committee for (*or* controlling) education in (*or* for)
the Borough of Croydon '. This usage is so common and
convenient as to be above suspicion. But newspaper
headlines (where the attributive nouns are great space
savers) sometimes set us a pretty puzzle. Here are half a
dozen selected examples:

PLAY INQUIRY CALL RENEWED (*DT*)

FESTIVAL MUSIC BROADCAST DISPUTE OFF (*O*)

TONBRIDGE CUP REPLAY LEAD (*DT*)

GRANDMOTHER MURDER CHARGE (*DT*)

FOUR-CLOCK TOWER DECISION (*DT*)

IS. 5D. MEAT RATION FEAR (*DT*)

(*e*) The gerundial adjective, that is, the verb form in
-*ing* used as a simple epithet to represent a preposition +
gerund phrase, is a valuable piece of telescoping which
follows the attributive noun pattern: a *walking* stick, a

[1] In *The Making and Meaning of Words*.

[2] A better form of the plural than 1930's.

[3] *Global* has another meaning: ' pertaining to or based on a group
as part of a whole ' from an obsolete meaning of *globe* = ' group '.
See Gowers: *ABC of Plain Words*, s.v. *global*.

swimming bath, a *running* track, a *booking* office (' for walking ', ' for swimming ', ' for running ', ' for booking '). The infinitive has a similar concise adjectival use in such expressions as ' a house *to let* ', and ' There is nothing *to say* '.

2. *Noun into Verb*

(*a*) And here is the poem, to *example* Andrew Young's work, that needs no bush.—*JL*

(*b*) Galsworthy is a social not a psychological playwright, and his characters are, to a large extent, *typed*.—*NS*

The use of the noun and, more rarely, the adjective as a verb is common in modern usage, and was even commoner in older English. Abbott (*Shakespearian Grammar*) says: " It may be said that any noun or adjective could be converted into a verb by the Elizabethan authors, generally in an active [transitive] signification ". He gives among his examples: " This day shall *gentle* his condition " (' make him of gentle birth '); " *stocking* his messenger " (' putting him in the stocks '); " He *waged* me " (' paid me my wages '). The modern writer has no such absolute freedom; he is bound by the custom of usage that has developed during the past three hundred years or so. According to that custom, the use of *example* in sentence (*a*) in the sense ' given an example of ' is obsolete, except in the adjectival use of the past participle (*exampled*). In sentence (*b*), *typed* in the sense ' drawn as types rather than as individuals ' is certainly a neat compression of a phrase into a single word; and Shakespeare would have used it without a qualm. It is beginning to establish itself:

> His Desert poems, which had appeared in various periodicals, had already put him in danger of being typed as a " war poet ".—*S*

There is, in fact, a tendency in modern English to revive the Shakespearian freedom in this matter. Probably the influence of American has something to do with it.

Here are two more illustrations, both of the verb *fault* used in the sense ' to find fault with ':

(a) Sutcliffe batted beautifully, and his stroke play could not be *faulted* in the two hours before lunch when New Zealand had scored 71 for one wicket.—*O*

(b) It will not be everybody's notion of entertainment, but as a piece of craftsmanship it seems to me almost flawless, and I was so gripped, and excited, and moved to cheering by it, that I wouldn't try to *fault* it if I could.—*O*

Tennis may have suggested the use (' to foot-fault a player '). There is no reason to condemn it; it is in fact a revival of an old usage in Shakespeare and other Elizabethan writers.

However, it must be admitted that in some kinds of writing the noun-verb becomes a mere affectation:

(a) We had a set or two of country dances, a serene yet gay *patterning* on the lawn.—*JL*

(b) Watching the pageant of ships on the intense blue beyond the headland; hearing the surf that *creamed* on the rocks below.—*JL*

(c) It made no speeches and *peacocked* no tricks; edged into the home, asked for confidence, and got it.—*NS*

(d) Unless the British Government makes this clear from the start, it may very well be *pressured* during the Summer into consenting to a full-scale blockade.—*NS*

(e) The most zealous Communists, financed by the most foreign gold, and *propaganding* in the most capitalist lands, are not thus penalised for their faith.—*S*

(f) On one of them, a benign clear evening was *drifted* with honeysuckle.

I am not sure whether *drifted* is an example of a noun-verb. But if not, what is it, and what does it mean?

One modern Americanism is worth noting—' *stem* from ' = ' spring from ', ' originate in '. It is a noun-verb tele-scoping of ' comes or grows from the same stem as '. The phrase first came into English during the War, and now bids fair to establish itself. It was used, for example, in an official notice at the South Bank Exhibition in 1951: " From the ancient assembly in Westminster a family of Parliaments stems throughout the world ". And it is already a favourite with journalists:

. . . . the present boom stems from the fact that the City gentry expected the Chancellor's progressive redistributions.—*NS*

Virtually all the modern renaissance of the printing arts stems from William Morris and his band of apostles.—*T*

A few years ago their optimism might have stemmed from sentimental illusions about the nature of the Soviet regime.—*NS*

3. *Noun into Participle*

The use as an attributive adjective of a past participle formed from a noun is now accepted in English usage (*unscripted* talk, *matted* wicket). But Dr Johnson made his protest:

> There has of late arisen a practice of giving to adjectives derived from substantives the termination of participles; [1] such as the *cultured* plain, the *daisied* bank; but I was sorry to see, in the lines of a scholar like Gray, the *honied* Spring.

And Coleridge thundered:

> I regret to see that vile and barbarous vocable *talented*, stealing out of the newspapers into the leading reviews and most respectable publications of the day. Why not *shillinged*, *farthinged*, *tenpenced*, &c ? The formation of a participle passive from a noun is a licence that nothing but a very peculiar felicity can excuse. If mere convenience is to justify such attempts upon the idiom, you cannot stop till the language becomes in the proper sense of the word, corrupt. Most of these pieces of slang come from America.—*Table Talk*

But, like most of his notes on language, this is an example of his own muddled and incoherent thought.

4. *Jumps in Meaning*

Sometimes by telescoping a word takes on an associated meaning that is apparently remote from its normal meaning. A good example in English is *execute*. ' To *execute* [= do, carry out] the judgment of the court upon a criminal ' is

[1] What he meant by this, however, I cannot understand; *cultured*, by the way, here means ' cultivated '.

telescoped into ' to execute [= kill, hang] a criminal '.
The process, in a modified form, is common; that is to
say, a word often acquires associated meanings owing to
its power, often through metaphor, of concentrating in
itself the sense of a whole phrase. The word *contact* in
one of its modern uses is a good example. ' To *make*, or
establish, or *come into* contact with ', is a long-established
idiom; ' to *contact* ', where *contact* is an ordinary transitive
verb (' contact a person ') and *contact* (noun) = ' the person
contacted ' (' The Prime Minister is one of my contacts ')
are recent telescopings which we owe to standard American
usage. Some English dictionaries do not yet recognise
them, and they still offend the purists.[1]

5. *Each other, one another*

The expressions *each other, one another*, are convenient
telescopings: ' We wrote to *each other/one another* ' = ' Each
one of us wrote to the [an] other.' Purists make a distinction between them, using *each other* for two things or persons
only, and *one another* for more than two things or persons.
In spite of Fowler's rather perverse repudiation of it, this
distinction is a convenient one, though so often ignored
as not to have any real validity.[2] Fowler, for some odd
reason, condemns the construction in which *other/another* is
itself subject; we should write, he says, ' We know what
each the other wants ' not ' what each other wants '. This
is pedantry run mad. Englishmen use the telescoped
expression every day, and therefore it is modern English
usage. The possessive form of these compound words is
each other's, one another's.

[1] We are in deep water here. An hour with a good etymological
dictionary will serve to remind us what remarkable ' jumps ' in
meaning words sometimes take from language to language. The
curious reader may well begin with the following half-dozen, all of
classical origin: *cancel, ostracise, focus, cynical, examination, lunatic*.
But the subject is a vast one and is outside the scope of this book.
See *Good English*, p. 150.

[2] It must be confessed that SOED is even more downright than
Fowler; it has the laconic entry ' *e. other* = *one another* '. But the
older formal grammarians were equally definite on the other side.
Nesfield says: " *each other, one another:* Remember that the first is
used for two things, the second for more than two ". See general
comment on pp. 8-10.

6. *Sameness and Difference*

Peculiar difficulties arise when we wish to express briefly and succinctly that one thing is the same as, or different from, another. We usually resort to a kind of telescoping that is, to say the least of it, open to question. Here are a few sentences to illustrate the point:

> The layout of the books is similar, each page being of diagrams with brief explanatory notes.—*TES*
> But the attitude of the poets in the two wars is extra-ordinarily different.—*O*

Similar and *different* imply at least two layouts and two attitudes; and the plurals *books* and *wars* do not atone for their singularity. But to say ' The layouts/the attitudes are . . . ' does not solve the problem: it only leads to another implication, that each book has a number of layouts and each poet a number of attitudes. There is, however, a simple and on the whole satisfactory solution: ' The books are similar [*sc*. to each other] in layout ', ' The poets of the two wars are extraordinarily different [*sc*. one from the other] in attitude—'.

> More probably they agreed to share a volume because of a similarity in their subject-matter, which is macabre and ghostly, and of their method, which is leisurely but not digressive and has that moderation essential if the improbable is to be made acceptable.—*O*

The writer of this sentence is faced with, but does not solve, the same problem. Nevertheless the solution is easy; he merely needs a plural after the phrases ' similarity in/of '. The only difficulty is that *subject-matter*, being a collective noun, does not admit—at any rate, in normal usage—of a plural. He must, therefore, resort to a synonym: ' similarity *in* themes or subjects/ *of* methods '.

> This congestion could be greatly eased by the simple device of making food obtainable at a different counter from the coffee and tea.—*NS*

Here the problem is a little more complicated. The expression is a telescoping of ' making food obtainable at a different counter from that at which coffee and tea are obtainable '. But it is not justified. At least we must insist that, in this context, one counter differs from another counter (not from coffee and tea) in service, if not in glory; that is, the word *counter* must be followed by ' from that . . .'. A possible ending, to avoid awkwardness, might be ' from that devoted to coffee and tea '. But why not change the pattern of the sentence—' device of serving food and drink at different counters ', which is itself telescoped English for ' food at one counter and drink at another '?

> Perhaps the greatest tribute to the child's persuasion is the fact that one looks at the real Miss Joyce quite differently at the beginning and end of the picture.—*O*

Evidently what the writer meant to say was ' one looks at the real Miss Joyce in a certain way at the beginning of the picture and in another (or, a different) way at the end '.

7. *A Problem of Number*

The ' plural ' problem discussed earlier in this section (p. 49) sometimes arises in another form:

> Mr. Guinness's Hamlet enlists rather than compels our attention. It is far from being a great performance but it is a very intelligent one, and on the night when I saw it little deserved the harsh and in one case brutal verdicts delivered by some of my colleagues after the unlucky opening performance.—*S*

The writer, valiantly attempting an elliptical construction, gets into trouble with *verdicts*. He wishes to suggest that several verdicts (' by some of my colleagues ') were harsh and that one verdict was brutal; so he brackets the adjectives and puts the plural (*verdicts*) outside the bracket. But it will not do: *verdicts* cannot at the same time represent a plural and a singular. Oddly enough, *verdict* (singular) would stand; in a construction like this it is idiomatic in English to admit what may be called a distributive singular —the *verdict* being regarded as ' of each colleague in turn '.[1] So in the following sentence there is no need for the plural

[1] See *Good English*, p. 163.

(*shortages*) in the second half of the correlation; say, ' a shortage of nickel, tungsten etc.':

> This country is now facing not only a serious shortage of sulphur, a raw material essential to a wide range of industry, but also, as Mr. Strauss, the Minister of Supply, said last night, shortages of nickel, tungsten, and molybdenum, which are used in the making of alloy steels.—*DT*

8. *Same*

This is a convenient place in which to deal with the problem of *same*, as represented in the following two sentences:

> The young Rajah keeps a harem yet looks on it with the same disgust that he does on his over-indulgence in drink.— *O*
>
> Inspired by the near collision of Hermes with this planet in 1937, this dramatic end-of-the-world story is distinguished by the same originality of thought and dynamic writing which marked *The King of High Street*. —Publisher's Advertisement

Perhaps there is no problem, after all. Anyhow, Fowler ignores it, and SOED admits the relative clause construction illustrated here. But it is possible to argue that in this usage we have telescoped expressions for: ' with the same disgust as that with which he looks [or *does*] ', ' the same originality of thought and dynamic writing as that which marked '; and, having admitted that, to prefer *as* to any form of the relative pronoun as the surviving word. This has the advantage of recognising the normal relationship of *same* and *as*, and of getting rid of the complications that arise when the relative pronoun (as in the first sentence— ' the same with which ') is, or should be, governed by a preposition. However, this is a mere suggestion: the choice is even more than usually the writer's own.

(iii) ELLIPSIS

Ellipsis, which signifies in language ' leaving out ', ' shortening ' (not, as it were, completing the full circle, like an ellipse), is naturally a characteristic of the more complicated methods of economy already dealt with—bracketing and telescoping. The brief note here is intended merely to remind us of its common and simpler manifestations in language. We see (p. 144) that in simple linkings (with *and* and *or*) of more than two words or other sentence units the conjunction is expressed only once, before the last unit, the others being represented by commas. The formula is: *a*, *b*, *c*, and *d*, not *a* and *b* and *c* and *d*. So, too, the omission, in certain circumstances, of the relative pronoun[1] and of the conjunction *that* introducing a noun clause (' I thought he was going ') is a familiar English idiom. It is important, by the way, to remember that it is an idiom, and to avoid using the relative or the conjunction when it may (and should) be omitted. The sentence ' That is the book *which* you lent me ' is an example of stilted, not idiomatic, English. So is this:

> Dr. Edith Sitwell has presented him to the world in a biography that has all the affection that a mother might devote to an engaging but backward child.—*JL*

Sometimes *that* is not merely a stylistic but an actual intruder:

> L.M. (London) sends another word which he has discovered that he habitually pronounces wrongly.—*JL*

The conjunction is *which* in its peculiar double function;[2] it stands in relation to both verbs, *has discovered* and *pronounces*, and *that* is therefore superfluous.

So, too, when a writer hesitates between direct and indirect speech:[3]

> On the other hand, Keats, the most modest of artists on all normal occasions, was led to such a detestation of Pope that he wrote on one occasion that " Pope's verses are like mice to mine ".—*JL*

Either a comma should replace *that* after *occasion*, or *that* should be retained introducing indirect speech: ' that Pope's verses were like mice to his '.

[1] See *Good English*, p. 89.
[2] See *Good English*, p. 84.
[3] The reader may raise his eyebrows at this. See p. 39.

> Even then I remember that he was interested in educa-
> tion, not as a theory, but as something that he had to do
> something about.—*NS*

The sentence is a trifle ambiguous; but it seems that
the adverb phrase ' even then ' modifies *interested*, not
remember. If so, ' I remember ' is parenthetic and *that* is
superfluous: ' Even then, I remember, he was interested . . .'.

Simple ellipsis is a kind of syntactical shorthand, and
is perfectly legitimate as long as the shorthand is understood
by both writer *and reader*. Thus if I write ' The first candidate was weak on grammar, the second strong ' the reader
has no doubt or difficulty: he automatically supplies from
the first clause the missing words in the second. (The
previous sentence, by the way, is itself an example of
ellipsis.) Our familiar words *Yes* and *No* in answer to a
question are elliptical conveniences, and in the interplay
of statement and question or question and answer auxiliary
verbs often stand for a whole predicate that has been
expressed in a previous sentence—' Are you going to see
the Test Match? ' ' If it is fine, I *am*.'

Unusual ellipsis of connectives (that is, simple conjunctions) has become common in modern newspaper headlines:

TREES, HOUSES, FLOODED IN STORM
DEAF DRIVER, 80, MUST PASS TEST

The poets have always been licensed to use ellipsis
more freely than the prose-writers; but lately they have
so out-Donned Donne and out-Hopkinsed Hopkins in
elliptical writing that what is left of their poems is difficult
to understand. Robert Bridges remarks that Gerard
Manley Hopkins himself was never sufficiently aware of
his obscurity, which arose mainly from his habitual omission
of the relative pronoun as subject; and he adds the following
general statement:

> Writers who carelessly rely on their elliptical speech-
> forms to govern the elaborate sentences of their literary
> composition little know what a conscious effort of
> interpretation they often impose on their readers.

It is a warning that the ordinary prose-writer, even though

his sentences are not elaborate, would do well to take to heart. If ellipsis leads to obscurity it is an offence against usage.

It is highly probable that the new ellipsis of the journalists and the poets will have a permanent influence upon the syntax and idiom of the language. After all, most of the constructions illustrated in this chapter have the effect of condensing into a word a whole prepositional phrase; and as those constructions become (as they are becoming) commoner, so the use of prepositions tends to decline. Now and then, too, writers dispense with *and* and the definite article. One piece of shorthand has established itself in commercial and semi-official (if not official) English —*and/or*:

> Allowance for industrial and/or teaching experience will be made in fixing the initial salary.—Advertisement in *TES*

This means that allowance will be made for one of the following types of experience: (*a*) industrial (*b*) teaching (*c*) industrial and teaching. In utilitarian writing of this kind the construction is permissible—and, indeed, desirable; but as yet it has no place in literary writing. It is, however, to be avoided in joining subjects, since the number of the verb may present an insoluble problem:

> The President and/or the Secretary *are* ? *is* ? empowered to act.

In general, it may be said that the whole tendency of the language in syntax and idiom, as well as in the form (pronunciation and spelling) of its words, is towards economy or shortening. Possibly, with the increased and increasing impact of American idiom this tendency will become more pronounced; and doubtless it owes something to the paper shortage that has continued since the Second World War into the armed and precarious peace.

CHAPTER IV

CONSTRUCTION AND IDIOM

> To suppose that grammatical English is either all idiomatic or all unidiomatic would be as far from the truth as that idiomatic English is either all grammatical or all ungrammatical.—FOWLER: *Modern English Usage*

IN this chapter one or two of the commoner syntactical misconstructions and errors dealt with in *Good English* are further exemplified. For the most part the sentences are left to the comment and criticism of the reader, but notes and suggestions are given when special points or complications arise. The quotations given, discovered in good modern journalism without any particular search or trouble, prompt a very significant question—Are certain constructions which were considered loose in the ' pedantic ' period of grammatical rules and regulations[1] regaining their place in English today? There is a special note on this in the section (p. 57) illustrating current carelessness in the use of the participle phrase.

The second half of the chapter is devoted to examples, with commentary, of errors in idiom.

And-whichery

This construction, which has been common for two centuries, does not deserve the forthright condemnation in *Good English* (pp. 80–90). A few examples are given, however, in all of which except the first there are complications that illustrate certain dangers in using a conjunction before the relative.

> I hate old books in the sense that I hate books *printed before the present century* AND *which it would ' be a crime to deface '*.—S

The sentence quoted illustrates pretty clearly the reason

[1] See p. 8.

for this illogical construction and the difficulty of avoiding it. The writer is at pains to separate his relative pronoun from its apparent antecedent (*century*). If he leaves out the *and* the ambiguity of antecedent immediately arises; if he retains it he must, rather awkwardly, make his participle phrase an adjective clause ' books *which were printed . . . and which . . .* '.

> Nevertheless, it is perhaps not without significance that Belgium, which has a population of 732 to the square mile, and England and Wales, with about 750 to the square mile, and which are among the most densely populated countries in the world, have correspondingly high accident rates.—*Motoring*

Here a relative clause does actually precede the piece of and-whichery; but it qualifies only part (*Belgium*) of the double antecedent (*Belgium* and *England and Wales*) of the second (*and which*) relative clause. This is the construction:

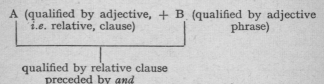

The purist will condemn the sentence; and even the anti-purist will admit its awkwardness.

In the following sentence there is a more serious error:

> There is something irresistible in this clever, clowning man with his unsteady Adam's apple—which he always[1] managed to nick every morning when he was shaving—and whose wits were never lacking.—*NS*

A non-defining relative clause, rather unnecessarily put in parenthesis, qualifying ' Adam's apple ', is joined to a defining clause qualifying *man*.

> It is much to be hoped that, given a fine summer, it may recover some of the freedom, not only good in itself

[1] An obvious piece of tautology.

but of which the highest level of English cricket stands
in most need.—*O*

The *but-whichery* is here entangled in the ' *not only . . .
but [also]* ' construction. However, reconstruction is not
difficult: we have only to keep in mind the essential balance
of correlatives; if *not only* is followed by a simple adjective
(*good*) so should *but [also]* be. Our sentence would, therefore, run: ' not only good in itself but necessary for maintaining the level . . . '. If the relative pronoun is used at
all it must occur once only, outside the bracket, and the
sentence should be amended accordingly: ' which not only
is good in itself but is necessary for maintaining the
level . . . '.

> They were now on what Eliza described as ' very proper,
> relation-like terms ', but which were perhaps, if anything,
> slightly more interesting than the terms between[1] most
> relations.—ELIZABETH JENKINS: *Jane Austen*

The antecedent of *which* is obviously *terms*; but this
has not previously been qualified by a relative clause—
so the *but* is superfluous. There is, however, some kind of
argument to justify the but-whichery: *what* is a compound
demonstrative-relative = ' that which ',[2] so that in the
previous clause there is at least a disguised relative—' they
were now on terms which Eliza describes as . . . '. But
the author, anxious to include the exact and full quotation,
did not in fact use this construction. She is not therefore
entitled to her *but*, especially as it can be omitted without
any other adjustment of the sentence.

The Participle Phrase

Good English suggests that the laxness of older writers
in their treatment of the participle (adjective) phrase was
by no means absent from modern writers as long as the
' loose ' phrase did not render the meaning ludicrous or
nonsensical. To judge from the following examples, the
modern journalist cares no more than Addison for the
logical relationship, based upon position in the sentence, of

[1] The reader may like to comment on this doubtful construction.
I have done so on p. 184.
[2] See *Good English*, p. 88 n.

noun and qualifier (that is, participle phrase). It is, indeed, possible that English today is swinging back to a freer syntax. The reader is invited to comment for himself, and make any necessary or desirable corrections. I have added a note here and there.

1. *The Misrelated Present Participle Phrase*

> Looking back on the books published in 1950, two stand out as unquestionably more notable than the others.—*DT*

> Looking back over its fifty years, the Borstal experiment could justly claim to be succeeding.—*NS*

> Taking the one on the *Home Counties* as typical, they are a marvel of freshness, compactness and intelligent anticipation of what the intelligent reader wants to know.—*JL*

> Looking at these footmarks with the dents and scars of the raindrops on the parched surface, the reality of a harsh, shimmering red and intemperate world returns for a moment.—JACQUETTA HAWKES: *A Land*

(This sentence was quoted in the *Observer* as an example of a style " both excellent and rare ". See also p. 41).

> Taking him merely on his own ground, an Eve of a great festival (and the Epiphany is, liturgically speaking, a greater festival than Christmas Day) is a fast, not a feast.—*JL*

> Following hard on the heels of the Tudor volume, the Falcon Press have now produced its successor covering the seventeenth century, which more than maintains the high standard already set.—*TES*

> Taking his own versions of attentions paid to Mrs. Campbell he would appear as philanderer and unfaithful husband.—*TLS*

It is presumably the reviewer, not the philanderer, who is ' taking his own (*i.e.* the philanderer's) versions '.

> He comes home on leave, and, meeting by chance Phillips, an influential figure in the world of inventions, his remarks made on the subject of possible improvements in the construction of " flares " lead to acceptance of certain of Randall's suggestions.—*TLS*

The longish phrase in apposition to *Phillips* has caused the writer to forget the qualifying participle phrase by the time he arrives at his subject.

2. The Misrelated Past Participle Phrase

Since it is active, the present participle and the phrase it introduces smack as much of the verb as of the adjective; and misrelationships such as have been illustrated above are the less obvious and the more pardonable. But the past participle, being passive, is more an adjective than a verb; so misrelationships of its phrase are easily recognisable and sometimes ludicrous. For all that, they do occur:

> Nominated by the Government, supported by the Opposition, elected by the votes of all members, his authority over the House depends on his election by that House. *T*

One would have thought that, after such a burst of rhetoric, at least something which (to echo Portia) would " pass for a man " might have been elected ' by that House ', not merely ' his authority '.

> And after half an hour he gained what Lancashire so badly wanted, the scalp of Barton, caught at short-leg off a defensive stroke.[1]
>
> Bought as an investment to give lasting pleasure, their fascination, I think, would pall.—*NS*
>
> Born in an age when our language was in solution but not at a temperature to crystallize, Fortune chose him as a nucleus.—NEVILL COGHILL: *The Poet Chaucer*
>
> But I also enjoy new wine, if I can get it fresh and strong and local, seated in the midday heat under a trellis of the very vine from which the grapes come.—*S*

Not even the comma after *local* will ensure that the writer, not the new wine, is seated.

3. The Unrelated (' Hanging ') Participle Phrase

In all three quotations the participle phrase is so placed as to be related to an impersonal (or ' dummy ') *it*:

[1] See also p. 114.

Leaving aside all reference to the greatest sayings of all, it may be remarked that the ancients well understood this passion for overheard speech.—*JL*

Knowing how their promise was fulfilled, it is impossible to discover, with detached honesty, what promise they show.—*S*

The book is moving and well-written and while not necessarily agreeing with Captain Liddell-Hart that "it is one of the most remarkable war novels that have yet appeared," it is certainly much above the average standard.—*NS*

In the last sentence we have not the simple participle (adjective) phrase but a participle phrase turned adverb by reason of an introductory adverbial conjunction (*while*). The relationship is, therefore, not with the subject (noun, pronoun) but the verb. This sentence should run ' while not agreeing . . . I think ', the phrase modifying *think*.

Not—nor

This ' double negative ' construction is discussed and illustrated in *Good English*.[1] Examples of it are to be found in the Questions at the end of this book (p. 190). Here is one which is interesting because the writer has used the same construction twice in a short passage, first incorrectly and then correctly:

He does *not* build a cosmology, *nor* inflate his verse with abstract words. And although he is a priest of the Church of England, he does *not* dogmatise *or* dress his ideas in ritual.—*NS*

The first sentence has also a superfluous comma. Correct: ' does not build a cosmology or inflate . . . '.

Superstition and Prejudice

Most people are (sometimes painfully) aware of two ' grammatical ' injunctions—(*a*) that they should not split an infinitive and (*b*) that they should not end a sentence with a preposition. The first they usually manage to obey, since, being aware of the danger and apprehensive of the explosion, they never write an infinitive without

[1] pp. 64, 65

scaring away any intrusive adverb or adverb phrase that might threaten to separate what should be, if not joined, at least contiguous. The second they sometimes (quite unwillingly) disobey, since in some expressions the preposition is by the custom of language forced to the end.

Of the split infinitive *Good English* has said all that is necessary, except perhaps this—that, after all, the two elements in the modern infinitive have not become a single entity (they are not, for example, joined by a hyphen), and that until they are an occasional modest split with a single adverb only may be justified.

As for the preposition at the end, it arises chiefly, and necessarily, in sentences where the relative pronoun is unexpressed: ' That is the room I slept in '. Other uses arise from and justify themselves by that.

The real case against the preposition at end lies in the etymology of the word itself: *pre-* is so familiarly ' before ', even to the non-Latinist, and *-position* means what it says. But the argument from etymology is sometimes a dangerous one. Latin prefixes are doubtful guides to English constructions. For example, even when we use the word *subscribe*[1] in the literal sense, we do not associate it with the English equivalent preposition *under*: we subscribe our names *to*, not *under*, a letter. So with *inspire* (' breathe into '). Chaucer has:

> Inspired hath in everich holt and heeth
> The tendre croppes

—' hath breathed the tender crops (= flowers) into every wood and heath '. But we say ' inspire a person *with* a thing ', not ' inspire a thing *in* (or *into*) a person '.

It is in deference to etymology that people condemn the phrase ' *under* the circumstances '. *Circumstances*, they argue, means literally ' things standing round '; *under* is therefore a particularly inappropriate preposition, and *in*, though not ideal, is to be preferred. Fowler describes this and any other argument against ' *under* the circumstances ' as puerile. It is not so much puerile as vain. ' *Under*

---

[1] The normal use of *subscribe* (' *subscribe* to a charity ') is, of course, a development of the use with the etymological meaning (' write under ').

the circumstances ' has established itself in English idiom; ' *in* the circumstances ' is merely the proud variant of those who remember their ' grammar ' not wisely but too well.

Sometimes the argument from etymology concerns a native word. Neville Cardus in his *Autobiography* tells the following story:

> I once tried a gesture in a scene with him [C. P. Scott] that arose out of a question of English usage. In my hurry one night to send up the Miscellany column to the composing-room, I allowed a contributed paragraph to get into print with ' from thence ' in it. As soon as I saw the paper next morning I knew I was, as they say, ' for it '. Scott went through every column lynx-eyed, all excepting the market reports. Sure as death, he tackled me without delay. His whiskers clove the air when I entered his room. " You should know by now," he said with infinite charm and menace, " that the term ' from thence ' is not English and is therefore banned from the *Manchester Guardian*. A man might as well say ' to thither '."

The remarkable thing is that Cardus himself was bluffed by the prejudice of his august chief. True, *thence* means ' from there '. But ' from thence ' has long been, and still is, good English, and ' to thither ' is not. There is nothing more to be said.

Even the writers on language sometimes come under the etymological spell. Fowler, for example, calls etymology to his aid in a confused condemnation of *meticulous*[1] and of *intrigue* as verb (' I am *intrigued* by . . . '). He also argues, with as little logic, against certain hybrids, especially scientific terms, because they are made up incongruously of (for example) English words linked together by a classical particle or rounded off with a classical suffix. He says that since *speed* and *meter* (< O.E. *mete*, ' measure ') are both English, the word *speedometer*, in which the linking *o* is a Greek particle, is a ' monstrosity '. But *speedometer* is the English word, and Fowler's suggested *speed-meter* is not. It is a pity that the word which Evelyn used, when he saw on a coach a device to measure the miles, did not survive to settle the question even before it arose. Evelyn called it ' a way-wiser '.

[1] See *Good English*, p. 196.

Preposition and Apposition

The superfluous *of* or *as to* after ' the question ' is illustrated and commented upon in *Good English*.[1] Here is an
example of the simple error:

> The question of how far he will succeed cannot be
> answered now; David Gascoyne is only thirty-four.
> But he has attempted something more, perhaps, than
> any[2] poet of his generation, something perhaps beyond
> his capacities.—*NS*

In the following sentence the construction is more
complicated. The writer is not using the normal idiom
' the question ' because he has qualified *question* with an
adjective (*unresolved*). Nevertheless the *of* is superfluous;
but we do not quite get over the difficulty by merely
striking it out:

> This is the unresolved question of how the Korean war
> is to be brought to an acceptable conclusion, and, in the
> meantime, how it is to be related to American over-all
> policy.—*O*

The sentence is better reconstructed like this:

> This [that is, something already mentioned] is the
> unresolved question [or, preferably, problem] of the
> Korean war—how it is to be brought to an acceptable
> conclusion, and, in the meantime, how it is to be related
> to American over-all[3] policy.

That's two of his questions, as Hamlet might have said,
but the construction will pass.

Sometimes *doubt* and *question* are confused:

> There was some doubt in people's minds as to just how
> far this scheme would really solve the problem of
> accommodation and social life for overseas students
> and whether all classes of students would stand to
> benefit equally.—*NS*

Both words require an indirect question (noun clause)
directly in apposition; that is, *as to* must go. We have to
choose between (*a*) ' There was some question just how

[1] p. 158.   [2] See p. 211.   [3] See p. 148.

far this scheme . . .' and (b) ' There was some doubt whether this scheme . . .' Since (a) more adequately represents the writer's meaning than (b), it is the obvious choice.

Usage does not easily tolerate the preposition + noun clause formula, though sometimes, in practice, the construction can hardly be avoided. In this sentence the appositional clause, as with *question*, is to be preferred—that is, the *of* after *story* should be omitted:

> And then I met Frank Pick and felt sure that I was right when I heard the story of how Mr. Duff Cooper as Minister of Information took him to see Winston Churchill as Premier.—*NS*

Even better: ' the story of Mr. Pick's introduction to Winston Churchill as Premier by Mr. Duff Cooper as Minister of Information '.

And here *question* and *measure* are so muddled in the writer's mind that he deviates into nonsense:

> The measure of whether you will enjoy it or not, is how much you enjoy Shakespeare's low comedy.—*NS*

All he really means to say is ' You will enjoy it [the play concerned] if you enjoy Shakespeare's low comedy '. But since he hankers after a proportion sum he embarks on the difficult and doubtful idiom with *measure*. If he insists on *measure* he must reconstruct the sentence in some such way as this: ' The measure of your enjoyment of it [the play] is your enjoyment of Shakespeare's low comedy ': that is, you measure one enjoyment by the other, which acts as a kind of standard gauge or measuring-rod.

Consider and Regard

> The American penal system comes in for special attack: the English system Dr. Wilson considers as a model.—*TLS*

The idiom with *consider* and *regard* is dealt with in *Good English*.[1] This sentence is merely given as a reminder and a warning. But in the following sentence matters are not quite so simple:

[1] p. 158.

> It will be recalled that when ' Red ' Lewis heard that his wife, the formidable and dominant Dorothy Thompson (known to her admirers in England as " The Presence "), was considered as a candidate for the U.S. Presidency, he said he hoped she would be elected because it would give him an opportunity of writing " My Day ".—*NS*

Here (unless it simply means *regarded*) the word *consider* has a quasi-technical meaning, and the normal idiom goes by the board. But there is still confusion: the choice lies between the two expressions (*a*) ' was proposed as a candidate for ' and (*b*) ' was considered for candidature at the U.S. Presidential Election '. At an interview a candidate is considered (by, for example, a Committee) *for a post*, not, superfluously, *as a candidate*.

Choice and Alternative

Under the following incorrect sentence, four possible correct constructions are given which illustrate the difficulties and the dangers with these two words:

> The choice, as Mr. Angus Maude expressed it, is to do everything (or nearly everything) somehow or to do the most important things really well.—*TES*

(i) ' The choice is *between* doing . . . and . . . doing '
(ii) ' The alternative is to do . . . *or* . . . to do '
(iii) ' The alternatives are to do . . . *and* . . . to do '
(iv) ' We must *either* do . . . *or* . . . do '.

In the next sentence the problem is complicated by the elliptical bracketing (see p. 37):

> Here the broad choice is to reduce either the quality or the quantity of education provided.—*TES*

If *choice* is used the preposition *between* must follow, and that in turn involves a plural or a double (*a* + *b*) object;[1] we should have to amend, therefore: ' the broad choice is between reducing the quality and reducing the quantity '. But this tends to blur the real meaning of the sentence. It is better to drop *choice*, and use the simple alternative construction: ' We must reduce either the quality or the quantity of the education . . . '

[1] See *Good English*, p. 38.

To sum up, here are the idioms:

> the choice is between A and B
> the alternative is A or B
> the alternatives are A and B.

MIXED IDIOM

One of the commonest errors in writing is the confusion of two (or more) idioms—what is called in *Good English* ' mixed idiom '. The following representative examples illustrate some of the more subtle dangers and problems:

Flirting with Comparatives

(a) Perhaps no other twentieth century writer except Wells could conjure into his characters bouncing, inescapable vitality.—*TT*

(b) His genius was not of another kind from his own folk, but a heightened degree of the language of the fields.— *TLS*

(c) The scene is a New York lodging house, the water-front on a hot summer night, and the vast prospects in the minds of two young people who are discovering (from a different point of view than in Mr. Mosley's book) the landscape of love.—*JL*

(d) No sooner there but Shelley has rushed off to Cuckfield, in Sussex, partly to raise funds and partly to meet Elizabeth Hitchener, the schoolmistress.—*JL*

In the first two sentences the writer flirts with a comparative and then deserts it for another love; in the third he deserts another love for the comparative. To come, as the excellent Salanio (or was it Salerio?) said, to " the plain highway of talk ":

(a) In the first sentence *other* should, like all comparatives, be followed by *than*. But it is better omitted; then *except* can be retained after the negative *no*.

(b) Ellipsis (pp. 51 ff.) has complicated this sentence. If the comparative (*another*) is to be used, then the sentence will run: ' of another kind *than* that of his own folk '. But this is scarcely English. The writer's other love was *different*, but again the ellipsis

cannot stand: ' was different from that of . . .' However, the whole sentence is so woolly that it qualifies
for a place in Chapter IX.

(c) In spite of Fowler's rather perverse note on the
subject, *from* is the preposition that follows *different*
in modern English usage. At any rate, *different* is
not a comparative, and therefore cannot be followed
by *than*. Again, the ellipsis is awkward. Open out:
' *from* a different point of view from that in . . .',
though the two *froms* are admittedly awkward.

(d) No sooner *than*, not *but*.[1]

Among and Between

> It is a rare experience to meet, among the flood of
> competent fiction, a novel written in full consciousness,
> by the whole person, just as a good poet writes.—*JL*

> These were the leaders only; among the rank and file
> marched many men with names as memorable. Among
> so rich a treasure the selection of single dramatists must
> depend on the caprice of the critic.—C. V. WEDGWOOD:
> *Seventeenth Century Literature*

Strictly, *among* like *between* demands a plural object.
There is something odd about ' among the flood '; and the
half-dead metaphor only accentuates the oddness. The
two examples in the second sentence are passable; that is
to say, they cannot be condemned outright. But since
among implies plurality, and since there is the obvious and
safe alternative (*in*) it is difficult to see why a writer should
tempt Providence with *among* + singular. Say ' in the
flood/rank and file/so rich a treasure '.

> Historians are not thinking enough of the problem
> which will, among other things, put Penguin Books out
> of business.—*NS*

> From this comes, among other things, the clear sense of
> colour found in them.—*O*

These sentences are not open to criticism; they are
quoted merely because they happen to contain a recognised idiom, ' among other things ', which defies logical
analysis. How can a thing—the thing you are talking

1 See *Good English*, p. 90.   2 See p. 34.

about—be among *other* things? It can't, and that's the end of it; but the idiom has been sanctified in use. Fowler is silent on the matter, though he discusses the parallel (s.v. *of* [7] ' You are the man of all others '. There is, of course, nothing to be done about it; like some other idioms, ' among other things ' laughs at logic.

> Among contemporary novelists, he is the standing justification for that much overworked phrase, a good craftsman, and one imagines him testing and fitting the pieces of his book together like a gunsmith.—*NS*

This is rather more subtle. The point is this—What is the reader led to expect when a sentence begins ' Among contemporary novelists'? Surely, that the writer is going to pronounce upon the virtues or vices of a particular novelist. It is, therefore, important that the *one* should be stressed in contrast to the *many*; and the sentence should read 'Among contemporary novelists, *he* is the only *one* who justifies', or, more dramatically ' he alone justifies'. In any case, if the verb *to be* is used, the complement must be *novelist* or an equivalent noun; ' among *novelists* he is a *justification* ' is nonsense.

Between with the plural has much the same significance as *among*: there is only the finest distinction between ' *among* the trees ' and ' *between* the trees '. But it is worth while remembering that, because the root of *between* (and its poetic variant *betwixt*) is the *tw*[-] of *two*, purists will not allow the construction ' between *a*, *b*, and *c* ' (on the analogy of the legitimate ' between *a* and *b* '). But unless in the expression ' between the trees ' the plural is always assumed to mean two trees only, there seems to be little in the prohibition. The construction is fairly frequent in modern usage. Here is a typical example:

> It [the conference] will be between the representatives of the men now on strike, their employers and the union officials.—*TES*

And since there is no obvious alternative (*among* won't do), the construction in this context is justified. After all, idiom and usage are stronger than etymology. A man may halt between *three* as well as between *two* opinions.

Inflict and Infuse

These are such old and familiar confusers of ordinary men that it is comforting, even if a little surprising, to find them wrongly used by practised writers. However, here are one or two examples:

> But they could not help infusing it with something of the ideals and convictions they themselves held.—*TES*

> And it is not difficult to distinguish between the poet who infused an old subject with contemporary meaning . . . —C. Day Lewis: *The Poetic Image*

The choice is between ' *infusing* something *into* it ' and ' *imbuing* it *with* something'.

> Alas, this is a promise which is never fulfilled, and we are inflicted with fifteen pages of wrangling ecclesiastical dispute. Perhaps clarity is the most conspicuously absent of all good qualities.—*O*

There is a simple confusion of *inflicted* with *afflicted*, the correct word here. If *inflict* is used, the sentence should run: ' and fifteen pages of wrangling ecclesiastical dispute are inflicted upon us'. The constructions are: ' *afflict* A *with* B ', ' *inflict* B *upon* A'. It is worth while remembering two or three other similar pairs:

> *fill* A *with* B : *instil* B *into* A
> *replace* A *with* B : *substitute* B *for* A
> *prefix* A *to* B : *preface* B *with* A
> *force* A *into* B : *enforce* B *upon* A
> A *implies* B : *infer* B *from* A

Sitting on the Fence

In the following sentences the writers have confused fixed, conventional idioms. After each example the idioms so confused are set out, usually without comment. It is not quite true to say that both or all will be equally suitable to the context, since here as elsewhere in language the law of synonyms operates. The writer has still to make his choice, remembering that no two idioms can have precisely the same use and significance. One thing is certain—he cannot avoid choosing by merely sitting on the fence. To mix the idioms is, as Theseus put it in an illogical idiom of his own, " the greatest error of all the rest".[1]

> And you will spend hours of delight browsing through its pages wherever the mood takes you.—Advertisement for *Chambers's Encyclopædia*

' Browse *in* ' *or* ' glance (read, look) *through* '.

> A highly ambitious lighting-plan, erratic in execution, certainly did not show them at their best light, and the stage-management appeared to be overwhelmed by the occasion.—*O*

'At their best ' *or* ' in their best light '.

> A lovely middle-aged mother, in company of one of her contemporaries and admirers, goes at his suggestion to hear him lecture at her son's University.—*JL*

' In company with ' *or* ' in the company of '.

> He goes to the point of insisting on Shakespeare's plays being performed either in steady daylight or in a steady light representing daylight.—*TES*

' Goes to the length of ' *or* ' makes a point of '. The reader is invited to comment on the gerund construction in this sentence.

> And Miss Peggy Simpson, who had a little let us down as Violet in the first act (not harsh or hard enough by half), came nearer up to the mark in the scenes with Hector's father.—*NS*

' Came nearer to the mark ' *or* ' came more nearly up to scratch '.

> This is the third edition, brought up to date down to the " Atomic Age " in science and engineering, and including 250,000 words on the Second World War.—*NS*

' Up to date ' *or* ' down to the "Atomic Age " '. The expressions (they are scarcely idioms) in this sentence

[1] See p. 210.

are not mixed. In an excess of zeal the writer has two separate time phrases where one would do. This would not matter so much—indeed, one could justify it on the grounds that he is intent on making his meaning doubly plain—but for the incongruous association of *up* and *down*.

> There is not so much as a single comma, colon or full stop in the whole 300 pages.—*TLS*

' Is not so much as a comma ' *or* ' is not a single comma '. A nice point: but they are separate expressions, and are more effective kept apart.

> The boot isn't only on the one leg there.—RANDOLPH CHURCHILL, in a broadcast.

This is typical of mixed idiom in speech. We are all guilty of it occasionally, since we have no time to ponder and revise, but use words, constructions, and idioms as they come. Here, it would seem, the speaker has a hazy notion of one or two figurative expressions incorporating *leg* or *foot*—' not a leg to stand on ', ' to stand on one's own feet ', ' the boot is on the other leg '. And out of these he fashioned a new but inadmissible idiom of his own.

> And how curious the cool air with which Mr. Hughes relates all these curiosities, stepping aside from time to time to cock a sidelong glance at Welsh nationalism, or life in a hospital, or a scene in the park ! He compels on the reader his own acceptance of all this: it is only on reflection that something alien, something artificial, seems to linger in memory.—*O*

' Cock a snook ' or ' cast a sidelong glance '.

In the second sentence there is, it would seem, a mixture of two such expressions as: ' thrusts on the reader his own acceptance ' and ' compels the reader to accept '. But it is hard to say definitely. The whole passage is so hazy as to have little distinct meaning.

> But soon he and Bedser had fallen to the teasing length of Tattersall, and with Surridge far out to sea with Hilton Lancashire were finally left with 39 runs for victory an hour before lunch.—*T*

'At sea' *or* 'far out of his depth'.

> These things are said not to cast the shadows of dirty linen on holy ground.—*JL*

We can only guess what expressions or idioms were in the muddled mind of the writer of this incredible sentence. I venture a suggestion: 'cast a shadow over', 'stand on holy ground', 'wash dirty linen in public'.

> Major Legge-Bourke surely hits the right nail on the head by advocating that we should give these unfortunate victims moral encouragement.—Letter in *The Times*

'Hits the nail on the head' *or* 'is on the right lines'.

> As for *A Doll's House*, once again one found oneself completely subdued to the old ogre's spell.

'Subdued by the old ogre' *or* 'under the old ogre's spell'.
There is a similar confusion in the following sentence, where a verb (*matched*) is imposed upon a simple preposition + noun phrase:

> The singing and dancing of the other rompers are unimpressive matched by American standards, but the show is broad-based on Emney; that foundation-member does not fail.—*O*

'Matched with those of the Americans' *or* 'by American standards'.

> Nothing misses his eye and in this, as well as in his vivid prose, he reminds me of G. W. Stonier who has already made a reputation.—*JL*

'Nothing escapes his eye' *or* 'his eye misses nothing'.

> It is needless to say that the dustman Doolittle is more than safe with Charles Victor.—*O*

The idiom is 'Needless to say, the dustman ...' It is a parenthetic phrase—that is, the following clause is not

[1] See p. 76.

a noun clause depending on it; so ' needless to say *that* ' is not English. The alternative here would be ' It is unnecessary to say that . . .[1] '.

> And you must be hard put, for the moment, to find (or invent) another stick to beat the United States.—Letter in *NS*

' It must be hard for you to find ' *or* ' You must be hard put to it to find '.

There is a similar confusion in the following sentence:

> The reader is often hard put to know what precisely is happening.—*TLS*

' Is hard put to it to know ' *or* ' finds it hard to know '.

> Uncertain as are the prospects of a Persian acceptance of Mr. Stokes's proposals, it would have been helpful to his fellow-countrymen if they at least could have been provided with a clearer picture of his offer.—*DT*

The expression ' uncertain as are ' is an idiomatic inversion which should be followed by an actual or implied antithesis—' this much is certain ', ' the situation is nevertheless clear '. There is no such antithesis here, and the inversion is therefore unjustified. The writer means simply 'As the prospects are uncertain '.

---

[1] Constructions with the various forms of *need* are worth noting:
  (a) *Verb*
    He *need* not take the examination.
    Why *need* you worry about it?
This is the abnormal uninflected *need* in negative and interrogative sentences, followed by the infinitive without *to*. The normal, less idiomatic, forms require *to* in the infinitive: ' He *does* not *need* (or *needs* not) to take the examination '; ' Why do you *need* to worry ?' In the following (negative) sentence the *to* in each infinitive is superfluous:
    He says of mass democracy that we need not to defend it so much as to create it.— *O*
  (b) *Noun*
    If *need* be . . .
    There is no *need* to . . .
  (c) *Adverb*
    Needs must when the devil drives.
    He must *needs* fling his wicket away.

> But he did initiate informally and with some diplomatic irregularity a bogus "feeler" about fresh negotiations which the British Government had no recourse but to reject.—*DT*

The writer means 'had no option but to reject'. It is difficult to see how the normal idiom 'have recourse to' could have meaning in this context.

> There is an audience for the classics, provided stars be laid on, and there are many who will take anything French as being a masterpiece without question asked. —*O*

'Take for (a masterpiece)' *or* 'regard as (being)' *or* 'consider (a masterpiece)'. 'With no questions asked' *or* 'without question'.

> In the fourth place, Freya Stark follows the example of her predecessors in devoting to clothes, cosmetics and jewellery the importance which, in the life of any explorer, they ought to occupy.—*O*

'Devote attention to' *or* 'give, assign importance to'.

Confusion of Verbs

In the following sentences confusion of thought has led to the choice of the wrong verb. The verb concerned is italicised:

> *The Petrified Forest*—Robert Sherwood's play, with Bette Davis, Emlyn Williams, Gary Merrill—*obliged* me to miss the first fifteen minutes of a controversy *Does the Law of Marriage Need Reform* ?—*O*

This use of the verb *oblige* with an indirect personal object and the infinitive is now archaic, and confined to legal language, where *oblige* has its original Latin meaning (*obligare* = 'to bind'). The passive, 'I was obliged', belongs to modern usage; but it is important to remember that it cannot be associated with an instrument or agent —that is, we can say 'I was obliged to go' but not 'I was obliged by him to go'. The writer of this sentence should have used *compelled*, or, by reconstructing the sentence, the idiomatic passive of *oblige* noted above: " Having

heard *The Petrified Forest* through to the end, I was obliged
to miss . . . ".

> The author *delves* back into the origins of printing and
> *takes* issue with some of the oft-repeated orthodox views,
> and he describes the latest methods of illustration to
> which we often see references but seldom get an ex-
> planation.—*JL*

Adam delved and Eve span, but *delve* in normal modern
usage is always figurative; the stock phrase is ' delve into
the past '. And whether literally or figuratively we do
not ' delve *back* into '; probably the writer means simply
' goes back to '. In the second clause he confuses ' takes
offence at ' and ' joins issue with '. His final error is to
omit ' of which we ' before *seldom*—or (more idiomatically)
an *of* at the end of the sentence (' but seldom get an explanation of ').

> The conscious brain, by which we are human and in
> God's image, is something that should always *occupy us
> with* wonder and even worship. Words, in themselves
> an act of faith because they link us to each other and to
> the past, help to make that relationship.—*JL*

In this context *occupy* means ' busy, keep engaged '
(COD); but this is scarcely the writer's intention. He
meant ' should always *fill* us with wonder and even *inspire*
us to worship '. The rest of his sentence is equally woolly
and vague. Why are words an act of faith because ' they
link us to each other '? What relationship do they help
to make?

> Profiting by these aspects of infinity, he has been able
> to *endure* the arduous industry entailed by his researches
> and to write an interesting and useful book about a man
> who lacked ethical or even intellectual attraction.—*O*

A man may endure pain, hardship, or even toil, but not
industry; toil is, in fact, the word here, especially as the
stock epithet *arduous* is used.

> Their youth, their initial innocence, the dewy verse in
> which they make known their love, *approach* them more
> closely to Romeo and Juliet than to any other pair.—
> C. V. WEDGWOOD: *Seventeenth Century Literature*

This causal use of the verb *approach* (='make [them] approach') is now archaic. SOED gives an example from Scott: ' He approached to the fire a three-footed stool '. But normally *approached* is followed by an indirect object or an object governed by *to*.

> He did something of the kind to English poetry, *enfranchising* the coming generation from French and Italian leading-strings.—C. V. WEDGWOOD, *Seventeenth Century Literature*

Enfranchise is an ' absolute ' verb; it means ' give freedom (to) ' or ' make free ' in general, not from any particular thing.   Certainly it is not used, as here, with a semi-metaphorical figure (' from leading-strings '). The possible verbs are *freeing, loosing*.

> In the second section he *examines* how his ideas, prejudices and sympathies were the product both of his own temperament and of the climate of his age.—*O*

The verb *examine* should have a noun as object, not a noun clause.   Substitute *tells*, or amend: ' examines his ideas etc. to show how they were . . .'. So also *advocating* in a sentence on p. 72. *Advocate* should have as object a verbal noun or a noun, not a noun clause: ' advocate the giving of moral encouragement to ' or ' advocate the moral encouragement of '.   The following sentence contains a similar misconstruction with *congratulated*:

> Professor Macdonald is *to be congratulated* that he has not found it necessary to obtain a visa from the Kingdom of Dullness to endorse his passport to scholarship.—*JL*

The correct construction is ' congratulated on not finding it necessary '.

> But his main contacts with Shelley *sum up* to one of the most extraordinary series of experiences in the history of human relationships.—*JL*

The writer means *add up*; *sum up* is an intransitive or transitive ' particle ' verb (see p. 95)—' To sum up, his main argument was . . .'; ' We can sum up his main argument in this way . . .' It means ' make a *summary* (rather than a *sum*) of '.

> We have waited long for this difficult enterprise to be *attacked*, and it is a pleasure to say that it has been carried through with notable success by a New Zealander, Mr. C. E. Carrington, already known through his services to the great Cambridge History.—*JL*

An enterprise is *undertaken* not *attacked*; and once having been undertaken, it may, as in the second clause, be carried through.

> . . . the anti-Catholic laws of Elizabeth, which had not been *repealed* from the Statute Book.—*DT*

Repealed is an absolute verb; the appropriate verb here is *removed*. If ' from the Statute Book ' is omitted, *repealed* of course may stand.

Stereotypes

(*a*) But in reviews, hard pressed for space, it may often seem that the best novels are the most carped about, while lesser books, admirable in their more limited intentions, achieved unqualified praise.— *O*

(*b*) In brief, what has occurred is a sharp division in the Cabinet between the Morrisonians and the Bevanites which has been for the time, at least, amicably patched up.—*NS*

(*c*) A lot can be said in sixty words, and if this column had been the author it would have suffered umbrage. —*Punch*

(*d*) Why women were shy of glasses may be because[1] they loomed so large on elderly male noses.—*T*

(*e*) So it is with the little fellow in *A Breeze of Morning*, whose devotion to his elder sister Ann is so impressive that it is bound to break bounds and carry him on the flood to some other adoration outside the family.—*JL*

(*f*) To exclude our patron saint from the Festival merely because his finest portrait is the work of a foreign artist would be to cut off the nose of merrie England to spite a dead Italian's face.

There are certain idioms (often associated with particular and peculiar words) that are, as Lamb said of certain books, " great Nature's stereotypes ". They are, in fact, clichés;[2]

[1] See p. 211.   [2] See *Good English*, p. 167.

but only clichés in the good sense that they are stereotyped phrases without any alternative or substitute, and preserve something which would otherwise have been lost: they exist, that is, in their own right. One such—'a moot point '—is used on p. 25. Six others are exemplified in the above sentences, but they have all been carelessly remembered and unjustifiably tampered with by the writers. They are:

(a) carp *at*. This, at any rate, is the modern usage. In earlier days *carp* was often used intransitively (= ' talk querulously '). Nowadays only a critic carps (at); hence the fixed phrase ' carping critic '. SOED says that *carp* is associated with *cark*, which gives us another isolated cliché, ' *carking* care '.

(b) The only thing that can be metaphorically *patched up* is a quarrel—not a war, or a contest, or a division or anything else of this kind. A division, rather oddly, may be *healed*.

(c) *Umbrage* is a word that has forgotten or outlived all its literal and early metaphorical meanings (shade, protection, hint [=shadowy appearance], pretext, suspicion), and survives only in two half mysterious, but rather delightful, stereotyped idioms ' to *give* umbrage ' and ' to *take* umbrage '. Certainly, ' *suffer* umbrage ' is not English; so this column which so acidly and so shrewdly criticises others might for once criticise itself.

(d) The phrase ' loom large ' is a stereotyped idiom; *loom* (COD) means ' appear indistinctly, be seen in vague and often magnified or threatening shape '. It is used of *e.g.* a tree or a motor-car seen through fog, or metaphorically of *e.g.* an experience or an ordeal. These glasses merely ' *seemed* or *appeared* so large '.

(e) A river (for such metaphorically the little fellow's devotion appears to be) may break its bounds or burst its banks; but ' break bounds ' (without a qualifying possessive) is a stereotyped idiom meaning ' escape from restrictions ', and used generally of men or animals.

(*f*) The stereotype or fixed idiom is ' cut off one's nose to spite one's face ' (= ' indulge pique at one's own expense ', COD). But you cannot spite another person's face by cutting off your own nose.

Some writers modify such stereotypes without doing them any real harm, like this:

> Or perhaps it would be truer to say that he is known but not deeply felt and that we are *at a respectful loss* when we are told of his pre-eminence in Russian literature.—*NS*

> This would indeed be a *pretty kettle of budgetary fish.*—*NS*

> The *judicial cat* has once more found its way [*i.e.* ' been put '] among *the etymological pigeons.*—*IL*

But on the whole the practice is not one to be recommended.

Geometrical Idiom

(*a*) The real discussion centres round the relation of rearmament to foreign policy.—*NS*

(*b*) This picture, which is set in a women's D.P. camp in Italy, centres round the case of an unmarried Jugoslav girl.—*O*

(*c*) His fellow countrymen will certainly have noted and appreciated the fact that he centred himself in his own Glasgow and never, like Sir James Barrie for instance, " came South ".—*NS*

(*d*) However, Professor Valentine is scrupulously fair, and his numerous footnotes provide leads to a variety of viewpoints.—*TES*

(*e*) From a wider standpoint, our fuel difficulties in this country must be seen as part of a world problem.

(*f*) Yet this very inability to see things except from her own narrow angle enhances the historical and social value of her *Journal.*—*O*

"And so ", said Bully Bottom to the woolly and incoherent Peter Quince, " grow to a point." Idiom, too, has its points; some of them are exemplified in these six sentences. Centre *round* is threatening to establish itself as a legitimate idiom; but it represents an odd confusion

of the (centre) point and the circumference. True, ' centre
on ' does not bear logical analysis, but it is the better
idiom, and is therefore to be preferred by careful writers.

In sentence (*c*) the writer has been betrayed into the
indefensible ' centre *in* ' because mentally he confused
' established himself *in* ', ' devoted himself *to* ', and ' centred
himself *on* '.

The other three sentences merely suggest one or two
curious questions:

(i) What are *leads* to a viewpoint? Clues? Encourage-
ments? Directives?

(ii) Is it true to say that *viewpoint* is, for the most part,
used literally, and ' point of view ' used metaphorically?
Would ' points of view ' be better in this sentence?

(iii) Can the utterly non-Euclidian conception of a wide
(or wider) stand*point* be justified, even in metaphorical
idiom?

(iv) What geometrical picture does the phrase ' from a
narrow angle ' suggest? ' To see a thing from a particular
angle ', ' to see a thing from a narrow angle '—are these
idiomatic phrases equally justifiable?

The reader is invited to think on these things. My own
comments are on p. 184.

Miscellaneous

And here are a few odd confusions, with comments, to
end the chapter.

> That would be better than nothing, but our summer is
> brief, and who knows but the writer of this review may
> not find his opportunity to walk discreetly away from
> the office on a Wednesday or Thursday when the sunshine
> promises a blessed match at Guildford or Chichester?
> It was hard to get over the extinction of the county
> matches at Leyton.—*S*

The ' writer of this review ', thinking no doubt of that
' blessed match at Guildford or Chichester ' with the senti-
mentality which has afflicted writers on cricket since the
early days of Neville Cardus, has omitted a *that* between
but and *the*, and then by making his verb (*may find*) negative
has said the exact opposite of what he intended to say.

> With this echo of Calvary, the book proceeds to show the equally parallel intrigue, cruelty, indifference, and bewildered worship involved both before and after the event of the public hanging.—*JL*

Here, the writer means that the intrigue, cruelty and the rest of it were the same before as after the public hanging. But first he puts *equally* in the wrong place; then, possibly realising this error, adds a superfluous *parallel*. The irony of it is that the sentence would be perfectly sound if he omitted *equally parallel* altogether.

> The authentic locations are there, so far as regards locations in this country.—*O*

The writer thought vaguely of the introductory ' as regards ',[1] combined it with ' so far as ', and made nonsense. He means, probably, ' so far as it concerns ' or ' so far as locations in this country are concerned '.

> Thoughtful persons of all kinds must be asking themselves anxiously which are the elements in civilisation which make it worth while the heavy price we seem to have to pay.—*NS*

This construction with *worth* needs care. The thing to be remembered is that the verb ' to be worth ' is in a peculiar way transitive—that is, it demands an object; and when that object is not an actual noun or verb part (gerund), we have to supply a ' stock ' object, *while*, which is the old word for ' time '. So we have, in certain circumstances, a recognised formula, ' to be worth *while* '=' to be worth *the time* spent on it '. Now we are apt to go wrong in two ways. If we express the sentence ' Getting up early is worth while ' with the impersonal or ' dummy ' *it* as subject,[2] ' getting up early ' is still the real subject, and *while* has to be retained as object: ' It is worth while getting up early ', not ' It is worth getting up . . .' But if the pronoun *it* is real, that is, if it represents an actual thing, the sentence will have a simple construction like this:

> The prize is a substantial one. It [=the prize] is worth working for.

Here *it* is the real subject and ' working for ' is the object

---

[1] See *Good English*, p. 145.   [2] See *Good English*, p. 24.

of worth; the temptation is to insert a superfluous *while*. The pronoun *it* (not subject, by the way) in the sentence originally quoted is real (=' civilisation '); so the *while* is superfluous: ' which make it (civilisation) worth the price we seem to have to pay '.

> And if Sussex need bowlers, Middlesex must still rely mainly on players of an older vintage.—*O*

The antithetical *if* is a favourite with journalists, who, like the writer of this sentence, often use it loosely. We can always test the construction by using instead the normal conjunction of antithesis, *but*. Thus this sentence would run something like this:

> Sussex need bowlers but Middlesex need batsmen (or fielders, or a wicketkeeper).

In the sentence as it stands, there is no true antithesis at all; the idiomatic *if* is, therefore, inadmissible.

Here is a sentence in which the construction is legitimately used:

> If it was Donne who affected the shape and nature of their ideas, it needed Jonson's robust personality to throw down for future English poets the restrictive barriers of Italian rhetoric.—C. V. WEDGWOOD: *Seventeenth Century Literature*.

(' Donne affected . . . but Jonson's robust personality was needed . . .'.)

And here are one or two examples for the reader to comment on :

> (a) If the spectacle of Mr. Spender chasing off to Spain, half-committed to the Left-wing cause, but equally impelled by private moral guilt about the fate of a friend, seems to the austere observer feckless, irresponsible and an example of moral frivolity, that is only half the story.—*NS*

> (b) Nevertheless, it will be a great thing to win the toss and if Brown, who has done so only three times in 13 Tests, is overdue for another success it is no more than even odds that he will gain it.—*S*

(c) If in his relations with his " good Blake " he blundered into immortality, his real services to Cowper, both as friend and biographer, really do entitle him to modest fame.—*NS*

(d) If the chapters on marine life are the most absorbing, the accounts of seasonal changes, of currents, tides, storms and human exploration are interesting enough. —*O*

(e) This dangerous chivalry is present at all levels; if it finds its perfect flowering in Mrs. Thirkell's heroines, I suspect Elizabeth Bennet of being the thin end of the wedge.—*NS*

My own comments are on p. 184.

CHAPTER V

WORDS

And as nails well fastened are the words of the collectors of sentences.—*The Book of Ecclesiastes* (R.V. *marg.*)

" I WISH," said Coleridge, " our clever young poets would remember my homely definitions of prose and poetry; that is, prose = words in their best order;—poetry = the *best* words in the best order." It is not a good specimen of his wisdom, but it does serve to remind us that words cannot be treated in isolation, except in respect of their sound and spelling.[1] We must see them at work before we can define or recognise either their meaning or their function. And that in turn reminds us that in these respects no two words can be identical—that ' synonyms ' have only an approximate correspondence. Theoretically only one particular word is appropriate in a particular context. Whatever the ' homely definition ' of poetry may be, that of prose might be well amended as ' the right words in the right order '. For the writer, scratching uneasily with his pen, that rather begs the question. But it is a maxim he does well to remember, all the same.

Writing, too, must reflect the changes that happen to words in meaning and use. In the continual traffic of language words are lifted up or cast down; they come into fashion and then go out again; they graduate from the colloquial to the literary language; they lose or gain a figurative significance; they take on a new relationship with other words in the sentence. They are, in fact, living things, with all that that implies for those who use them, whether in writing or in speech.

It is impossible in this section to do more than illustrate with a number of representative examples what may be called contemporary usage in words. The matter of

[1] And even not always in respect of these. We should have to know the context before we decide between *beach* and *beech*, or *présent* and *présent*, or *lives* (verb) and *lives* (noun).

synonyms is treated adequately in *Good English*,[1] and is only touched upon as occasion arises in this book. In any case, here one cannot go beyond stating and emphasising a general principle. But the use of certain individual words where it raises points of difficulty or interest is commented upon. For convenience, a rough classification is made; but there is not—indeed, there cannot be—any systematic treatment. The reader will merely be warned by the examples I have chanced upon in ordinary reading, without any deliberate or organised search, to have a dictionary by his side when he himself sits down to write, and a Fowler (or some other alphabetical reference book) not far away.

' Bad ' Words

> But the writer too often uses bad words—*wee*, *whilst*, *songster*—instead of good words—*small*, *while*, *thrush*.
> —From a review in *O*

By ' bad words ' the reviewer means those which have only a precarious survival as archaisms, dialect forms, and pseudo-poeticisms. They are not actually dead, but they are at their last gasp—and therefore not fit for the hurly-burly of modern usage. Of the three he quotes, *songster* is the most alive, and indeed might conceivably be the right word in certain contexts. A sentence on p. 44 illustrates a context in which it might legitimately be used.

It is odd how some words (*songster* is among them) become tinged with a kind of false emotional effect, and fall into a semi-archaic twilight; *folk*[2] and *lore*, either together or apart, are examples—they are both good Saxon but, rather inexplicably, doubtful English. For a similar obscure reason the phrase ' God's acre ' for the ordinary English *churchyard* has never established itself. Probably the more utilitarian *cemetery*, *crematorium*, and *necropolis* have added their weight against it. A little group of words associated in the main with the time of day are pseudo-poetical waifs and strays: *eve*, *morn*,

[1] pp. 179-81.
[2] Though with the revival of folk dancing, *folk* (at any rate as a noun-adjective) has taken on a new lease of life.

forenoon (legal, rather than poetical—one is summoned to a court at 10.30 o'clock in the forenoon), *dayspring*, *sundown*, *sennight* (for *week*), and all compounds with *-tide*. *Wee*, which has a reasonably honest English ancestry, still lives in Scottish use, like *bairn*, which (as *bearn*, ultimately from *bear*) was also once good English; south of the border ' wee bairn ' is a sentimentalised monstrosity. Such words as *mickle*, *kirk*, *braw*, *cotter*, *bonny*, which crop up from time to time in writers who vaguely remember the Scottish classics from Scott to the Kailyarders, are better sent back to Scotland.

Whilst is an apparently unnecessary variant of *while*. There are similar pairs: *among—amongst*, *amid—amidst*, *on—upon*, *though—although*, and, as Fowler suggests, it is strange that one or other in each pair has not dropped out of the language. But the fact that it has not is only another proof of the extraordinary richness and flexibility of English. We do not use *whilst* for *while* or *amongst* for *among* on any conscious or formal principle; we are prompted to it by the suggestion of sound, ease of pronunciation, or some subtle verbal association. And while (or whilst) this is so, both words will remain—though probably not for long.

Near Misses

In each of the following sentences there is a word (italicised) which is so slightly off the mark that the error would not be noticed in a casual reading. But in language, as in other departments of life, a miss is as good as a mile.

> I never recovered from its implausible prologue—in which a young man whose wife was in child-birth was persuaded to sit down and listen to the rest of the programme. If he was forbidden to be *restive* in such circumstances, I was most certainly not.—*O*

For *restive* the COD definition is: " (of person) unmanageable, rejecting control; (*erron.*) restless ". Probably the writer has used the word erroneously here; he means *restless*. The two words are not, by the way, of the same derivation.

> " Hamlet " is a long play which has generated such *longitude* of comment as no other play in the world has ever produced.—*O*

Longitude is nowadays a term so exclusively geographical that it is unwise to use it in any other context. As a simple synonym for *length*, the COD marks it ' *joc.*'; and that, perhaps, is this writer's excuse, since he seems to be attempting a rather feeble pun on *long* and *longitude*. Otherwise he would more naturally have said ' such a mass of comment '.

> Miss Black adds that Anouilh works in stimulating company and lists nine French Grade A dramatists. Let the worshippers worship: I want better proof than " Point of Departure " before I fall on my *appraising* face.—*O*

The writer apparently refuses to worship (' fall on his face ') like the others. The expression is an odd one ; but it is reasonable to suppose that if *face* is to be qualified at all it should be by a word like *praising* or *approving*, not *appraising*, which means ' estimating critically '.

> The only feature in the document which rescues it from complete *inanition* is its refusal to concede anything to Bevanism.—*DT*

It is just conceivable but hardly likely that the writer meant *inanition*, whose normal meaning is ' emptiness from want of food ', though it is also used figuratively. The appropriate word in this context would be *inanity*.

> Quite a number of them are inclined to fancy they are writers; but when their jewelled prose, which looked so well among the agency reports and the editorials, is served up in the form of a book, the *misunderstanding* becomes clear.—*NS*

A misunderstanding is a taking of things in a wrong sense, or an incomplete understanding of (a person). The writer means more than that here: he means ' their mistake '.

> Mr. Alan Webb was the triumph of the evening, as a *balmy* baronet whose plan it was to impersonate Boney and order the French troops home.—*NS*

The use of *balmy* in the sense ' wrong in the head ',
' slightly mad ' is comparatively common. But it is worth
while recording that the real word is *barmy* (from *bearm*,
' yeast '—therefore, ' frothy '). COD quotes the slang
phrase ' barmy in the crumpet '.

> Then when these two had added 53 Laker miss-hit an
> off drive and was caught at deep mid-off.—*O*

The prefix *mis-* is often and not unnaturally confused
with the word *miss*, as in this sentence. Normally, it
has the sense ' amiss ', ' badly ', ' wrongly '—it is not a
negative prefix like *dis-*. A mishit, therefore, is a faulty
hit; *miss-hit* represents a contradiction in terms. Even a
Test cricketer could not miss and hit the ball at one and the
same time. In *misfire* the confusion is in reverse. Here
a direct negative is implied, and *misfire* should probably
be (COD) the compound word *missfire* or *miss-fire*.

> Yet he is summed up in Mr. Pearson's *unkindly* comment,
> " He seldom interfered with his cast unless they got
> between him and a box ".

There is (are?) an adjective *kind* and an adjective
kindly, between which the distinction is a fine one; in
general, ' a *kind* thought ' implies something more lasting,
less casual, than ' a *kindly* thought '. The adverb from
kind is *kindly*, and that from *kindly* (though in fact it is
hardly ever used) *kindlily*. Oddly enough, *unkindly* is
rarely, if ever, an adjective. In this sentence, if the writer
wanted to tone down the epithet *unkind* he should have
used the normal modification ' rather (or somewhat) unkind
comment '.

> The singularity of its richly secluded landscape, the
> aberrant charm of its vernacular building, so *distinctive*
> from the grey or tawny limestone of its neighbourhood,
> and the memory of a great man of little fame.—*S*

Distinctive is an ' absolute ' word meaning ' having
distinction or a particular character '. Here the writer
means *distinct*.

> The *undoubtable* distinction of *Spaces of the Dark* is one,
> I think, more of promise than performance.—*O*

The adjectival and adverbal derivatives of *doubt* are *doubtful*[*ly*] (adjective, with its corresponding adverb), *doubtless* (adverb), *undoubted*[*ly*] (adjective, with its corresponding adverb—negative forms only). *Undoubtable* and *undoubtably* are not recognised English words. For *undoubtable* here read *undoubted*.

> In recent years there has been a steady *import* of novels dealing with the special moral and psychological problems that worry Americans in Europe, and English readers may by now be pardonably tired of the subject.—*NS*

The act of importing is *importation*, and that which is imported is an *import*; *importation* is the word required here.

> The author of this tale, a young American settled in England, *purports* to have followed up a few clues as to the possible identity of the unknown woman, and he tells her life-story.—*JL*

The verb *purport* is a difficult one. It is normally used of documents, letters, etc. in the sense ' profess '—' The letter purported to be writted by Oliver Cromwell ', ' The document purported to contain the truth about the mutiny '. Fowler, in a somewhat confused note, says that sometimes, though rarely, the subject may be a personal noun, but only when the person is considered in relation to his speech and actions as a kind of living document. He gives as an example " The Gibeonites sent men to Joshua purporting to be ambassadors from a far country ". The ' author of this tale ' in the sentence quoted is not thought of in any such way; *purport*, therefore, is the wrong word. Substitute *profess*. Notice also ' a few clues to ', not ' as to '. See p. 63.

> The book is written with a firm skill, a *surety* of touch which seems wasted on anything so unlovely as this stupid life.—*JL*

Except as an archaism, especially in the phrase ' of a surety ' (=' certainly '), *surety* means a pledge, usually in a legal sense. The writer here means *sureness*.

He had an extraordinarily fine head; and the spectacle of its upturned majesty, on the summit of Primrose Hill, while he paused and *inveigled*, with pounding gamp, against the imperialism of Cecil Rhodes or the cooking at his club, brought even the most *irrespectful* urchins to the sense of an occasion.—*TLS*

In general " The Spanish Gardener ", which *inveigles* a full portrait into the outlines of a sketch, is a mature accomplishment.—*O*

Inveigle is probably a corruption of the French *aveugler*, ' to blind the senses ', and now means ' to cajole, deceive, entice ', with a person as object. Unless the printer was at fault, the writer of the first sentence is guilty of a downright malapropism. He meant *inveighed* (<Lat. *invehere*, whose past root gives us *invective*). What the second writer means is a mystery. One might possibly inveigle *a person* into *doing* a thing; but ' inveigles a portrait into the outlines of a sketch ' has no recognisable meaning in English usage, ancient or modern.

The first writer's urchins were not *irrespectful* but *disrespectful*. *Respect* has a separate negative prefix for each of its three different suffixes:

*dis*respect*ful*:	'wanting in respect'	
ir [in] respect*ive* of :	'not having regard to',	
	'independent of'. The word is generally used adverbially nowadays: 'The game will be played irrespective of the weather'.	
*un*respect*able* :	'not respectable' *e.g.*, in appearance or dress	

It is from these television workers that I have sought for nearly three years to conceal the apathy, *disinterest* and often open hostility towards the new medium which exists in some quarters of Broadcasting House.—NORMAN COLLINS, as reported in *DT*

The common confusion of *disinterested* and *uninterested* is discussed and exemplified in *Good English*. *Uninterested* has no corresponding noun; *disinterested* has *disinterestedness*; *disinterest* is a ' no-word '. In this context the speaker meant ' lack of interest '.

> The latter is embellished with woodcuts by Joan Hassall, such *atmospheric* little pieces, so superbly made, that a critical article should be written about these alone.—*JL*

We speak of the atmosphere of a play, a meeting, or even a book. But the adjective *atmospheric* has not yet progressed far enough from the literal to the metaphorical to be used appropriately in such a context as this. Recast: ' little pieces with such atmosphere and so superbly made that . . . '. The " stammering ' construction with the commas is irritating and unnecessary.

> His scene, wherever it may be set, is always *meticulously* observed.—*O*

Fowler's rather petulant condemnation of *meticulous* as " this wicked word " is commented on in *Good English*. True, the journalist is still fond of it, but his very fondness has caused the etymological limitation of meaning (' over-scrupulous in a timid way '—Latin, *metus* ' fear ') to be largely ignored, or abandoned altogether. Eric Partridge says that it is erroneously used to mean ' careful of detail in a praiseworthy manner '. If this is true (as strictly it is), the word is wrongly used in the sentence quoted. Fowler—on firmer ground later in his article—suggests helpfully that *meticulous* should be ' a negative complement to *punctilious* '. But few of us remember the distinction. In this sentence ' punctiliously observed ' would be better ; but *meticulously* scarcely causes even a pedantic shrug of the shoulders nowadays.

> The *necessity* of both art and nature to painting and poetry is the subject of the next chapter.—*TES*

The (very awkward) construction with *necessity* would be something like this: ' The necessity for painting and poetry to have/contain/be governed by art and nature '. For *necessity* substitute *indispensability*. The two constructions are:

> necessity for a + infinitive of verb —→ b (object).
>
> indispensability of b to a.

> He knows, and knows intimately and in detail, the
> *articulation* of the human spirit in its hunt for power
> and possession.—*JL*

For *articulation* the COD definition is "act, mode,
of jointing; joint; articulate utterance, speech; consonant".
The only one of these senses suitable to this context is
' articulate utterance '—but the association with a human
spirit on the hunt is by no means clear.

> And it is comic, with a gusto, ceaseless invention and
> an *intransigence* of exposure that one must go back to
> *Volpone* to match.—*NS*

The word *intransigence*, now much in favour, implies
obstinate opposition to overtures of peace or reconciliation.
In this sentence the writer means nothing more than
remorselessness.

> As to occupations, St. Helens is, as near as *maybe*, a
> ' company town ' with 18000 at work in the glass
> factories and five thousand miners travelling to *nearby*
> *pits*.—*NS*

A simple confusion of the adverb particle *maybe* (American, but gaining ground in English; normal English,
perhaps) with the verb tense ' may be '. The fusing of
near and *by* into a single word is still resisted by the purists.
But there is nothing against it, especially when *nearby* is
an epithet adjective, as here.

> The Hotels Executive *respectively* inform passengers that
> in the interests of national economy they have been
> reluctantly compelled to withdraw the Restaurant Car
> Service from this train.

This is not a near but a bad miss. The Hotels Executive
mean *respectfully*.

> This story of the war in the Atlantic, as seen by the
> crews of a corvette and a frigate, is indeed in the old
> heroic tradition, where the enemy is not only the U-Boat
> but the sea personalised in the title, and the human
> *protagonists* embody the simple heroic virtues. Each
> character is firmly fixed.—*O*

[1] See *Good English*, p. 188.

It is an ironic twist that has made Mr. Strauss, as
Minister of Supply, one of the chief *protagonists* on the
Government side in the rearmament controversy.—*S*

On the second of these two sentences a correspondent
wrote to the Editor:

Now the Oxford Dictionary defines the word ' protagonist ' as follows: " From the Greek *protos*, first; *agonistes*,
combatant, actor. A leading personage in a drama; the
principal character in the plot of a story; a leading
personage in any contest; a champion in any cause ".
From the above definitions I would suggest that there
could be only one protagonist. It might be argued with
regard to the last definition, taking the word ' champion '
in its widest sense, that there might be more than one
champion, but in its original sense a champion means
" the winner of a contest ".

Fowler thunders against the common journalistic use of
the word, reminding us that it probably arises from a
confusion of the prefix *pro* ' on behalf of ' and *prot[os]* ' first '
and the belief that the word is the opposite of *antagonist*.
But, after all, many a word from Latin and Greek has
gained a meaning in English which does not square with
its original significance. We are not yet justified in
condoning this loose use of *protagonist*; but it may easily
prevail.

No doubt there are many detailed improvements in
organization of which our average businesses are *susceptible*, particularly in the sphere of labour relations—
greater reliance on foremen and easier promotion . . .—
TLS

There are two constructions with the word *susceptible*: a
matter may be susceptible *of* proof or *of* a certain interpretation, and a person may be susceptible *to* colds or flattery.
In this sentence, for *susceptible* substitute *capable*; the
average businesses are capable (not susceptible) of improvement.

Prefixed Particles

The gross humour, though given with skill and relish,
does not *overlie* the wit.—*O*

The position of Mr. —— ——, whose interpretation of his duties and responsibilities as ' administrator ' seems to have *underlain* a good deal of the trouble, is likely to be clarified in a further statement by the Board of Governors.—*S*

The verb *lie* is intransitive, and *lay* is transitive. In these sentences a prefix (*over*/*under*) is added, and the resultant verbs appear to be transitive. But the intransitive form (*lie*) remains. The reason is that the prefix is not adverbial but prepositional in effect; or, to put it another way, the objects (*wit*, *deal*) are governed not by the verb itself but the disguised preposition:—' lie over the wit ', ' lie under a good deal '. The transitive verb (*lay*) is followed (not preceded) by an adverb particle: ' lay out so much money ', ' lay in a stock ', ' lay down the law '. There is no compounding of the verb and the particle, except in one or two special meanings. We have, however, the noun *outlay*.

English is very rich in what may be called ' particle ' verbs—verbs, that is, which are so linked as to be almost compounded with a following adverb. Thus, ' give *in*/*up*/*out* ', ' keep *in*/*out*/*up* ', ' take *in*/*up*/*out* ', ' write *up*/*down* ', ' set *down*/*in*/*out* '. In this way intransitive verbs develop transitive compounds, and rather subtle distinctions arise. Thus in the phrase ' look up the street ' the verb is simple and intransitive, *up* being a preposition governing *street*; but in the phrase ' look up the reference ', the verb has become ' compounded ' with a following adverb particle (' look up ') and is transitive.

There is a tendency in modern English to extend, following American usage, the idiom by which a simple verb is reinforced by an adverb particle, mainly for emphasis. A well-established example is ' keep on ' for *keep*, and a more modern one ' beat up ' for *beat*.[1] As usual, the guardians of language are rising up in protest; but since the idiom is not new, an extension of it seems natural, if not inevitable.

It is interesting to note that Eric Partridge in *Usage and Abusage* (*s.v.* ' Tautology ') gives a list of tautological

[1] Of course, older senses of ' beat up ' (' beat up an egg ') are not referred to here.

phrases, based on a book *Words Confused and Misused* by the American writer Maurice H. Weseen. Among them are many particle verbs, including the following: *drink up, eat up, finish up, follow after, hurry up, lend out, gather together, link together, meet together, open up, polish up, rise up, settle up, swallow down.* But all these particle verbs are well established in English, and each has a significance that differs from that of the corresponding simple verb. In one or two of them there is apparent tautology ('rise up', 'follow after'), but in most of them there is none at all; if tautology implies repetition (as it does), what tautology is there in the phrase 'drink up'? These expressions, and others in the list, are in fact important contributors to the wealth and flexibility of the English vocabulary and the richness of its idiom. To treat them with even faint disapproval is to flout the genius of the language

This sentence sets us wondering a little:

> Jill continues to reveal herself a liar and a slut who hopes to have her cake and eat it, and James, of course, *loses out* in the end, but makes the discovery that he was wrong to try to impose his own morality on Jill.—*O*

But this piece of intensification is common in American; and there is no real reason why it should not enrich our English vocabulary.

The following sentence illustrates an opposite type of idiom, the omission of the pronoun object in a reflexive verb, leaving the verb intransitive:

> . . . who, unable satisfactorily to *adjust* to the American way of life, tries to kill herself. After much psychological probing . . . she finds herself able to *readjust* to life and to the initially uncouth but fundamentally idealistic young doctor.—*O*

On this I make no judgment except this, that it is an adjustment of syntax which may well establish itself in English.

Aggravate and Enhance

In *Good English*[1] the use of *aggravate* in the sense 'tease',

[1] p. 179.

' irritate ', is noted, and I ventured to prophesy that it would establish itself in our usage. Here is a sentence in which *aggravate* has neither this meaning nor the recognised legitimate meaning ' increase (an evil) ':

> Nothing could more obviously be likely to aggravate Anglo-U.S. relations.—*NS*

The possibilities are: ' upset *or* endanger Anglo-U.S. relations ', ' aggravate the differences in Anglo-U.S. relations' and (with the vulgar sense) ' aggravate the Americans '.

The verb *enhance* also requires care, and in much the same way. It can have only one type of object—a word representing the abstract quality of worth (*worth, value, effect*). In the following sentence for *enhanced* write ' improved upon ', or (keeping *enhanced*) recast, ' enhanced the effect of the book ':

> This was an extremely good feature, and for once I felt that dramatisation even enhanced the book that was adapted.—*NS*

New Words

" Then M. Duhamel," wrote Sir Harold Nicolson, in a recent article,[1] " much to the delight of his admirers, employs new or forgotten words. Such is the way that language ought to be treated by those whose business it is to handle, massage, refurbish and rejuvenate the thing. I have often used words that do not occur in the Oxford English Dictionary even under the designation *arch.*, and I feel refreshed when I have done so. I do not mind very much if I receive letters from doriphores asking me what ' hypoulic ' means. It may happen that one of the words I invent may fifty years from now be adopted by some distinguished writer and will figure in the 2051 edition of the OED as ' hypoulic: rare '."

That is well said. There is no more fatuous and harmful activity of the pedant than resisting new inventions. Sir Harold's implication that the language requires refurbishing and rejuvenating is apt. The present impact of

[1] *Spectator*, 17 August, 1951.

American is all to the good, since there are signs that English is sinking into a somewhat inadventurous complacency. There is no danger of a glut of them. Only those will survive which fulfil a purpose and (more important) have in them something of the genius of the language. It is too early to prophesy concerning Sir Harold Nicolson's *doriphore* and *hypoulic*; perhaps his own explanation will ensure their inclusion in the 2051 edition of the OED.

Of recent inventions, *skylon* for the architectural symbol of the South Bank Exhibition in 1951 is likely to be a survivor of the Festival. It is strange how often when we want a name for a new thing we go back and (to use Sir Harold's term) refurbish an old word: *railway*, *broadcast* and *roundabout* (on the roads) are examples of this. So in quite recent times *airstop* has been adopted (rather illogically on the pattern of *bus stop*) as the term for a helicopter station—a fact which prompted the following verses to a helicopter:

> Since *helico* and *pter* are not
>   In English quite at home,
> And airstop is your landing-spot,
>   Not helicopterdrome.
>
> Should we not then rechristen you,
>   Among aerial things,
> Either, let's say, a winged-screw,
>   Or else a screw-with-wings?

Sometimes an old word takes on almost by accident a particular meaning. A good example is *appeasement*, which means in general 'pacification'. But since the thirties of this century, when British politicians attempted to come to terms with the European dictators, especially at Munich (1938), the word has been used in a bad sense.

There were attempts to find some high-sounding term for what are called 'traffic lights' or more tersely and simply 'the lights'; but nobody ever attempted to give a Greek name to the instrument which we call in good round English a loudspeaker. A little time ago, with the popularising of television, there was some discussion concerning the appropriate name for one who sits down and looks. Probably *viewer* is the answer; it is already beginning to establish itself:

T—D

Not content with inflicting it on evening audiences, the B.B.C. is now extending the suffering to matinée viewers.—*O*

A Short Miscellany

Here are a few miscellaneous inventions of novelties or revivals I have come across in recent reading:

I was still at college, and *tangling* with the works of the Reverend Laurence Sterne, when I discovered the invaluable properties of the word a-moral.—*O*

I cannot recognise the verb *tangle* in any of its meanings. Can this be a pleasant Carrollian portmanteau word for, say, ' dallying with ' and ' tangled in '? Anyhow, it is neat and expressive, and deserves to survive.

And, though Lewis Carroll's book cannot be so neatly *procrustated* . . .—*JL*

From the context it would seem that *procrustated* means adjusted to two contrasted conditions. If so, it is made (probably on the model of *procrastinate*) from *Procrustes*, the robber of Greek legend who, by lopping or stretching, fitted lost travellers to his famous bed.

This was the edition (now out of print) perused by *omni-legent* later Victorian and early Edwardian children.—*S*

The prefix *omni-* may be added, presumably, to any Latin root. I have never seen it prefixed to *-legent* before; but no doubt it is used here because *omnivorous* (in its metaphorical sense) had not quite the meaning intended.

The fog over the early nineteen-hundreds is due to two causes—nostalgia and the camera. Mr. Gore's *Scrapbook* vividly illustrates the *occlusive* power of the second of these powerful influences.—*S*

Occlude is a specialised word for ' stop up ' or ' close '; but the dictionaries have no knowledge of *occlusive:* Does the writer mean ' blotting-out (with fog) '?

> But despite the glitter of her *ambience*, Letty Landon's life was sad.—*O*

Oddly enough, though there is an adjective *ambient* meaning 'surrounding' in a somewhat ethereal sense ('the ambient air'), there is no noun *ambience*. Here it is invented either consciously or unconsciously as a word for 'surroundings' or 'environment'. But it cannot be said to be necessary.

> The publishers refer, by the way, to "passages of passionate intensity". The phrase should not, I hope, mislead readers into expecting *impruderies* untypical of the child-like, almost puritanical writer.—*O*

Pruderies we know and *improprieties*, but what are *impruderies*? The shameless revelations of an imprude?

> By the end of the book Jefferson Hogg is a presence, if not a person; the ironical, tender North Countryman who, after flirting with Shelley's *impossibilism*, Shelley's revolutionism, became a conservative.—*DT*

The COD (1950) knows no such word. But it is a useful one. Shelley was an *impossible* fellow in the half colloquial sense; and *impossibilism* is an appropriate noun to represent that peculiar quality; *impossibility* has another meaning.

> Mr. —— was an *activist* in the trades union movement during the General Strike.—*S*

An activist is a 'practical idealist'. *Chambers's* (1943) gives "*activism*, a philosophy of practical idealism, originated by Rudolf Eucken (1846-1926)". But COD (1950) ignores both *activism* and *activist*. As a term for one who, while actively working in a movement, clings to his ideals, the word seems to be useful.

The rapid political and sociological changes in the world today are having a great effect on language, especially on its vocabulary. New words are needed, or old words have to be invested with new meanings. To condemn a word merely because it is unfamiliar in form or use is to indulge a foolish prejudice. The ultimate question is, Is it necessary?

CHAPTER VI

METAPHOR

Sir Andrew: What's your metaphor?
——*Twelfth Night*

Since metaphor is not only, or chiefly, an ornament but an integral part of language, our use of it is largely unconscious. Unless we are deliberately striving after some particular rhetorical effect, especially in formal speech, we do not consciously initiate and develop a figure through a whole sentence or paragraph. Poets still do in their obscure and difficult way; and now and then a politician mixes a metaphor as of old. But even mixed metaphors rarely have the former picturesqueness and abandon. Here are four excellent specimens discovered by the late R. W. Jepson, who courteously gave me permission to quote them:

> The Middle Danube Valley is a seething cauldron of discontent so that at any time a spark applied to the tinder might result in an outbreak leading to a world conflagration.

> I suggest to them [*i.e.* the party opposite] that they should reflect again, and reflect deeply, before burning their boats on the slippery slope that leads to disaster.

> He was opposed to a fence round Japan and letting her stew in her own juice, as it would create a festering sore with permanent explosive tendencies.

> She hoped the Secretary of State would see his way, without seeming to climb down to Congress, to build a bridge so that the new constitution might have a chance of being launched in an atmosphere of greater goodwill.

But for the most part the modern specimens evoke a superior smile rather than a hearty and sympathetic laugh. Listening to the wireless a month or two ago, I heard a noble lord complain of "an avalanche of small bills sent up by the Commons". It promised something, but petered out into mere incongruity. *The Times*, aided and abetted by Mr (now Sir Winston) Churchill, came nearer to the old standard in this sentence:

> Mr. Churchill devoted much time to unravelling the motives which surrounded the Government's action. He ascribed it to a party manœuvre by the Prime Minister to placate his 'unhappy tail'. By this he meant the Socialist left wing, which had been forced to stomach unpalatable political fare in other directions.

But this sentence itself, after all, only reminds us of that process in language by which the metaphorical is, as it were, assimilated to the literal, and the original image loses its figurative force. This Dr I. A. Richards has discussed at considerable length and profundity in *The Philosophy of Rhetoric*. There is an excellent summary of his argument in Partridge's *Usage and Abusage* (s.v. *Metaphor*). As far as the ordinary use of metaphor in prose is concerned, the important thing to remember is this, that we have to recognise and distinguish three types—living, half-dead (or half-living), and dead.[1] If a metaphor is dead, there is no further trouble; it has become part of the literal language. But many apparently dead metaphors have a spark of life left in them, especially when they are associated in the same sentence with living metaphors. The writer of the above sentence quoted Sir Winston's metaphor 'unhappy tail', associated it with a wing, and gave that wing, by implication of the word *stomach*, digestive organs. It is possible, however, to argue that 'left wing' (of a political party) and the verb *stomach* in its abstract sense (='put up with') are dead metaphors. But in this context—associated, that is, with Sir Winston's living (or, at any rate, half-living) metaphor —they come incongruously to life.

So in the following sentence *off-shoot* of itself is a dead metaphor; but its association with the following live metaphor ('showing its paces') brings it to life again:

> Last week the Old Vic interrupted their own season to

[1] See *Good English*, p. 169, and Fowler, MEU, s.v. *Metaphor* 1.

> give us the chance to see their off-shoot, the Young Vic,
> showing its paces in *The Merchant of Venice.*—NS

True, the whole expression is still rather more dead than
alive, but its completed metaphor, in which an off-shoot
shows its paces, is indubitably mixed. Since the racecourse
figure, in which the Young Vic ought properly to be called
a filly or a foal, is scarcely appropriate, it is better to let
the metaphor unmix itself by almost (if not quite) expiring
in some such harmless horticultural phrase as ' off-shoot . . .
blossoming forth '.

The examples given below are roughly classified. They
illustrate the difficulties and the dangers of metaphor,
whether conscious or unconscious.

1. *Conscious*

In these passages the writers or speakers consciously
ventured (we may imagine) on a particular metaphor and
endeavoured to develop it logically to the end. The first
is quoted from a speech of the Public Orator at Oxford,
as reported by *The Times*:

> Our poet here is almost the only singer; and by proving
> that song can please he guards the grain and fosters its
> secret growth and sees that it shall spring one day to
> harvest—the precious grain of song that our fathers and
> grandfathers knew and their fathers before them.

Here is the familiar figure of the seed and the harvest.
But it is difficult to understand why, if our fathers and
grandfathers and their fathers before them ' knew ' it, it
did not grow to harvest long before. However, apart
from that, the metaphor though trite is sound enough,
except that the verb *knew* (why not *guarded*, since apparently the grain was not lost?) tends to reduce it to the
literal—that is, the speaker reveals that he is thinking
not of the metaphorical grain but of the literal song.

In the next passage the writer seizes upon a metaphor
(or, rather, a simile not quite yet become metaphor)
concerning nuts. First of all a squirrel stores them.
Then, again in a simile, the nuts—hazel by this time—
have been stored (surely not by the squirrel?) in a bushel,

out of which somewhat acrobatically they ' tumble over
each other '.[1] Finally, in a metaphor, they are swept up
again ' into a neat little heap ', not, as we might have
expected, put back again into the bushel. The two similes
and the final metaphor have no vital connection beyond the
common factor *nuts*; there is, in fact, no real logical development of the figure. And all this merely to say that Mr
Lucas's wealth of quotation sometimes obscures his general
theme:

> It must be realised also that certain types of memory
> are condemned to storing quotations as a squirrel stores
> nuts. Mr. Lucas possesses this type of memory; we
> should not be disconcerted if his allusions, instances,
> illustrations, images, contrasts and parallels tumble over
> each other like a bushel of hazel nuts spilled upon the
> floor.
>
>   *   *   *
>
> However much I enjoy these capacities, I admit that
> they may obscure the importance of what the author has
> to say. Only when the hazel nuts have been swept into
> a neat little heap can one discern the thesis that Mr. Lucas
> has in mind. —*O*

The next writer is obsessed with the metaphor of *crutches*,
which with elegant variation[2] he refers to later as ' artificial
aid ' and ' elementary forms of support '. Why being
' soiled and shiny ' should affect their efficacy is not clear;
and it is certainly difficult to understand how they could
' improve a welter '. The third sentence is cloudy. We
are left wondering whether the crutches are two facts or two
types of narrator—a reminiscing invalid and a madman:

> *A Grove of Fever Trees* leans too heavily on its technical
> crutches. And they are two crutches soiled and shiny
> already from constant use by other writers in need of
> artificial aid. One is the fact that its first person
> narrator is a reminiscing invalid. The other is that this
> narrator is Mad, so that Anything May Happen. It is
> only fair to say that the welter of melodrama in an
> isolated white settlement in Zululand is improved even
> by those elementary forms of support.—*NS*

In the following sentence indignation becomes tentatively

---

[1] See p. 48.   [2] See *Good English*, p. 146.

('as it were') and by implication a kettle standing 'permanently on the hob'. No doubt, since it has stood there permanently, it has boiled over (not *overboiled*, by the way, which is scarcely English). But this is not stated definitely enough to justify the phrase 'with equal suddenness' in the second sentence. No suddenness has been mentioned in the first; the kettle boiled merrily, it would seem, all the time. Or rather, in the first sentence there is no real kettle to boil; indignation stands, 'as it were', on the hob, but it is still indignation (not a kettle) that is directed against something:

> His indignation, which stood, as it were, permanently on the hob, was directed against precisely those things which are usually considered proofs of virtue in his time. But it was an indignation which overboiled with equal suddenness at some fresh proof of bureaucratic iniquity or at recollections of the mishandling of a minor problem by Lord Rosebery's Cabinet.—*TLS*

The writer of the next sentence is haunted by death and bones. A psychologist or the latest analyst of imagery and semantics would find in him a good subject. First, the fun of the evening is embalmed; but since the bouquet has evaporated, apparently only bare bones are left to be embalmed. Not that the writer says this; he falls back rather feebly on the literal 'for the record'. In the last sentence *volatile*, no doubt, harks back to the evaporated bouquet, and rather disappointingly forgets the embalmed bones:

> After the party the company would disperse home, where they would try to embalm the evening's fun in private diaries and correspondence. But by then the bouquet of the jokes had evaporated and only bare bones remained for the record; the essence of Smith's comic genius was volatile.—*NS*

And here is a sentence in which the writer cleverly sustains a metaphor from golf. It is open to criticism only on the grounds that it too lightly assumes a knowledge of golfing terms on the part of the general reader:

> Swinging colossally, they top poems into the long grass of the listener's impatience, loft them into the bunkers of his

boredom, cut them into the gorse-bushes of his bad temper.—*O*

2. *The Half-dead*

In each of the following sentences there is a metaphor which is just alive enough to cause trouble. I have italicised the metaphorical word, or words, concerned and added brief comments.

> Where the author indulges in the literary dabblings of his hero, however, the *going* is mawkish and unreal.—*JL*

A metaphor from racing, in the stock phrase ' the *going* is good '. But the *going* is never mawkish or unreal: the author's style or theme may be.

> It marks the conflict between public and private life which is one of the *key* themes of our age and which, on many *levels*, has been most *fruitful* in Mr. Spender's life as a writer.—*NS*

There is just enough metaphor left in these three words to make their coming together incongruous. For *key* say *chief*, and for ' on many levels ', which is a vogue phrase (like ' at top level ') with no very obvious meaning here, say ' in many aspects '. The *key* metaphor is incongruous, too, in the following sentence:

> This ironic *twist* to the end of the story has a certain artistic effect: it ends the book with a fine flourish, but I think it is *out of key*.—*DT*

How does a twist become out of key? Substitute the harmless and quite dead ' out of place '.

> But in the end the *view* we get of Stevenson's youth has *balance*, *warmth* and *charm*, and perhaps if it does not *go very deep*, it is none the worse.—*TLS*

Normally, *view* is a ' dead ' metaphor—a ' synonym ' for *idea*, *opinion*, *thought*. But when a view is credited with ' balance, warmth and charm ', and described as not going very deep, what metaphorical life there is in it rather uncomfortably obtrudes itself. So in the following sentence *viewpoint* comes to life in its odd role as a ' flattener-out ':

> Yet, in these stories, we have distinctions of profession, income, accent and racial origin, but they are all *flattened out* by the writer's *viewpoint*.—O

See also p. 184.

> It is not this Coleridge who is admired: but Coleridge in another of his *roles*, a *garb* more attractive to the modern eye, that of the uncommitted candid inquirer. —O

The apposition has the effect of equating a role with a garb. But the half-dead metaphor thus gratuitously thrown in is quite unnecessary. Omit it, and amend: '. . . roles, more attractive to the modern reader '.

> If too much is attempted at once, of ruinous inflation *swamping* the entire venture . . .

Passable, perhaps, since *inflation* in its semi-technical financial sense is metaphorically dead. All the same, *swamping* jars; it makes us conscious, for some reason, that *inflation* means a ' blowing up ', and that the association of the dead (*inflation*) and the half-dead (*swamping*) is an unfortunate one.

> Let us hope that public interest, although slow to be fully *kindled*, will yet be roused enough to prolong the run.—*TT*

If *kindled* (='set on fire ') is really metaphorical then *fully* is unnecessary; but the writer really means, using the same type of metaphor, ' although slow to burst into full flame '. But for the sake of his sentence pattern as well as to avoid metaphorical confusion he should have been content with ' slow to be fully roused '.

> Into his *net* come all sorts of the strangest Church monuments, signed, very often, by forgotten sculptors who, when their works are ranged together, become real personalities.—*NS*

The metaphor from fishing is, no doubt, rather more

dead than alive.   We admit 'into the net' anything
(including abstractions) that the net could conceivably
hold; that is to say, we are not conscious of the literal
net, which is the origin of the metaphor.   But the idea of
admitting a Church monument causes the metaphor to
become embarrassingly alive.

> Yet the ubiquity of the spirit of competition, which
> *crops* up even in the mildest of men, suggests that it
> is part of the data of the moralist's problem which he
> must seek to *bend* to his purpose and not to eradicate.
> —*TES*

This sentence, with its doubtful pronouns, might well
qualify for a place in Chapter IX.   (To what nouns are
which [line 1], *it*, and *which* [line 3] respectively related?)
The metaphors are only just alive, but a spirit which
crops up and data bent to a purpose are oddities.   In this
context even *eradicate* (lit. 'root up'; Lat. *e-* 'out of',
radix, 'root'), metaphorically long dead, stirs a little
uneasily.

> The flashback method may irritate, and given the
> harsh subject, I should have liked to see its harshness
> made more *rasping*, not *dipped* in the melancholy of a
> *low-keyed* photography.— *NS*

They are all half-dead—*rasping*, *dipped* and *low-keyed*;
and the general effect is one of blurred confusion.   The
writer has played at metaphor, and played very badly.

The Incongruous

> The book is about two English students at Trinity
> College, Dublin, who are faced with the dilemma of
> finding themselves in a dangerously neutral country
> during the war.—*JL*

Dilemma is a Greek word meaning 'double assumption':
it implies a compulsory choice between two things, what
are metaphorically and picturesquely called the 'horns of
a dilemma'.   It follows, therefore, that *dilemma* is something more than a synonym for *difficulty* or *problem*.   The
two horns have to be indicated on which a man finds

himself somewhat vaguely and uncomfortably perched. In this sentence there is no such ' double assumption '; the unfortunate students face a problem, not a dilemma. The reader is invited to pronounce upon the following sentences in both of which the dilemma's two horns are much in evidence:

> The football players had to choose; to lose games or to lose examination marks. It was possible to evade one horn of this dilemma by getting illegal help in the examinations. It was impossible to evade the other horn, to avoid getting beaten by the Navy or a great civilian university.—*S*

> It is a fascinating and impressive story, arousing emotions as mixed as those which placed his own age on the horns of a dilemma, poised between Nature and the urge towards Improvement.—*JL*

My own comment is on p. 185.

In the following sentence there is a picturesque but incongruous variant of the *dilemma* metaphor:

> Ten years ago Mr. George Barker's book of poems *Lament and Triumph* hoisted him on to the knife-edge between promise and achievement.—*TLS*

We cannot but feel sorry for the unfortunate poet. To sit or lie or stand on a knife-edge must be uncomfortable enough; and to be *hoisted* there like a sack of coals (even by a book of his own poems) must have been humiliating as well as uncomfortable. And what exactly was the knife-edge doing *between* promise and achievement?

> This may be a shallow view; but insistence that one is in deep waters has been known to end on the rocks. —*TLS*

View again (see p. 105). The incongruity here lies in the association of the ' water ' metaphor with three separate and unrelated noun forms: the *view* is shallow, *one* is in deep waters, *insistence* ends on the rocks. One image has illogically and inconsequently suggested the other. Say, ' insistence is sometimes dangerous '.

> From Mr. Roy Harrod's recent biography we have

been able to acquire a full knowledge of Keynes's fascinating character and to obtain a comprehensive view of the coruscation of his intellect, observing the wide-lit avenues and twinkling side-streets stretching their tentacles into the night.—*O*

Here again metaphorical suggestion has been at work. Out of the dead metaphor *coruscation* came the rather ornate image of the avenues and side-streets, and that in turn suggested the figure of the octopus; ' with its wide-lit avenues and twinkling side-streets ' would be quite enough without the tentacles.

Though writers as scholarly and sensitive as Maurice Baring and C. M. Bowra have given us translations, we are still left with a skeletal poetry that has lost some of the indispensable verbal blood, the play of vowel upon vowel, the mysterious call of association or disclaimer between word and word.—*NS*

The only point to be made here is that a skeleton (' skeletal poetry ') would surely have lost not some of its verbal blood, but all. Here is another anatomical curiosity:

When Wellington had to resign as Prime Minister, the artery of political information on which Harriet's diary had come to depend ceased to pump, her own interest slackened.—*JL*

It is the heart that pumps, surely, not the artery.

Instead the P.M. tempered the wind to these shorn lambs— 235,000 would be called up, but only for a 15 days' refresher course—and turned the heat on the national purse.—*NS*

The ' temper the wind ' metaphor is passable if Z reservists may be figuratively called ' shorn lambs '. But the question arises whether the next metaphor ' turn the heat on ' has any connection with it. Is it, for example, an antithesis? Presumably the heat is a bad thing for the national purse. But why? In brief, what does the metaphor mean?

I never cease to maintain that what is mostly wrong with wireless is that there is far too much of it, that the harassed scriptwriters and producers are harnessed to a remorseless conveyor-belt.—*O*

Whatever may be the state of the harassed script-writers and producers, it is safe to say they are not *harnessed* to a conveyor-belt; they may conceivably be on it.

> Miss Manning is one of the few women novelists who can tell a story seen through masculine eyes without leaving a trace of lipstick on the cup.—*NS*

This modern metaphor means, I suppose, or implies in ordinary English ' as if she herself were a man '. The incongruity arises mainly from the association of the masculine eyes with the feminine mouth.

> . . . and hopes (poor fool) to resolve his psychic diffi-culties, by taking them along with him and looking at them with the needle eye of loneliness.—*JL*

> The abyss between patriotism, which urges us to save our money, and self-interest, which commands us to spend, is becoming too wide for frail human nature, and like the Gadarene swine we are plunging down the inflationary slope.

> Where in the cloud of restrictions with which we are encompassed is one to draw the line?—*TLS*

The common element in these three sentences is an echo of a Biblical expression, faint in the first and clear in the second and third. " It is easier for a camel to go through a needle's eye "—but what is a needle eye, how does one look with it, and what has it to do with loneliness? Is there also a faint suggestion of *needle* (adj.)=' sharp ', ' closely contested ' as in ' needle match '? Or does *needle* mean simply ' sharp '? The second writer pictures an abyss so wide that for some inexplicable reason we are all impelled to plunge into it—that is, if the inflationary slope really belongs to the abyss. Moreover, through a simile (introduced no doubt to jog the reader's memory) the Gadarene swine join us in the plunge. But they, surely, had no notion of an *inflationary* slope?

The third writer remembers the famous passage about the cloud of witnesses (Hebrews xii. 1), and then suggests drawing a line in the cloud. There is no way out of it; the writer must begin again, and would do well to throw the metaphor overboard.

> The web of European civilization seems to have been
> slung between the ideas of Christianity and those of a
> half-secret rival, centring perhaps (if you made a system)
> round honour.—WILLIAM EMPSON: *The Structure of
> Complex Words*

A hammock might be slung, or a net, but surely not a
web—especially in this context. But even if it were, how
then could it afterwards centre round[1] anything?

> Next in importance is the secondary school, which
> takes second place only because if primary schools
> fail to lay the foundation secondary schools are stymied
> at the start.—*TES*

Under the new rule, golfers will soon not be stymied at
all, but they never were stymied by their opponents' failing
to lay a foundation.

> The material is immense, yet Mr. Troyat has managed
> to give to all the innumerable personages the appropriate
> touch of significance, and to turn a sea of people and
> places into something clear and comprehensible.—*NS*

> There are grand stories of medical courage in face of
> this sea of ignorance.—*JI.*

Shakespeare made Hamlet say " Or to take arms against
a sea of troubles "; and since his day the sea metaphor
has been variously used and abused. The writer of the
first sentence seems to vaguely remember[2] the familiar
metaphorical cliché ' a sea of faces ', and then tries to
graft on to it a quite different idea—the idea of turbidity
and confusion (contrasted with clearness and compre-
hensibility). To the second writer the sea spells not
confusion but massive opposition, as indeed it did to
Shakespeare. Both writers may (with Shakespeare) be
excused if we grant that *sea* has progressed past the mere
metaphorical into the symbolic. Nevertheless, both would
have done well to avoid the metaphor (or symbol). The
first could have said ' a *medley* of people and places ', and
the second might have resorted to an adjective like
incredible or *abysmal*.

[1] See p. 79.   [2] Bang!

Part of Mrs. Thirkell's art is to show how the aristocratic spirit can sail through that morass unsmirched.—*JL*

The publishers of this encyclopædia have always swum manfully against the swarming tide of specialists.—*NS*

Impervious to the impact of other temperaments, and even of events, he swims through the storm, and wins the election.—*JL*

The same kind of confusion occurs in the above sentences —sail through a *morass*, a *swarming* tide, *swims* through a storm (for ' battles through ' or ' faces').

It is a fascinating and curious exploration in which we follow him. Its pitfalls are many, but we come through in little disarray and in general accord with the author.—*TLS*

Exploration, and especially fascinating and curious exploration, is not usually associated with pitfalls; with difficulties, perhaps, and dangers. Perhaps these are what the author had in mind; one would scarcely ' come through ' a pitfall.

If[1] the reader is left feeling that *Dead Man Over All* somehow lacks the final spurt which should sweep such a book to its climax, I think that this is a disadvantage which is indigenous to the author's method.—*NS*

' The final spurt ' is a metaphor of the racecourse—or of the track. But how it can sweep anything to a climax is certainly difficult to understand; a sweeping spurt is an oddity. There is nothing for it but to drop the whole muddled expression and begin again, using either some such phrase as ' somehow never achieves success ' or dropping into expressive slang, ' somehow fails to ring the bell '.

Some of those who were not invited to broadcast evidently suffered attacks of sour grapes.—*RT*

The disappointed would-be broadcasters may have suffered an attack of sickness, indigestion or bellyache— the result (we may imagine) of eating sour grapes—but scarcely an attack of the sour grapes themselves. In

[1] For *if* see p. 82.

modern idiom one cries ' sour grapes ' like the fox in the fable, disparaging for others what one cannot attain to oneself. There is no question of eating them, still less of being attacked by them. Probably this wrong notion arose vaguely from the Biblical image, " The fathers have eaten a sour grape, and the children's teeth are set on edge " (Jeremiah xxxi. 29). It is the second, not the first, half of this sentence which has given us an idiom.

> . . . . our industrial life which was going at half mast before the war.—Mrs BARBARA CASTLE in a broadcast.

Confusion of metaphor is very common, and in some degree excusable, in speech, where expression of thought in language has to be immediate, without the opportunity of preparation and revision. The speaker here meant either ' going at half speed ' or ' was at half cock '; but was beguiled by the irrelevant image of the flag at half mast.

> Nor does the style make things easier, since it is a ponderous machine which grinds out, as it were by accident, a vivid piece of writing on every twentieth page or so, and then lapses again into the Dark Ages of verbosity.—JL

It is difficult to see how a ponderous grinding machine can lapse into ' the Dark Ages of verbosity ', whatever that may mean. There is no mixed metaphor here, as there was in Mr Churchill's reference during the last General Election to " two party machines baying at each other ". The incongruity arises only because the writer forgets the machine by the time he reaches the end of his sentence.[1]

> The history of criticism is tangled, often repetitive, confused by cross-currents, and Professor Atkins has once more deserved our gratitude by sorting out the threads during a period, with a thoroughness readers of his volume on English Renascence criticism will recognise.—S

Into the main metaphor, that of tangled threads, the writer has introduced first a piece of quite literal language (' often repetitive ') and then an entirely different metaphor (' confused by cross-currents ').

[1] See *Good English*, p. 172.

> The irony of the story is quickly mined, and we see it taking shape as the book proceeds.—*JL*

Dashing away with the smoothing iron? It is incredible that a responsible reviewer should imagine that *irony* has any connection with *iron*; but, unless I misinterpret the verb *mined*, the incredible is, nevertheless, true.

> This dangerous chivalry is present at all levels; if it finds its perfect flowering in Mrs. Thirkell's heroines, I suspect Elizabeth Bennet of being the thin end of the wedge.—*NS*

The thin end of the wedge may do many things, but scarcely, like Aaron's rod, burst into flower, or cause anything else to burst into flower. But the sentence, which is included in the *if* puzzles on p. 83, is muddled throughout. Perhaps it means: ' I suspect that Elizabeth Bennet is the inspiration of that dangerous chivalry which is very common in novels and finds its perfect flowering in . . .'. This is merely a guess. I don't know.

> And after half an hour he gained what Lancashire so badly wanted, the scalp of Barton, caught at short-leg off a defensive stroke.

The participle phrase here qualifies *scalp* (see p. 59). An odd mixture of the literal and the metaphorical seems to have finished Barton off altogether. And there, with his scalp well caught at short-leg, we may appropriately leave both him and the subject of metaphor.

CHAPTER VII

SPELLING

Orthography means neither more nor less than the very humble business of putting *Letters* together properly, so that they shall form *Words*.—COBBETT: *A Grammar of the English Language*

IN an excellent article on Simplified Spelling[1] R. A. Piddington stated as his first main point that "English spelling is not as difficult as it is made out to be", It is indeed remarkable that men of the intellectual standing of Robert Bridges and Bernard Shaw should have missed that simple if surprising truth, and indulged in dreams of reforms that, as Mr Piddington points out, would make confusion worse confounded. True, our etymological system has its drawbacks, since it often obscures and sometimes flouts the correspondence of sound and symbol; and it is arguable (indeed, I advanced the argument in *Good English*) that it would be a good thing to return to the loose, almost anarchic, practice of pre-eighteenth-century days. But that is (perhaps fortunately) out of the question. Systematic and artificial reform on Shaw's or some other lines would appear at first sight to be a reasonable solution of the undoubted difficulties. But this is impracticable, not only because there is no English Academy to initiate it and sanction it, but also because it is next to impossible to devise an adequate and consistent phonetic system. Mr Piddington illustrates this by quoting a paragraph from a would-be reformer in which *camels* is spelt phonetically in two different ways (*kamelz, kamels*), and *worrying* is rendered as *worriing* instead of *wurriing*. The simple truth is that (even apart from such inconsistencies) you cannot have a standard phonetic spelling based on a pronunciation which is by no means standard.

So we come back to spelling as it is. And here Mr Piddington makes another telling point:

[1] *Daily Telegraph*, March 24, 1951.

Another widespread delusion is that those who find English spelling deceptive are the victims of its arbitrariness: in other words, that they try to spell logically and that their efforts are not accepted. Far otherwise; investigation reveals the root of their trouble to be a blurred visual memory, on which they unthinkingly rely. Frequently their erroneous efforts are further from being phonetic than the standard spelling, as in ' tenis,' ' whent,' ' Goilath the Gaint,' ' lentgh,' ' sliper,' ' thier,' and ' dectetive '.

To this day, owing to some confusion in childhood, I myself always hesitate between *dairy* and *diary*. In short, the eye plays a great part in the spelling especially of short and familiar words; and since this is so, phonetic has no advantage over etymological spelling.

In *Good English* I hinted at two possible and natural reforms—the standardisation of the *-ise* ending in verbs so that we no longer have to hesitate between *-ise* and *-ize*, and the dropping of the *u* in nouns ending *-our*, as in American. Most writers—especially those who have no Greek—carry out the first reform for themselves, but are often thwarted by the printers. The second has been a slow process in English (we have *terror, horror, governor*, all of which were once spelt with a *u*), and merely needs quickening up by a few journalists and novelists with confidence and vigour enough to defy convention.

It is important that we face the real difficulties and are not bothered with mere trivialities. Time and time again the Saxon *gh* words (*bough, cough, right, rough* and the rest) are quoted as the outstanding symbols of the difficulty of English spelling; and much is made of ' silent letters ', as in *gnaw, knot, sword, psalm* and *solemn*. But in fact to an Englishman these words present no particular problem. They are part of his heritage; he scarcely notices their pleasant eccentricities.

These are, perhaps, his two most urgent questions— When do I double a consonant before a suffix? When do I write *-er* and when *-or*, when *-ent/-ence* and when *-ant/-ance*? And here, I must confess, I am impatient for reform. I wish the answer to the first question could be Never. We should not then be bothered about the number

of *r*s in *occurrence* and the number of *l*s in traveller.
The answer would always be the same. Of course, there
would still be double consonants in root words, and two
consonants would still come together by assimilation or
directly as the result of adding a prefix or a suffix (*suPPose,
iLLegal, diSSatisfaction, witHHold*). And I wish we could
make the second question unnecessary by adding a new
symbol to the alphabet—an *e* upside down (ə), for example,
to represent what is usually called the neutral vowel.
Then we should write *actər* and *bowlər, resistənce* and
insistənce without anxious thought.

But these are Utopian dreams. We have to face the
fact that since our spelling is etymological, some knowledge
of etymology is necessary to cope with it. And indeed if
the important Latin and Greek roots and affixes together
with a number of French words that are familiar in English
word forms were systematically taught in the secondary
modern schools, spelling would (I think) improve. If, for
example, we know the Latin roots *scio* ('know') and
scando ('climb') we are not so likely to go wrong with
words like *conscious, science, descend.* Meaning and form
are brought into relationship, and spelling is by that process
made easier.

An argument often advanced against spelling reform is
that it would tend to sever the close tie of English with the
Classical and Romance languages. Thus if *nation* is spelt
nayshun its root connection with the Latin *nasco, natus*
('be born') and with the French *nation* is quite obscured.
The argument is a strong one; with an artificial phonetic
alphabet, English would to some extent sacrifice her
advantage of having a large vocabulary common to the
other languages of South-western Europe, and would almost
certainly lose her chance of becoming a world language.
Nevertheless, it can be overstressed. I read an article the
other day in which the writer (Dr Henry Bett), from
whom I borrowed the above example (*nation*), discussing
this very matter, complained that to write *dout* for *doubt*
would obscure its origin in the Latin *dubitum.* So it would
—or rather, so it did; for *doute* was the ordinary English
spelling right up to the Renaissance, when the *b* crept in
again as a sign of the original Latin, and it is the spelling

in modern French.[1] There is, thanks partly to Dr Johnson, too much etymology in English spelling. But for better or worse it is our spelling, and we have to make the best of it.

And that brings us back to reality. Though English spelling (as Mr Piddington says) is not so difficult as it is made out to be, there is no denying that it has its snags and inconsistencies. There is no short way to the mastery of it, no spelling without tears. The speller has to do, in the main, two things: (i) train his eye to ' see ' a word, especially a word (often Saxon in origin) which has something odd or difficult about it; and (ii) build up a (long) word mentally on the prefix-root-suffix pattern, remembering what spelling adjustments may happen at the joins. Thus if he has to spell *unnecessarily*, he will begin with *necessary*. This is one of the root words which he has to ' see ' in his mind's eye: *c-ss-a*. If he knows the Latin adverb *necesse*, so much the better. Then, adding the prefix *un-* he is bound to get two *n*s; and if he tacks the adverb suffix *-ly* direct on to *necessary* (*necessaryly*) the very look of the word, let alone any remembered rule, will tell him that *y* turns into *i*.

A few reminders and extra notes are added here:

acq-   In *acquaintance*, *acquit* and *acquiesce*, where assimilation is not complete.

æ   This ligature[2] has almost disappeared in modern English spelling. We keep it in a few Classical proper names (*Æneas*, *Cæsar*), but for convenience in writing usually separate the symbols (*Aeneas*, *Caesar*). It survives, the ligature untied, in *aeon* and *aesthetic*. *Mediaeval* is at present in the transition stage; many people spell it with the simple *e* (*medieval*),

[1] For an interesting reference to this see *Love's Labour's Lost* v. 17 ff.

[2] ligature   A ' binding ' of two letters together (æ, œ).
    digraph   The combination of two letters which represent one sound—*ch, ph, ea, ee, ou*.
    diphthong   The combination of two vowel sounds in one—*fruit, white, ale, go*. It will be seen that sometimes a diphthong is represented by a digraph and sometimes by a single vowel. The word *diphthong* is often loosely used for digraph and ligature.

as in the now established *primeval*. Fowler makes the safe prophecy that the simple *e* will in the end (and very soon) prevail.

aero-   A Greek combination form from the noun *aer* (' air '). We have it in *aeroplane, aerodrome, aeronaut* and several other less common words connected with the science and practice of flight. But the English form is used in *airship, aircraft, airfield* and *airport*. There was an attempt at one time to popularise *airplane* (which is the American spelling); it failed, but unfortunately gave rise to the confused spelling *airoplane*.

al-   The Arabic definite article (*the*), prefixed to certain words that have spelling difficulties, chiefly *alchem/-y/-ist, alcohol* (= 'the stain ') and *alkali* (= ' the calcined ashes '). In *alchemy* the *ch* is hard, as in modern *chemist*, because of confusion with the Greek words *khemia* and *khumeia*.

ante- ⎫
anti- ⎬   *Ante* is a Latin prefix meaning ' before ', and is used in such compounds as *antecedent, antechamber, antedate, antediluvian* (' before the flood ') and *antenatal*; *anti* is a Greek prefix meaning ' against ', and is used in such compounds as *anti-aircraft, anti-climax, anticyclone, antiseptic, anti-socialist* (usually as adjective, ' anti-socialist propaganda '), *antidote* (= ' a medicine given against poison '). But notice *anticipate* (' grasp beforehand '), where the *e* of *ante* has become *i*.

aqu-   The Latin word for ' water ' is *aqua*; but notice the English spellings *aqueduct* (' conveyance of water '), *aqueous* (' watery ').

-ar   The agent suffix (or apparent suffix) *-ar* has various and rather complicated origins. Note *-ar* (not *-er*) in the following words: *vicar, exemplar, burglar, pedlar, beggar, liar*.

ay   Verbs ending in *ay* add *-ed* direct to the stem (*played, delayed*), except *lay, pay,* and *say* (*laid, paid, said*). For the general rule concerning vowel + *y* see *Good English*, p. 238.

b   At the end of some words *b* is silent (*dumb, comb, limb, climb*), and in the middle of others (*debt, doubt*). Usually this *b* results from deliberate etymological spelling in comparatively modern times—that is, representing by a symbol a sound that was long since lost. Thus Milton's spelling of *dumb* is *dumm*; and the common spelling of *doubt* (Lat. *dubitum*) and *debt* (Lat. *débitum*) in older English was *doute* or *dout, dette* or *det* (compare the modern French *doute* and *dette*).

c   Hard (= k) before the 'guttural' or throat vowels (*a, o, u*) and soft before the 'palatal' or front vowels (*e, i*).   One or two points are worth remembering:

(a) If we add a suffix beginning with a guttural vowel (e.g. *-able, -ous*) to a word ending in *-ce*, the *e* remains to keep the *c* soft (*traceable, serviceable*).

(b) If a word ends in *-ic* a *k* is added to keep the *c* hard before a suffix beginning with a palatal consonant (*trafficking, trafficker*); if the *k* is not added the *c* becomes soft (*music — musician, mystic — mysticism*).

(c) Note the (hard) *c* in *arctic, antarctic, character*.

ch   In nearly all words where *ch* is hard (= k) it is derived ultimately from the Greek X (= *kh*).   Here are a few miscellaneous examples:

Greek	English
khoros ' song and dance '	*chorus, choir, chorister*
khronos ' time '	*chronicle, chronometer* (' time-measurer '), *chronic* (' lasting ', ' lingering ').
knasma from } *khasko,* ' gape ' }	*chasm*
kharakter, ' an engraving stamp ' }	*character*
pakhus ' thick ' } *derma* ' skin ' }	*pachyderm* (' a thick-skinned quadruped ').
psukhe ' breath ' ' soul ' }	*psych* —⟨*ology* / *ic* / *iatrist*⟩ (See also under *p*, p. 125.)
stikhon ' line ' (of verse) }	*distich* a couplet (in verse).
khrusos ' yellow ' ' golden '	*chrysanthemum* (' golden flower ') *chrysalis, chrysolite*

The word *ache* has a hard *ch* in modern English pronunciation.   In Old English the verb was *acan* and the noun *æce*; both were later spelt *ache* and pronounced with a soft *ch*, like the name of the letter H. Shakespeare puns on this in *Much Ado About Nothing*:

> *Beat.*   By my troth, I am exceeding ill.   Heigh-ho!
> *Marg.*   For a hawk, a horse, or a husband?
> *Beat.*   For the letter that begins them all, H.

Doctor Johnson wrongly derived the word from the
Greek *akhos*.

The prefix *arch*, from Greek *arkhos*, ' chief ', is pronounced with a soft *ch* when in well-established compounds (except *archangel*): *archbishop*, *archdeacon*,
archduke.   But in what the COD calls ' literary ' words,
it has a combinative form *archi-* or *arche-* with hard
ch: *architect*, *archetype* (' original type or model '),
archidiaconate, *archipelago*.   The words *archive* and
archaic have the hard *ch*, being derived not from
arkhos, but from *arkhaios*, ' old '.

cr   Note *crystal*, *crypt* and *cryptic*, not *chr-*.

ct (=x)   Fowler and others prefer the etymological spellings
connexion, *inflexion*.   The SOED says dogmatically
(and quite wrongly) that this spelling " is most used
in England ".   But since the simple verbs are *connect*,
inflect, and since the parallel forms *deflexion* and
reflexion have almost (if not quite) dropped out of use,
it seems reasonable to forget the Latin forms in *x*
(*connexus* etc.) and stick to the forms that show
obvious relationship with the normal verb: *connection*,
inflection, *deflection*, and *reflection*.   The distinction is
as unnecessary as that between *-ise* and *-ize*.   Note,
however, the two forms *reflective* and *reflexive*, between
which there is a difference in meaning.

de- ⎫
di- ⎬   The following spellings should be noted.   In each
dis- ⎭   word the prefix is divided from the root by a hyphen
only to stress the correct formation:

DIS- satisfied
      semination
      sent/sension
      service   These words therefore have
      sever   a double *s* at the begin-
      simulate   ning: *dis-s*
      sociate
      suade/suasion

DE-   sist
      spair
      spise/spite   not *dis-*
      spoil
      stroy/struction

In modern spelling *dissyllable* is usually spelt thus, with two *s*s; but the prefix is really the Greek *di-* (' two-', ' twice '), and the spelling should be *disyllable*. The same prefix is seen in *distich* (see p. 120). Note *di-lapidation*, not *de-lapidation*, the prefix being a shortened form of *dis-*.

e, ee   This little group of words should be carefully memorised:

	but	
proceed	but	*accede*
succeed		*intercede*
exceed		*precede*
		procedure
		supersede

ei   For *ie* and *ei* see *Good English* p. 241.
Notice the *ei* in *height* and *sleight* (of hand).

e (final)   The final -*e* is sounded at the end of certain words derived from the Greek and of one or two other foreign borrowings: *apostrophe, epitome, syncope, anemone* (Note: *n-m-n*); *recipe* (Latin); *reveille* (' revalli '— French); *dilettante* (Italian).
For mute final *e* see *Good English* p. 237.
Note: *unmistakable, likable*, following the rule that final muͭe *e* is dropped before a suffix beginning with a vowel, except when *c* and *g* have to be kept soft before, *a, o, u*.

e (medial)   Note *cemetery, monastery*, but *laundry*. Even the writers or the proof-readers sometimes trip up:

It is stocked with hotels and restaurants and launderies.—*NS*

-er   See *-or*
exc-   Words with soft *c* following *ex-* are worth noting: *exceed, excess, excel, excellent, except, excerpt, excise, excite*. Note *escape*, not *excape* or *exscape*, and *ecstasy*.

f   (i) In modern derivatives from Greek the Greek symbol (*ph*) is kept: *photograph, telephone, epitaph, philanthropy* (note: not -*phy*), *phantom, asphalt, asphodel* (not *ash*-). In *fancy* and *fantastic* the *f* has now prevailed; *fantasy* usually has *f*, but may be spelt *phantasy*.

(ii) The old guttural *gh* (see p. 123) is sometimes pronounced as *f*: *rough, cough, tough, enough, draught*. In the eighteenth century the *gh* in *though* had the *f* sound; eighteenth century texts often have the spelling *thof*.

(iii) *Off* is merely a stronger (usually adverbial) form of *of*. Notice the spelling of *sheriff* (shire + reeve) and *bailiff*.

(iv) For *f* > *v* in noun plurals see *Good English*, p. 239.

for-
fore-
Note *forbears* (verb) = ' abstains ', ' refrains ', but *forebears* (noun) = ' ancestors '; *forgo* = ' abstain from ', ' do without ', but *forego* = ' go before ', especially in the past participle as adjective (' a *foregone* conclusion ').

g
(i) Like *c*, *g* is hard before guttural and soft before palatal vowels. If we add a suffix beginning with a guttural vowel to a word ending in *-ge*, the *e* remains to keep the *g* soft (*outrageous*, *pageant*, *manageable*).

(ii) *Give, get, begin, geese, gild* are examples of Old English words in which the hard *g* has been carried over from other forms—*gave, got (gat), began, goose, gold*. These words also have hard *g* : *geyser, gibberish, gibbous* (moon), *gill* (= ravine, sometimes spelt *ghyll*; and part of fish), *gillie* (Scots attendant), *giddy, gig, giggle, gimlet, gird*.

(iii) Initial *g* is silent in *gnaw* (Old English), *gnome*, *gnomon* (of sundial), and *gnu*.

gh
(i) For the Old English guttural see *Good English* p. 230 and under *f*.

(ii) Note initial *gh* (pronounced like hard *g*, without aspirate) in: *ghost* (*aghast, ghastly*), *gherkin, ghetto, ghoul*. For *ghyll* see above.

gu-
As a compound symbol (pronounced *g*, hard) *gu* is common—*guarantee, guard, guide, guess, guest, prologue, rogue, vogue*. A word to note is *gauge*, not *gu-*.

h
(i) Initial *h* is not aspirated (' breathed ') in *heir, honour* and *hour*, and whenever the word which it begins is unaccented it loses most of its breath. Medial *h* is not sounded " unless the accent falls on the syllable that it begins " (Fowler)—not, therefore, in *philharmonic* and *forehead*. In the combination *wh-* where the *w* is sounded the *h* is now usually unaspirated—thus *which* is pronounced like *witch*. In *who* and *whoop* it is the *h* that is sounded, and the *w* is silent.

(ii) Notice the *hh* in *withhold*; but *threshold* has only one *h*, not *threshhold*.

i   For *i* and *y* see under *y*; for *y>i* see *Good English*, p. 237.

j and *g* In the spelling of a few words *j* and *g* (soft) alternate: *gibe – jibe*, *gerrymander* (from an American proper name, Gerry, Governor of Massachusetts) – *jerrymander* (by confusion with *jerrybuilt*), *gaol-jail*, *sergeant-serjeant*. In ordinary use *sergeant* belongs to the Army and the Police, *serjeant* to the Law. But oddly enough, *serjeant* is the official War Office spelling, in, for example, *Queen's Regulations*. Fowler says gravely that in the phrase ' Jack and Jill ' *Jill* should be spelt *Gill* (for Gillian). But in view of the need here for alliterative spelling as well as alliterative sound, this is pedantry run mad.

k   (i) See *c* and *q*.
(ii) Initial *k* before *n* is silent in many Old English derivatives, for example: *knee*, *knife*, *knock*, *know*.
(iii) Notice *kh* in *khaki* (not *kakhi*), and *gymkhana*.

l   This troublesome letter is dealt with in *Good English*, p. 241. It is often silent after a guttural vowel (*a*, *o*, *u*), especially before *m* and *k*: *alms*, *palm*, *calm*, *psalm*, *haulm*, *holm*, *folk*, *yolk*, *walk*; but is usually sounded after a palatal vowel (*e*, *i*); *elf*, *elm*, *shelf*, *golf*, *elk*, *film*, *kiln*, which we used to pronounce ' kil ' (without the *n*) in Kent, when I was a boy.

m   The *m*s are apt to be mixed up with the *n*s in *anemone*, *mnemonic* (where the first *m* is silent), *phenomenal* and *impermanent*. The confusion of *momentum* ('motion ', 'impetus ') and *memento* (='reminder ' 'keepsake ') goes deeper than spelling. *Punch* recently quoted: " After speeches the two national anthems were sung, and the two youngest boys and the youngest girl received momentums ", *Punch*'s comment was " Well, they shouldn't fidget ".

n   See *m*. When final it is silent after *m*: *solemn*, *column*, *hymn*, but when a suffix (other than *-ed*, *-ing*) beginning with a vowel is added to these words, the *n* is sounded: *solemNity*, *solemNize*, *hymNal*, *hymNology*, *columNal*.

The American *columnist* ('writer of newspaper column'), which has now established itself in English, hesitates in pronunciation between *columist* and *columNist*.

œ   This ligature is for convenience written as two letters *oe*, and is usually so printed. In some words, of which *economy* is the most notable example, the *oe* has given way to the simple *e*. The now popular word in ecclesiastical contexts, *ecumenical*, has shed the *oe* in common usage, though the latest COD (in spite of Fowler's recommendation twenty-five years ago) still pedantically sticks to *oecumenical*. Two special words to remember are those derived from the Greek *rheo* (='flow'), *diarrhoea* and *pyorrhoea*.

-or   The agent suffix *-or* is of Latin origin and is usually added to Latin stems. But the question when *-or* and when the English *or* has no definite answer. We have to learn by heart and by experience. One thing, however, can be said: *-or* is a 'dead' suffix (that is, the words in which it occurs are already established in the language), but *-er* is living, in that it can be added to any English verb which requires a permanent or *ad hoc* agent-noun. But this does not get us very far. For myself, I have a 'blind spot' in this matter, and tend to write, for example, *agitater*, *propellor* and *imposter*. Indeed, *imposters* was printed in a quotation in the first edition of *Good English* (page 154) not so much because of carelessness in proof reading as because of ignorance, madam, pure ignorance, to adapt a phrase of Dr Johnson. Unluckily, though there are a few 'doublets' (for example, 'coal *conveyor*' but '*conveyer* belt'), the choice has to be made, and the only way out of the difficulty is to follow the revolutionary suggestion I put forward on p. 117.

ou   For the suffix *-ous* and words ending in *-our*, see *u*.

p   Initial *p* "is silent as in Psmith", to quote one of P. G. Wodehouse's most famous characters. It is, in fact, silent in a number of Greek words (for example, *psalm*, *psychology*, *ptomaine*) which, since they form a group in the dictionary, are best studied there. *Receipt* (Latin, *receptum*) is a deliberate etymological spelling.

ph   See *f* (p. 122).

pp Notice the exceptions to the rule[1] for the doubling of a final consonant before a vowel: *worship, handicap, kidnap, horsewhip, sideslip.* Each one of these has *-pp-* (*worshipped, handicapped,* etc.).

q In all words except one or two proper nouns, of which *Iraq* is the most familiar, *q* is followed by *u*; the *qu* is pronounced *kw* at the beginning (*question, quite, quaver*) and middle (*loquacious, aquarium, iniquity*) of words, but *k* in the combination *-que* at the end (*cheque, picturesque, grotesque, unique, technique*). In a few words initial *qu* has the French pronunciation (*k*): *quay, queue, qui-vive, quoin* (' angle of building '); *quoit* and *questionnaire* hover between *k-* and *kw-*. *Eskimo* is an English spelling of the French *Esquimau.* Here and there a differentiation arises: *physique* (' bodily structure ') and *physic* (' medicine '); *mystique* (a recent word borrowed from French) and *mystic.*

rh The following spellings should be noted: *rhapsody, rhetoric, rhinoceros, rhododendron, rhombus, rhubarb, rhyme, rhythm.* There is no *h* in *rodomontade* (' boasting '), from *Rodomonte,* a character in *Orlando Furioso;* but an *h* follows the initial letter in *Rhadamanthine* (' incorruptible ') from *Rhadamanthus,* the judge in Hades.

sc The somewhat difficult *sc* (soft) has three main origins:

(i) combination with prefix (*discern* from Latin *dis-cerno,* ' sift '), sometimes with assimilation (*susceptible,* from Latin *sub+cipere, cept-* ' take '); *ascertain* is from French *a + certaine,* the *s* being intrusive, on analogy.

(ii) Latin words in *sc-* or Greek words that have come through French with soft *sc* or *s*: *science, conscious, omniscient* (Latin *scio,* ' know '), *ascend, descend,* (Latin *scando,* ' climb '), *scene* (Greek *skene,* ' tent ' through French *scène*). Note also *scissors, schedule* (pronounced *sh-* in English but *sk-* in American) and *schism* (pronounced *s-*). It is important to distinguish between *sceptic* (*sk-*) ' agnostic ' and *septic* ' poisonous '.

(iii) Latin verbs ending in *-sco: effervesce, acquiesce, quiescent* (from *quiesco,* ' be quiet, rest '), *disciple* (from *disco,* ' learn '), *obsolescent* (from *obsolesco,* ' grow out of custom ').

[1] See *Good English,* p. 234.

The temptation to put a *c* after the *s* in *absence* and *presence* must be resisted.

u   For *u* in words ending in -*our* (*honour* etc.) see *Good English*, p. 240; and for *u* after *g* see *gu*, p. 123.

w   Initial *w* is silent in the combination *wr* (*write*, *wrong*, *wring*) and sometimes in the combination *wh* (see *h*, p. 123). In the middle of some words (*Woolwich*, *Southwark*, *sword*, *two*, *answer*) *w* is not sounded. Sailors drop it in *forrard* ('forward'), and modern pronunciation prefers *toward* without the *w* sound. At the end of words (*shadow*, *hollow*, *gnaw*, *know*) *w* is merely another form of *u*, and is part of the vowel symbol.

x   See *ct* (p. 121) and *exc*- (p. 122).
Initial *x* is pronounced like *z*: *xylophone*, *Xanadu*, *Xavier*.

y   In certain words usage allows us a choice, *y* or *i*. Fowler carefully sorts them out, but it is wiser not to read his article, and to take what the gods give. The chief words, all spelt here with *i*, are: *cider*, *cipher*, *gipsy*, *lichgate*, *pigmy*, *silvan*, *siphon*, *siren*, *tiro*, *wich-elm*. Fowler includes *tire* (of a wheel) and recommends that spelling, relating it to its supposed derivation from *attire*. But *tyre* is the modern English spelling though *tire* is the American.
The letter *y* is, for some reason, so confusing to most of us that a short list of words in which it causes a (sometimes only momentary) difficulty is added:

analysis	bryony	gymkhana
synonym	dysentery	gyrate
anonymous	erysipelas	gypsophila
syllable	gyroscope	hypothesis
abysmal	glycerine	sibyl

z   For verbs in *z-ise*, -*ize* see *Good English*, p. 242.

CHAPTER VIII

PUNCTUATION

You will now see that it is quite impossible to give any *precise rules* for the use of these several points.—COBBETT: *A Grammar of the English Language*

THE question of punctuation is quite fully dealt with in *Good English*[1]. But the use of the comma is a matter for further argument; so I have devoted the main part of this section to the subject. Since there are few definite rules to guide us, we are all in this matter left very much to our own devices. Various modern writers on English usage have given wise counsel, especially Fowler (MEU), Partridge in *Usage and Abusage*, G. V. Carey in *Mind the Stop*, and V. H. Collins in an excellent article *A Vicious Fashion in Punctuation* published in *The Journal of Education* about ten years ago. I have referred to their recommendations in the following note, and have sometimes (but by no means always) followed their advice—rather shamefacedly taking out a comma here and putting in a comma there—when I was revising the punctuation of this book.

As an introduction to this main argument I give a few examples that have recently come my way of unusual or wrong punctuation with stops other than the comma:

This sharpness of impact—accentuated by the clarity of the voices, and the use of silence (the silent curtain, particularly)—are a mark of E. J. King Bull's work as a producer.—*NS*

This is parenthesis run mad. Dashes have a legitimate place in punctuation, but they are not to be used lightly. Here parenthetic commas should be substituted; the second parenthesis, in brackets, could then stand, as the commas effectively disguise the first. His dashes and commas so bemused the writer that by the time he reached his verb (are) he had entirely forgotten his undoubtedly singular

[1] pp. 101-31.

subject (*sharpness*).   This is indeed one of the minor
perils of parenthesis—that, itself being an aside, it tends
to divert the writer from the plain highway of syntax.

> Mr. Hesketh Pearson's book is very different from Miss
> Patch's record of her work; he is, at once, idolatrous
> and telling.   (He notes, for example, the touch of
> pedantry in Shaw.)—*NS*

It is safe to say that only very rarely should a whole
sentence be set in parenthesis.   In this example the
meaning would be neither more nor less clear if the brackets
were taken out.   But in fact the writer does require, or
imply, a kind of parenthesis exemplifying the quality of
'tellingness' in Mr Pearson.   The best punctuation would
be '. . . and telling—he notes, for example, the touch of
pedantry in Shaw'.   Even this leaves a slight ambiguity,
but not such as to mislead or inconvenience the reader.

> Miss Brenda Bruce is the backbone, both of *How He
> Lied to Her Husband*—a joke against *Candida*, and of
> *The Admirable Bashville*, the boxing melodrama written
> in fake Shakespearean verse.—*NS*

Having marked with a dash the beginning of his parenthesis, this writer forgot to mark the end of it.   The
punctuation as it stands makes nonsense of the sentence.
But the remedy is simple: since the parenthesis ends at
Candida, the comma should be replaced by a dash.   Rather
oddly, writing on the use of the dash in *Mind the Stop*, Mr
G. V. Carey himself makes the same mistake:

> No wonder that in some quarters the dash has fallen
> into disrepute; but I still maintain that, if kept in its
> place—and I make one here for it for luck, it is a very
> useful stop.

Mr Carey should have made a place for two, the other
one after *luck*.   His championship of the dash deserves
support.   It is a graphic stop, and more than most can
reflect the nuances and subtleties of thought.

The schoolmaster has always been hard on the exclamation mark; and the result is that most of us fight shy of it

even when it is not merely desirable but necessary. Perhaps, however, his objection implied that though we could exclaim in speech we should not exclaim in writing —except now and then with a few old trusted friends like *Hurrah!*, *Oh!*, and *Alas!*. That is why when we do exclaim on paper we are so ashamed of it that we try to pass off the exclamation as a statement. The five sentences quoted illustrate the point.

(a) And how a fear of life and a hankering after what rhetoric was meant to evade, would haunt the child.—*NS*

(b) What an astonishing achievement, that Miss Campion should make a wry, masculine tragi-comedy out of this material; a poor half-white creature outside the law, in a world of lost hope and lustreless despair.—*JL*

(c) And how sad for a man of his upright disposition to have seen the shining flowers of Communist idealism crumpled by the slickness of the dialecticians and smeared by filthy Tartar thumbs.—*O*

(d) He was offered the Laureateship (given instead to Pye) and how happily he would have devoted himself to the task of writing occasional verse.—*NS*

(e) James Kirkup is a poet whose work is often difficult to grasp at first or even third reading; but how worth while the effort is when made.—*JL*

All are exclamations; but the writers are afraid of the exclamation mark, without which their sentences have no real meaning at all. Note that the comma after *evade* in sentence (a) is superfluous.

Perhaps, however, leaving out the exclamation mark altogether is not quite so bad a sin as putting one in in the wrong place:

To the *Observer* this statement of a truth that once-occupied Europe and Asia would regard as a commonplace seems—would you believe it?—an example of " hysterical fellow-travelling ! "—*NS*

The exclamation of wounded incredulity is the *New Statesman*'s not the *Observer*'s; the exclamation mark should therefore come outside the inverted commas.

> How far such a theme is from topical matters, especially the politics-ridden matters of our contemporary world (not that I believe the world, the flesh and the devil were ever less so!).—*JL*

Whatever this, to me incomprehensible, parenthesis may mean, the exclamation mark should certainly stand outside the bracket.

> But his selection raises the question: " What is the use of studying generalizations if the experiences on which they are based are ignored? "—*TES*

> But there are some excellent occupational songs, such as " I love my miner lad," " Johnny Sangster," and the delightful " Shoemaker."—*TLS*

If usage, aided and abetted by the printers, refuses to get rid of inverted commas as an unnecessary and intolerable nuisance, at least it should make up its mind concerning their effect on neighbouring punctuation. My own recommendations may be stated simply and briefly:

1. In the writing of conversation, where expressions like ' he said ', ' he asked ', either do not appear at all or are merely parenthetic, the quotation marks take priority. This means, in effect, that other punctuation marks stand *inside* the closing quotes.

2. Where a piece of conversation or a quotation occurs incidentally in a main sentence, it is enclosed in quotes with any other punctuation mark that may be necessary to it; but the rest of the punctuation is independent of it and dependent on the construction of the main sentence. This means (i) that the punctuation marks of the main sentence stand *outside* the quotes, and (ii) that, where a quotation happens to come at the end of a sentence, any punctuation mark inside the quotes should not be made to serve for the main sentence also.

Thus, using the two quoted sentences as examples, the first written in conversation form would be punctuated like this:

> " What is the use," we ask, " of studying generalizations if the experiences on which they are based are ignored? "

But as the sentence stands, the quotation is merely incidental. The main sentence is a statement: there should, therefore, be a full-stop *outside* the final quotes.[1]

In the second sentence the two commas and the final full-stop *inside* the quotes should all be *outside*. So also when titles are enclosed in quotes:

> There are the rarest instances of great works that have had immediate success—" Hamlet " and " The Importance of being Earnest." They are freaks. Successful new plays often have merit—" Richard of Bordeaux," " Autumn Crocus," " George and Margaret " were all good work.—*O*

The full-stop at the end of the first sentence and the commas in the second belong to the punctuation of the main sentence and should not therefore be associated with or part of the titles. In modern usage book titles are usually printed in *italics*, and this problem of punctuation does not arise.

The question-mark does not often present difficulties, except in its relationship to inverted commas. In the following sentence from *The Times Literary Supplement* the writer hesitates between a direct question and an indirect question, and inserts a question-mark to be on the safe side. But the question is really indirect; the *should* in each half must stand after *there* (' why there should be '), and the question-mark must go:

> You might just as well ask why should there be an editorial in *The Times Literary Supplement* making this suggestion as why should there be congresses discussing such things?

THE USE OF THE COMMA

1. *The Syntactical Comma*

It is convenient to begin with the least doubtful uses— to consider the function of the comma as a syntactical stop

[1] But see *Good English*, p. 118. If the main sentence is itself a question it is scarcely reasonable, and certainly not elegant, to have two question marks (? " ?).

with a definite relationship to the construction of the sentence.[1] In each of the following sentences the relative clause is *defining*,[2] and is correctly not separated from its antecedent (*success, problem, those*) by a comma. But the comma at the end of the relative clause stands between subject and verb and, in Fowler's phrase, tries " to separate inseparables ".

> The success which *Drawings and Diagrams for the Woodwork Class* has enjoyed, has encouraged the author to produce a companion volume for metal-work.—*TES*

> The problem, however, is that most politicians who would be ' acceptable ' here, would not be ' acceptable ' in Teheran to Nationalists.

> Those who are acquainted with Bergson's work to which Mr. Tyrrell makes frequent references, will be reminded of his conception of the intellect as a practical faculty.—*NS*

In the following sentence a comma separates a comparative adjective (*less*) from its conjunction (*than*); reduced to its simplest terms, the construction is: ' lies less, than '. Here the writer—possibly for the reader's sake—has paused for breath, and in defiance of the syntactical construction of the sentence has inserted a comma to indicate a ' rest ':

> His interest, however, lies less in the information which para-normal phenomena may or may not be supposed to give about another order of reality, than in the light which they throw or, rather, which their reception throws upon this one.—*NS*

The conflict between the syntactical comma and the comma indicating a brief pause or rest in reading is clearly illustrated in the next sentence:

> So, all that this first act proves in the end is that it was a mistake for an actor with so large a part as Mr Clements has, to undertake the production as well.—*NS*

In the simple construction ' it was a mistake for an actor to undertake ' a comma after *actor* is manifestly absurd.

[1] See *Good English*, pp. 102-6.   [2] See *Good English*, pp. 85-8.

The problem arises from the accident that the phrase qualifying *actor* ends in *has*, which without the comma would tend to link itself with the following infinitive; the eye would read ' has to undertake ' with *Mr Clements* as subject. A simple solution is to omit the *has*. If it is kept, the comma will have to stay. Eric Partridge (*Usage and Abusage* s.v. Punctuation) gives the example ' The only student I have ever met who never believed his ears was blind ', and says that a comma after *ears* " does away with the ambiguity ". I see no real ambiguity here; it would arise only if the subject and the verb were plural: ' The only students I have ever met who ever believed their ears were blind '. In general, punctuation for the convenience of the reader should not clash with the punctuation demanded by the syntax. The reader has to play his part; indeed, to over-punctuate is sometimes to underrate his intelligence and insult him.

In the following sentences the intrusive separating comma occurs because the writer has not recognised that his relative clauses are non-defining; there should be a comma after the antecedent in each sentence (*pages*, ' volumes by Havelock Ellis '). Two commas marking off an adjective clause or phrase do not separate verb and subject.[1]

> The opening pages which shrewdly describe the climates through which he passed in his youth, are admirable. —*NS*
> Those who are familiar with the other odd eighteen volumes by Havelock Ellis which deal with subjects not strictly coming under the head of psychology or social science or sex, know what to expect.—*TT*

In the first of the following two sentences the adjective phrase should probably be non-defining—that is, there should be a comma after *nation*; and in the second the phrase should probably be defining—that is, both commas should be deleted. As they stand, both sentences are a little ambiguous:

> The solidarity of the nation built up on the humane class-relations of the eighteenth century and hardened in the fires of war, could not be dissolved over night.—*NS*

[1] See *Good English*, p. 106.

> The manoeuvres, in relation to the Foreign Ministers Conference, have reached their last stage.—*NS*

There is no doubt about the next sentences. In each the relative clause is defining and both commas should go:

> The two American cousins, who write under this pseudonym, have long since overcome the stiff formality of their youth, and have been writing in their shirt-sleeves for the last ten or fifteen years.—*NS*

> It was the second of the two casts, who will perform Mozart's *Don Giovanni* under Mr. Eric Cundell's baton this week at the Guildhall School of Music in London and next week at Cambridge, that we saw and heard on Wednesday.—*T*

And here is an example of ' bracketing '[1] in which two phrases are related to a common phrase:

> Having said that, there is nothing but praise to add, and congratulations to the publishers for their courage, and to the editors and contributors for their intelligent labours in producing a work of such great potential value to a nation whose future depends not only on their courage but on their informed good sense.—*NS*

If both phrases are to have equal force there must be a comma after *labours*. This is the pattern:

```
publishers for their courage ⎱
and                          ⎰         in
editors and contributors for ⎰      producing
their labours                ⎱
```

Similarly, in this sentence a comma is required after *Truth* in order that the final participle phrase may qualify (as it is intended to do) all three items, not merely the last of the three:

> It consists of a series of extracts from philosophers, historians, statesmen, and others under such headings as Society and the Individual, Education, and Truth arranged in a manner suitable for form discussion.—*TES*

[1] See p. 36 ff., and *Good English*, pp. 62, 63.

Here the writer has obscured his pun (see p. 177) by the omission of a comma after *Edward*:

> Everywhere the country is alive to the Festival, building, as in Sheffield, a new restaurant, or, as in Leeds and elsewhere, reviving King Lear. But the spirit of this Festival is not Shakespeare's, but Edward Lear.—*NS*

The construction is:

$$\left.\begin{array}{l} \text{is not Shakespeare's} \\ \text{but} \\ \text{Edward} \end{array}\right\} \text{Lear}$$

The following sentence prompts the question, Who had the flighty daughter—the lodger or the woman smoker? If the lodger, the comma after *smokes* is correct; if the woman, the comma should be taken out—that is, the two verbs of the relative clause qualifying *woman* should not be separated (' who smokes and has '):

> He lodges in the house of a woman who smokes, and has a flighty daughter who does not appear until half-way through the book.—*JL*

2. *Comma and Semi-colon*

Partridge in *Usage and Abusage* notes " a recent revival, in literary prose, of the 18th century use of the semi-colon: that use which produces the effect of a stressed pause or of a rhetorical break ". He gives an example from a novel of 1936:

> And now we are coming to a clearing in the woods; a little glade, bright green with the soft moss-grass; in the centre of which glade a stream ran between two banks.

He goes further, and gives the following as an example of legitimate punctuation, merely remarking that it is " very literary ":

> He was; as all men knew; a scoundrel.

Indeed, he does not hesitate at the colon as a marker of pauses:

He was: as all men knew: a scoundrel.

But if these are examples of usage, it must be, I think, a usage that is not merely ' literary ' but abnormal. G. V. Carey in *Mind the Stop* takes approximately the same view as that taken in *Good English*, and treats the semi-colon as a kind of mid-way stop between the full-stop and the comma, useful for indicating a pronounced pause, or in certain circumstances for marking off the phrases in a long sentence. He does not, however, advocate the use of the semi-colon before the adverbial *so*, which he treats as a conjunction.[1] I was courteously taken to task by a correspondent for my attitude in this matter. He says that in the sentence ' I was tired; so I went to bed ' the semi-colon " splits up what amounts to one thought " and that in speech " there would be a very slight break between *tired* and *so* ". But I am unrepentant. We all have our whims about punctuation; one of mine is that a stronger stop than a comma (in other words, a semi-colon) should precede conjunctive adverbs like *so, then, therefore*. I have nothing to add to what I have said in *Good English* about the colon.

Here are half a dozen sentences in which a semi-colon or a colon should be replaced by a comma or some other stop:

> His method of bringing the scene to life is that of the pageant-master; marshalling his forces into significant groups, and sending them on stage to the sound of contemporary music, in the form of apt quotations: the technique may be held a trifle mannered but is undeniably effective.—*NS*

The semi-colon may stand, since the following participle phrase is only very loosely related to the main clause. I should, however, prefer a dash. The colon has no significance or justification at all; replace it with a full-stop.

> The quest is love; that love which is life itself, the command of a full understanding and acceptance; a humility in the face of circumstance, a renunciation of self-interest, and the final paradox of self-knowledge: the gain in utmost loss.—*JL*

[1] See *Good English*, p. 107.

This punctuation is of the type illustrated by Partridge and referred to in a previous paragraph. It is possible that it is used deliberately for effect, especially the second semi-colon, which precedes a phrase that seems to be either an afterthought or a climax. Again I prefer a dash for the first semi-colon; or in a sentence of normal pattern I should substitute a comma for the second, transferring the *and* from the penultimate to the last phrase: ' self-interest, the final paradox of self-knowledge, and the gain '.

> Unusual imaginative effort is needed if our sympathy for the victims of the Jamaican hurricane is to be backed by any real understanding of what hit them: something of which there is nowadays a little more chance of forewarning, but which still cannot be avoided or resisted.—*MG*

For the colon substitute a comma; since *something* is in apposition to *what* there is no need for any stronger stop.

> We all know them; sons, parents, friends; whatever the relationship, they doom it to frustration.—*JL*

The modern touch again. But the effect here is that of stammering. The voice in reading aloud would (I think) make an appreciable pause at *friends* and a brief pause at *them*. Appropriate punctuation is difficult. I should use comma, full-stop.

> (*a*) So the novel ends on a muddle, as it begins on one: only the joys of being alone will remain unaltered; and we, the readers, who like all percipient people knew from the beginning that this is the kind of book in which problems are set and not solved, can at last share in the real treasure trove of the journey.—*JL*

> (*b*) In Acacia Road, as at Glyndebourne, we stroll during the intervals in our host's garden; but there the resemblance ends. The Mermaid is not an opera house, but a small Elizabethan stage; portable, and capable of being dismantled and reassembled in 24 hours. Why, then, you may wonder, has it opened, not with an Elizabethan play, but with a Restoration opera: in fact, with Purcell's *Dido and Aeneas*, of which London has already seen two productions this summer?—*NS*

Here the writers have used the semi-colon and the colon indiscriminately. I suggest this punctuation: (*a*) full-stop, comma: (*b*) comma, comma, comma or dash.

Comma or No Comma

In an article already referred to, Mr V. H. Collins says:

> Teachers of English would be doing a useful and much-needed service by paying special attention to a practice in punctuation, which is today running riot not only in journalism but also in every type of prose writing, of inserting a comma between an adverb and an adverbial phrase and the words directly following it that it qualifies. The practice generally occurs at the beginning of a sentence.

He gives a dozen examples, of which I quote three:

> On his return, he consulted his solicitor.
> Of course, such an operation needs time.
> In this way alone, I had an advantage over my enemy.

He admits that commas are sometimes necessary, especially when the adverb or adverb phrase may have by chance another possible (*e.g.* prepositional) function which brings it into ambiguous relationship with what follows. There is an example in the first sentence of this section; if there were no comma after *to*, the *to* would tend at first reading to associate itself with the following noun (' article already referred to Mr V. H. Collins '). He himself mentions particularly *however, besides, further, after*, which may be used in more than one sense or as more than one part of speech. For example, the comma is necessary in the sentence " Further, violence often defeats its object " if *further* is intended to be an adverb, not an adjective.

Mr G. V. Carey advances the same argument in *Mind the Stop*:

> There is a not uncommon tendency to ' comma off ' all such words and phrases. I can see no necessity for doing so with words that can only be used ' absolutely ', or, shall we say, that cannot take on a slightly different meaning if closely combined with some other word or words.

He recommends that all such words and phrases, whether they are at the beginning or at the end of a sentence, should be ' commaed off ' only if there were any risk of ambiguity. I can see the force of Mr Collins's and Mr Carey's argument, which has at times influenced the punctuation of this book. But I feel they do not sufficiently recognise that these words and phrases are normally parenthetical, and that a comma or commas may legitimately be used to indicate such parenthesis. For example, I have put a comma after the adverb phrase in this sentence, since ' for example ' is a parenthetical phrase; without the comma the sentence would have a slightly different significance. The parenthesis is more, or less,[1] pronounced according to the intention of the writer; and the writer has the responsibility of deciding whether to comma or not to comma. I give a dozen examples, chosen at random from such magazines and books as I have at hand. In the comments C stands for what I think would be the ruling of Messrs Collins and Carey.

> Now, what should possess anyone, under those circumstances, to match the adjective with *otherwise* instead of *other*?—FOWLER: *Modern English Usage*

Omit first comma; keep the others. C—omit them all.

> Theoretically, the use of this stop should cause no difficulty at all; and, indeed, it does not to the experienced writer.—G. H. VALLINS: *Good English*

C would, I think, omit all these commas; I should be prepared to defend them all, though willing to omit the first. Without its commas *indeed* might be given its Welsh or BBC Quiz meaning ("Am I right? " " Indeed you are.")

> The commas in (xiv) and (xv) are superfluous, according to modern usage, though the extracts are from a contemporary writer.—G. V. CAREY: *Mind the Stop*

The first comma is superfluous. Mr Carey would (I think) agree, though in practice he ignores his own ruling.

[1] Note that this is different from ' more or less '.

It is not, of course, to the existing procedure that the Government and its supporters object.—*DT*

I should keep the commas; C would omit them.

In anticipation, I found the idea of the Third's devoting a week's programmes wholly to material written, produced or performed in 1851, exciting.—*NS*

C would omit the comma after *anticipation*; but if ' in anticipation ' is modifying the whole clause and not merely qualifying *I*, the comma is necessary. For the other commas in this sentence see p. 144.

In the past elections in similar circumstances have been precipitated by changes of side on the part of Members responsive to a new feeling in the country.—*DT*

A comma is necessary after *past*.

It is, strictly, amusing when, say, an H. G. Wells falls under his notice.—*TT*

The argument, however spirited, has sometimes become inept and, occasionally, downright silly.—*O*

The adverbs *strictly* and *occasionally* are probably intended to be parenthetical; if so, the commas are justified. But, owing to the commas both sentences have a ' stuttering ' effect. For ' inept and ' see below.

His brother Stewart was put on the B.B.C. the other day to say that all was well at Lake Success because, in spite of the delusions of a certain Left-wing weekly in Britain, no one in America really wants war.—*TES*

We will see them for two periods only each week; we know as well as they do that they are unlikely to work hard since, even by the end of the year, we will have failed to define for them the nature of their work.—*NS*

In these two sentences the comma-ing off of the adverb phrases has the effect of leaving the conjunctions (*because*, *since*) hanging in mid-air. The simple remedy is to take out the comma at each end of the phrase.

Constitutionally Mr. Attlee is perfectly within his legal
rights in refusing to resign in face of any hostile poll
other than that of the ballot box.—*DT*

Moreover politics, in so far as they represented a struggle
for power between Whigs and Tories, became meaningless, when the entire governing class, regardless of
Party, was lolling in luxury and prehensile of privilege;
while the manual labourers shivered with uncertainty
as regards their daily bread, and were only positive
about their poverty.—*NS*

This punctuation follows the ruling of C. I should
probably (if rather shamefacedly after reading C) put a
comma after *constitutionally*, and almost certainly after
moreover for the whimsical reason that to me *moreover*
without its comma looks like an adjective in this sentence.

It is important to remember that when a phrase or a
subordinate clause comes between an introductory adverb
or adverb phrase and the clause to which it is more or less
closely related, a comma is always necessary. I give two
examples, both from *Mind the Stop*. In the first Mr
Carey has and in the second he has not remembered this:

Actually, if the latter alternative were adopted, it would
be rather more natural to defer the inverted commas
still further.

On the other hand if any two items in a list should
really be in a specially close relationship, the ‘final
comma’ man, in order to indicate this, has merely to
couple them with an ‘and’ and drop the comma.

‘Bracketing’ Commas

The use of commas as a mark of parenthesis is discussed
in *Good English* and the punctuation with parenthetical
adverbs or adverb phrases is illustrated in the sentences of
the previous section. The following sentences illustrate
one or two other problems with ‘bracketing’ commas:

Newness or more properly up-to-dateness is in fact
the feature most noticeable to anyone glancing through
its pages.—*TES*

The *or* phrase is parenthetical or semi-parenthetical. It

should be commaed off. The comma enthusiast would go further: ' Newness, or, more properly, up-to-dateness, is, in fact, the . . .'. But this is to give the sentence measles.

> . . . U.N. strength in Korea—if as now seems likely the truce talks fail. . . .—*NS*

Better: ' if, as now seems likely, the . . .'

> Mr. Attlee may well feel that it is preferable not to run this risk, but to resign at a time, and on issues, of his own choosing.—*NS*

> The queue stood sullen and thirsty, irritated that one busy-body should presume to stand between them and their, possibly toxic, tea.—*NS*

The phrases ' and on issues ' and ' possibly toxic ' are not really parenthetical. The commas are a mark of affectation rather than of punctuation.

> A writer without a style like Trollope is interesting when he is writing about something interesting, flat when he is writing about something flat.—LORD DAVID CECIL: *Early Victorian Novelists*

The phrase ' like Trollope ' must be placed between commas; brackets would be better still.

CRICKET
THE FINAL TEST AT MELBOURNE

—T

Since only one Test match, not a series of Tests, was played at Melbourne, the phrase ' at Melbourne ' is parenthetical, and there should be a comma after *TEST*. If we expressed the phrase as a single noun-adjective we should write ' The Final (Melbourne) Test ', not ' The Final Melbourne Test '.

Lists

A difficulty in punctuation sometimes arises when two adjectives separately qualify a noun—' a tall, thin man ', ' a short, formal letter '. The following sentence will illustrate it:

> The Duke of York's Theatre, now all rosy rapture to
> the eye and thick, soft carpets to the feet, opened with
> a play which lacked the colour suitable to so rubicund
> a pleasure-dome.—*O*

The epithet *thick* is inadvertently associated with the eye
or the Theatre instead of with the carpets, or at first reading
appears to be left hanging in mid-air (see also p. 141).
But the comma between *thick* and *soft* cannot be taken
out, as ' thick, soft ' is not precisely the same thing as
' thick soft '. There is nothing for it but to put a comma
before the *and*.

G. V. Carey in *Mind the Stop* strongly advocates what
he calls " the ' final comma ' principle " in the formula
' *a, b, c,* and *d* ', saying that the omission of the comma
after *c* often leads to ambiguity in the last item or items
of the enumeration. This principle is equally valid for
enumerations of only three items—*a, b,* and *c,* not *a, b*
and *c.* In the following sentences I should put a comma
after *envy* and after *sapient*:

> The argument is that those who are suffering from
> power cuts must necessarily be filled with rage, envy
> and all unkindness when they see the blaze of lights at
> Piccadilly Circus or at the local cinema.—*TT*

> Boswell's picture of himself has indeed the accidental
> and unforeseeable quality of life which better organised,
> more sapient or more eloquent natures lose the moment
> they put pen to paper.—*NS*

And here, to end with, are two examples, one short and
the other quite long, of the excessive use of commas. The
second passage in particular is an eloquent argument for
those who advocate reducing commas to a minimum.
Most of these commas could go. I leave the reader to
determine which should survive:

> There is one answer, valid so far as it goes, in terms,
> strictly, of craftsmanship.—*NS*

> Already, before the New Ecclesiology came in with
> John Betjeman, guide-book language was, here and
> there, a private joke. That would be in the early

nineteen-twenties. I should say that, before then, the expressions ' E.E.,' ' Dec.' and ' Perp.' were never thought provocatively quaint but, on the contrary, so dull as to be as dull as anything could be—except, indeed, by those who used them, still, with the initiate's sense of knowing a little about something out of the ordinary.—*NS*

Although I have ended this section with an implied warning against excess, I heartily agree with Carey's suggestion that " the modern tendency towards economy in punctuation is going a little too far and that too little heed is being given to possible ambiguity ". That is well said. The insertion of commas indiscriminately at every little pause is a bad habit. But to follow blindly the slogan " Down with the comma! " is to ignore the fact that the comma is often a stop of important syntactical and idiomatic significance.

Hyphens

There is very little to add to the note called " The Hyphen Puzzle " in *Good English*. G. V. Carey in *Mind the Stop*, Eric Partridge in *Usage and Abusage*, and Sir Ernest Gowers in the *ABC of Plain Words* all fight shy of Fowler's unnecessarily complicated note in *Modern English Usage*, and give simplified guidance based rather on common sense (?common-sense—the query is also Carey's) than on function or the falling of the accent. Remembering that the main work of the hyphen is to join, either permanently or for the occasion, two or more words which are associated in use, we can arrive at the following working rules. The hyphen is used—

(i) To make fixed compounds of words which, though compounded in sense and by usage, have not yet coalesced as a single unit: *drawing-board, son-in-law, dog-rose, road-house, book-jacket*. There is a vast no-man's land here, since hyphenated compounds are always moving towards unhyphenated unity. Luckily there is no hard-and-fast rule. At any one time scores of words are in that state of transition when the writer can use a hyphen or not, as he pleases.

Here by way of example are some of the recommendations of the COD (1950) for compounds or phrase-associations with the noun *book*: *bookcase, bookman, bookseller, book-mark, book-maker, book-plate, book-keeper, book end, book token*. The three stages are well illustrated here—(a) unification, (b) hyphenation, (c) separation. But when does *book-maker* become *bookmaker* and *book end book-end?* There is no answer, except that in this matter (more even than in most) usage outruns the dictionary and defies the inscrutable custom of printers. But even the printers themselves are not consistent. For example, RCR and the COD give *hymn-book*, with a hyphen; but the General Catalogue of the Oxford Press prints the words separately (*hymn book*) in the text, and as one word (*hymnbook*) in the Index.

Of the hyphenated compounds given above, *book-keeper* is unlikely to lose its hyphen, which separates two *k*'s that would look odd if they came together (*bookkeeper*). Nevertheless, Carey points out that *public-house* is always printed *publichouse* in *The Times*, and that he " can never read this horrid word without wanting to run the *ch* together, as in *artichoke* ".

(ii) To make *ad hoc* compounds, in particular contexts; and especially to u ite two or more normally separated words that for the occasion make up an epithet adjective. Thus we write ' The biography was well documented' but ' a well-documented biography'; ' The regulation was enforced in war time ' but ' a war-time regulation '; ' the incident will never be forgotten ' but ' a never-to-be-forgotten incident '.

(iii) After certain Latin prefixes, especially *ex, vice, sub, non* (*ex-President, vice-principal, sub-lieutenant, non-starter*). Sometimes *re* is followed by a hyphen to indicate a specialised sense.[1] Sir Ernest Gowers (*ABC*) condemns the use of the hyphen to separate two vowels as in *co-operative, re-edit, re-adjust*, and rightly suggests that the hyphen should go, and that the second of the two vowels should be marked with a diaeresis, since " that is what a diaeresis is for "—*coöperative, reëdit, reädjust*. All the same,

---

[1] See an amusing example in *Good English*, p. 130, where *resigned* is used for *re-signed*.

the diaeresis is as strange as the cedilla to our eyes, which are likely to be misled by *coöp*, *reëd* and *reäd* as if the diaeresis were not there at all. Still, as Sir Ernest Gowers says, without the hyphen we should be saved from such eccentricities as *unco-ordinated* and *unco-operative*.

However, a few examples will be worth more than statements of rules that are so obviously and notoriously liable to exceptions. They are all chosen at random from the newspapers and magazines I happen to have at hand as I write this section. My comments are in the right-hand column.

the most unself-conscious aplomb	The hyphen 'breaks' the word at the wrong place. Write either *un-selfconscious* or *unselfconscious*.
Anti-Opencast Mining Campaign	The campaign is against (*anti*) opencast-mining; write therefore *Anti-Opencast-Mining*.
to centre over much on obvious limitations	*overmuch* (adverb)
war time drabness a performance of the right mannered gaiety	Hyphen needed: *war-time, right-mannered* (epithet adjectives).
11-year-old children	correct: epithet adjective
upper middle-class life	for *upper-middle-class*
quiz-mania crossword-craze fantasy-idea a prep.-school cap a hand-held camera war-film heroics	These are half a dozen examples of *ad hoc* hyphenating.
front-doors	No hyphen. But *indoors* and '*backdoor* influence'.
'Good will was blinded by egoism'	*Goodwill* (one word)
'with a good humour that strikes a corresponding good will from the audience'.	In the second quotation *good* and *will* are, perhaps, deliberately separated to balance *good humour*, which has not yet achieved a hyphen.

The overall allocation of resources.

A new and very popular word, resisted by Sir Ernest Gowers; spelt, as here, without the hyphen—*overall*.

motor-car

COD (1950) gives *motor-car*, with the hyphen (the normal form), but *motor bicycle* without the hyphen. Again I don't know why.

Descending with a bump to the ordinary-sordid, but carrying with us something of an afterglow, we have in Dal Stivens's first full-length novel a brutal, over-long exposure of tough contemporary life in Sydney.

There are four examples: (i) an *ad hoc* telescoping of ' the ordinary and the sordid ' or ' the sordidness of the ordinary '; (ii) one word (*afterglow*) in modern dictionaries; (iii) correctly hyphenated epithet adjective; (iv) one word (*overlong*) in *Chambers's, but often* with hyphen, as here.

anonymous children of pre-twentieth-century England

Correct. The second hyphen is often wrongly omitted.

Madly complicated free for all . . .

From a review of a crime story; hyphens are necessary, *free-for-all*. Crime reviews have a jargon of their own, in which the remarkable noun *whodunit* has established itself and now threatens to become standard English.

appearing one hundred and eighty-odd years after it was written

one-hundred-and-eighty-odd

Free Church Motor Policy

Unless Free Church is hyphenated (Free-Church) there is a chance of misunderstanding here—*free* may qualify *policy*.

the ironingroom
his deathwound
telegraphpoles
turfcoloured bogwater
grownup people
the easychairs

Half-a-dozen examples from an early novel of James Joyce (*Portrait of the Artist as a Young Man*). They point the way, perhaps, to a more general practice of dispensing with the hyphen in compounding words. Cf. *whodunit*, above.

The Apostrophe

The following sentence (from Empson's *Structure of Complex Words*) illustrates a common difficulty in the use of the apostrophe:

> This becomes an attack on the Ogden and Richards *Meaning of Meaning*.

The writer has, in fact, avoided the difficulty by skating round it. Ogden and Richards are joint authors of *The Meaning of Meaning*. If one of them had been the sole author, there would have been no apostrophe problem: ' Ogden's (or Richards's) *Meaning of Meaning* ' is a normal and natural English construction. But how with apostrophes can we make them both possessive? Shall we write ' Ogden's and Richards's *M of M* ' or ' Ogden and Richards's *M of M* '? Neither solution is satisfactory; so by a recognised ' dodge ' in English the writer turned the two proper nouns into adjectives, just as we turn ' *table*'s leg ' into ' *table* leg '. A similar difficulty arises sometimes with nouns in apposition: ' the secretary, Mr Smith's umbrella '. Since the apostrophe *s* to indicate the possessive has a very limited use, it is a safe rule to avoid all apostrophe problems by resorting, as the writer does, to an alternative construction.

A Note on ' Modernist ' Punctuation

Many modern poets and some modern novelists have a punctuation of their own. In its extreme manifestations the ' stream of consciousness ' style, with its deliberate ' flow ', dispenses with the full-stop. Certain parts of Joyce's *Ulysses*, for example, have no stops at all:

> I suppose theyre just getting up in China now combing out their pigtails for the day well[1] soon have the nuns ringing the angelus theyve nobody coming in to spoil their sleep except an odd priest or two for his night office the alarmclock next door at cockshout clattering the brains out of itself let me see if I can doze off 1 2 3 4 5 what kind of flowers are those they invented like the stars the wall-paper in Lombard Street was much nicer——

[1] = we'll.

On the other hand, in the style that represents thought or even narrative and description in jerks, each telegraphic phrase has its own full-stop separating it from the next:

> And we got down at the bridge. White cloudy sky, with mother-of-pearl veins. Pearl rays shooting through, green and blue-white. River roughed by a breeze. White as a new file in the distance. Fish-white streak on the smooth pin-silver upstream. Shooting new pins.
> —JOYCE CARY: *The Horse's Mouth*

But it is too early yet to predict what influence these aberrations will have on conventional punctuation systems. See also p. 183.

CHAPTER IX

THE TURGID AND THE TURBID

> Turgid, whether applied to ink in a bottle, or oratory, or a river, means swollen. The river now in spate (turgid) may, during a summer drought, shrink to a muddy trickle, which would probably be turbid.—Letter in *John o' London's Weekly*

IN this section I have given, with commentary, sentences and passages that are turgid, or turbid, or both. On the envelope in which I originally collected them I pencilled, for my own reference, the title 'General Cloudiness'. They illustrate that kind of ' fuzzy ' writing in which there is no true correspondence of thought and expression; in which, that is, the reader cannot quite ' get at ' what the writer means. Some of them are turgid, swollen with that kind of intellectual bombast which never rises to gusto; and all, in their various ways, are turbid. The signs of their turbidity are for all to see: a lack of precision in the use of words, an uncertainty of idiom, a disregard of the normal sentence relationships, a casualness of phrase, and (now and then, but rarely) a defiance of the fundamentals of syntax.

Here, to begin with, are a few brief turbidities and turgidities in which some awkwardness or illogicality of expression blurs the meaning:

This volume contains all the short stories which Melville is known to have written, and collects them for the first time in one volume.—*O*

' The volume collects in one volume '—an odd process. Recast: All the short stories which Melville is known to have written are collected for the first time in one volume.

It becomes a habit with critics to botanize among books, trying to place them, noting their derivations and origins. This does good professional service, and in the long run adds to the general structure of letters, disciplining both critics and authors toward an appreciation of tradition.—*JL*

(i) Having ventured on the *botanized* metaphor, the writer should have sustained it with some such phrase as ' trying to classify them, like flowers, in their species '.

(ii) How does one discipline anybody *toward* a thing? ' Discipline *in* an appreciation ' might pass.

It is evident that comparatively few electors have yet thought out clearly the correlation between foreign policy and re-armament on the one hand, and, on the other, the rising cost of living and the imminence of shortages in the shops.—*NS*

The writer is talking about correlation, but the phrases ' on the one hand ' and ' on the other' imply separation or antithesis. If, however, he takes out these phrases he encounters a difficulty of bracketing: ' between $(a + b)$ and $(c + d)$'. The three *ands* cause ambiguity and confusion. Recast: ' have yet considered clearly how a and b are related to c and d '.

They were made within a couple of years of one another; both start the wriggle of a tender-farcical excursion through the landscape, the commotion thrives, and vanishes.—*NS*

We can only assume that this has some meaning; it is difficult to find it.

This has now been reprinted by Sheed and Ward (10s. 6d.) with slight modifications in spelling and the use of archaic words to make it easier for modern readers.—*JL*

There is an odd ambiguity in this sentence. The bracketing is ' modifications in (spelling and the use of archaic words)', but only a comma after *words* will ensure that the second item does not detach itself and join incongruously with the final phrase.

He began, surprisingly enough, as a critic of painting besides being a book-reviewer, the former in Edmund Yates's fashionable weekly, *The World* (of which William Archer was the dramatic critic) and the latter in the old *Pall Mall Gazette*.—*JL*

When he became a critic of painting was he already a book-reviewer? If so, how did he *begin* as a critic of painting? The confusion, and the awkwardness of ' the former ' and ' the latter ' could be avoided by a recasting of the sentence: 'He was, surprisingly enough, a critic of painting in . . . *The World* . . . He was also a book-reviewer in the old *Pall Mall Gazette* '.

If the will has been destroyed by a parent like Lord Auchinleck, it may be replaced by a shiftless melancholy, an abeyance of spirits, and from that bewilderment all life afterwards will seem an unreckonable hallucination, when a high-blooded young man is engaged ingenuously with it.—*NS*

The false equation (' shiftless melancholy' = 'abeyance of spirits ' = ' bewilderment ') and the verbiage of the end of the sentence should go. Recast : ' and, because of this, all life afterwards will seem a hallucination to a high-blooded young man '.

In her daily search for some tiny needle of good news in the haystack of the bad, the house-wife reads, amid the new inevitable schedule of up-and up prices, that real cream will soon be available.—*O*

The writer is, no doubt, entitled to his rather trite metaphor (but why ' *tiny* needle '?); he must, however, sustain it by substi-tuting *finds* for *reads*. For *amid* say *in*, and take out the commas; *inevitable* might well go, also.

Living his private life publicly (I mean without reserve), arrest-ing public life tactlessly with the private instance; ingenuously, unguardedly, compulsively mix-ing the two together, Mr. Spender took the Fool's part in the distracted comi-tragedy of duty which was played out in that decade.—*NS*

For the punctuation of this sentence see p. 215. I cannot find the meaning of ' arresting public life tactlessly with the private instance ', or the force of the adverb *compulsively*.

And here are some more sustained examples:

1. I found his judgments a little hard towards all that is pleasurable in literature, even if that pleasure belongs to the strange, the remote, the fantastic or even the disorderly. It is thus that life has gained taste and sensitiveness and the strange enrichments which cannot be defined easily within the concepts of good and evil.—*JL*

(*a*) First, the idiom is mixed (see pp. 66 ff.). The writer cannot make up his mind upon

(i) I found his judgments a little hard *on* all that is pleasurable . . .
(ii) I found his judgments *of* all that is pleasurable a little hard . . .
(iii) I found his attitude *towards* (preferably *to*) all that is pleasurable a little hard . . .

Of these either (i) or (ii) is permissible, but not a mixture of the two (judgment *towards*). Sentence (i) is open to a hair-splitting criticism. The purist would say that the person judging (the *judge*, *you*), or the result of his judgment expressed indefinitely (*it*, *that*), may be a little hard on somebody or something, but not the judgment itself. It is a nice point, and one that has its interest for the fastidi-ous writer.

(*b*) The equating of 'that pleasure' with 'all that is pleasurable in literature' is unsound; the two phrases are not even roughly synonymous. But there is no difficulty. For 'that pleasure' it is possible to substitute *it* (= 'all that is pleasurable') with no more ambiguity than is usually associated with pronouns.[1] In this clause, too, the second *even* is unnecessary, though permissible if the writer really requires it for emphasis.

(*c*) 'It is thus . . .': How? In what way? The word *thus* is in origin a demonstrative pronoun, and demands all the care that should be given to ordinary demonstratives.[2] It must have a definite and particular relationship with the theme of the previous sentence or phrase. In this passage there is no such relationship; *thus* is a mere vague convenience.

(*d*) 'The strange enrichments which cannot be defined easily within the concepts of good and evil': This is full of sound, if not of fury; but what (to echo the quotation) does it signify? 'Defined within the concept'? Can it possibly mean no more than 'cannot easily be described as either good or evil', or does it refer to some mysterious no-man's-land between the two?

2. Moreover, the possibility must be entertained that it will become necessary to cut educational expenditure in the near future. This might happen under pressure of a severe economic crisis, and it certainly should not be done without weighing the claim of education against those of the other social services.—*TES*

The first sentence is merely verbose in a somewhat formal way. There is no great harm in this, but shortening is easy, and would make the statement more direct and forcible: 'Moreover, we must face the necessity of cutting educational expenditure very soon'. In the second sentence the pronouns *this* and *it* are difficult, or at any rate doubtful. Apparently they refer to the same thing—but what? Can it both *happen* and *be done*? Actually, the two pronouns refer to different things; in the amended sentence above, *this* would relate to *necessity* and *it* to *cutting*. It is safe to keep *this*, but the *it* should be replaced

[1] See *Good English*, p. 73.   [2] See *Good English*, p. 78.

by an appropriate noun: ' and [?but] the cut should certainly not be made '. Why the *claim* of education and *those* of the other services? Probably some kind of attraction has been at work. Say either ' *claim* and *that* . . .' or ' *claims* and *those* . . .'

3. He lived on the kind of eminence inhabited by the great Victorians, Huxley and Spencer and Mallock—an eminence upon which there was plenty of room for idiosyncrasy, ample self-confidence, and a breadth of intellectual activity on the plane of pleasure which refused to exclude such subjects as faith, doubt and fear, (for from all these he extracted positive enjoyment), while at the same time his romanticism and his love of good gossip brought him down to the common playgrounds of humanity with a frequent and delightful rush.—*TLS*

(*a*) The structure of the sentence is double: ' He lived on an eminence . . . while at the same time his romanticism . . .' But this is completely obscured and the whole sentence rendered meaningless by the punctuation. The long parenthesis begun with the dash after *Mallock* should end with a dash after *enjoyment*. For *while* see p. 29.

(*b*) The parenthesis itself is ambiguous. At first sight the phrase ' plenty of room for ' governs the three following nouns, *idiosyncrasy, self-confidence* and *breadth*, not *idiosyncrasy* alone. But though the verb is singular (*was*), they may be separate items (*plenty—self-confidence—breadth*) as a multiple subject. Even then, what is a breadth of activity on a plane of pleasure standing on an eminence? Is this something out of the higher geometry? The antecedent of *which* is doubtful; it is probably *breadth*, though there are three other nouns between it and the relative. After all this, the parenthesis inside a parenthesis matters very little; it is awkward and unnecessary all the same.

(*c*) A minor point: say ' frequently brought him down ' instead of qualifying *rush* with the adjective *frequent*.[1]

4. There is an obscure period in Boswell's youth when he joined the Roman Catholic Church. We do not know whether passion, giddiness, his irrational fears, or his

[1] See *Good English*, p. 47.

tendency to melancholy, moved him to this step. But native canniness got him out of the scrape which socially and materially would have been a disaster in that age and we can be grateful that the confessional did not assuage what Puritan diarising has preserved. For that confession contains more than an account of his sins; it contains his sillinesses, his vanities, moods, snobberies, the varying temperatures of his aspirations.—*NS*

(*a*) In the two separate lists of Boswell's qualities and failings the writer is peculiarly inconsistent in his use of the possessive *his*. The first of the two sentences is better without it ('irrational fears or a tendency'); the second requires it once only, with the necessary reconstruction at the end: 'his sillinesses, vanities, moods, snobberies and aspirations'. If the qualifying phrase 'of varying temperatures' means anything, it can follow *aspirations*; but a simple participle-adjective like *varied* would serve—'his varied aspirations'.

(*b*) For the intrusive comma after *melancholy* see p. 133.

(*c*) To preserve the logical pattern of the last sentence 'an account of' should follow *contains*.

(*d*) The attempted antithesis at the end of the third sentence is wrecked by the use of the word *assuage*. There is no justification for the meaning 'tone down' in a context like this; and in any case the natural opposite of *preserve* would be *lose* or *destroy*. As it is, the writer, contenting himself with a totally inappropriate word, leaves the interpretation to the reader.

5. If he has any affinity, I should think it must be with Gilbert White, for his work, like the prose of *Selborne*, leaves one with a sense of being present in the face of a deep content, a true humility, and a happiness of spirit that has saturated into the very depths of this man's nature, tincturing even the inevitable griefs and horrors from which no individual can escape, and touching them with gratitude.—*NS*

(*a*) Mixed idiom: 'being present in the face of' is intelligible, but odd; it seems to be an amalgam of 'being present at' and 'being faced by', neither of which would be suitable to the context. The phrase could, in fact, be omitted—

' with a sense of a (or better, *the*) deep content, true humility, and happiness of spirit that *have* '. Possibly the author meant *have* for *has*, but more probably he forgot his treble antecedent.

(*b*) *saturated*: The writer begins an idiom and a metaphor that he cannot see through to the end; *saturated—tincturing —touching* evidently have some full, or at least semi-metaphorical force; but the imagery is not sustained. Moreover, ' *saturated into* ' is not English; *saturated* is a simple transitive verb. But ' saturated the very depths ' will not do; substitute ' soak into '.

(*c*) The idiom ' touch . . . with ' is one that implies a contrast or balance: we say, for example, ' joy is touched with pain '. Here, therefore, *gratitude* is inappropriate; what the appropriate word is it is difficult to say—*content-ment*, perhaps, or even *delight*.

This is a good (or bad) example of the type of sentence in which the language never precisely expresses the thought; the idiom, the image, the word, and the construction are all a trifle off the mark.

> 6. And so all his novels have the critical tone of experiments in autobiography. They are, more watchfully than in other novelists, the lives of possible selves. Detached writers are often more truly sensitive to the spirit of their time than the committed : revolution, war and *coup d'état* left him energetically disgusted. He became indifferent. What did persist with him was the sense of campaign: his psychology is generalship.—*NS*

A piece of reviewers' jargon that is almost too good to be true. The reader is set what is called nowadays a ' comprehension test ':

(i) What particular critical tone have all experiments in autobiography? Explain the difference between an autobiography and an experiment in autobio-graphy.

(ii) Elucidate the phrase ' more watchfully ' in this context.

(iii) Estimate the number of selves possible to the novelist referred to. Is it equal to the number of (*a*) his lives, (*b*) his novels?

(iv) Define (a) ' detached writers ', (b) ' committed
     writers ', and add a note on what you consider they
     are detached from, and committed to.
(v) How does one become ' energetically disgusted '?
     Outline the connection between disgust and indiffer-
     ence.
(vi) Solve the equation ' His psychology is generalship '.

No answers are given elsewhere in this book.   There
are none to give, except perhaps to the first question.   The
writer probably means simply ' all his novels are like
experiments in autobiography '.

> 7. What so deeply impresses me is the power of observation
>   in the author; of sympathetic observation that stores
>   up in his memory every play of circumstance, every
>   quirk of nature, every significant accident, and gradually
>   links them together to make the portrait of a man who
>   began his life as a shy, rudderless youngster, and emerged
>   into a career of public service that won him a knighthood,
>   a brilliant wife (what a horrible harpy she turns out to
>   be, yet even with her one is made to understand and
>   to condone), and finally threw it all up because this,
>   too, had turned to dust and ashes.—*JL*

There is nothing to criticise in the first half of the sentence
except perhaps the use of the inadequate semi-metaphor
links; *fits* or *arranges* (without *together*) would be better.
But after that the sentence goes to pieces:

(a) It is a peculiar evolutionary process by which a ' shy,
rudderless youngster ' emerges into a career; ' and emerged
into a responsible public servant who won . . .' is a simple
and suitable amendment.

(b) Evidently the reviewer was going to make a considerable list of the author's winnings; but he had only
mentioned two, a knighthood and a brilliant wife, when
he was side-tracked into the parenthesis.   So we hold our
breath and wait for the others in vain.

(c) That the subject of the last clause (' finally threw
it all up ') is the relative pronoun *who* is disguised by the
intervention of the parenthesis and by the *and* introducing
the second of the three co-ordinate clauses (' who *began* and

emerged and *threw* '). There is a faint ambiguity resulting from awkward rather than faulty construction.

(*d*) The parenthesis itself hovers between exclamation and statement. The sentences would be better divided with an exclamation mark after *be*. In the second clause both the infinitives are transitive; they should not be followed by *with*. The correct construction would be: ' one is made to understand even her, and to condone her shortcomings '. Perhaps, however, the infinitives are used absolutely here—that is, *with* = ' in the case of '.

> 8. In contrast with the usual over-simplification of modern novels, *Christina Claimed* is successfully written on several coalescent levels. It is a conversation piece, an accurately and subtly observed reportage of a post-war social scene we have not yet met in serious fiction. But the book is also a moral study of character on an almost heroic scale, for the thread of the story is Christina's enforced realisation that detached discrimination is ultimately valueless and that her duty lies in total emotional involvement.—*O*

Throughout the sentence the expression is loose and fuzzy:

(*a*) The contrast is between modern novels, not over-simplification and a particular novel: amend—' In contrast with modern novels, which are usually given to over-simplification, *Christina Claimed* is . . .'.

(*b*) Certainly ' written on several coalescent levels ' sounds well, but what does it mean? Would not ' coalescent levels ' become or be, in fact, one level?

(*c*) The adjective phrase ' accurately and subtly observed ' should be placed (between commas) where it belongs, immediately after and therefore qualifying *scene*.

(*d*) The author means not ' the thread of the story ' but the central or main theme. No doubt he was thinking vaguely of ' lose the thread '.

(*e*) ' is Christina's enforced realisation . . . involvement ': The reader is invited to paraphrase this passage. My own attempt is on p. 185. Nevertheless, it has its attractions: Mr Polly would call it *verboojuice*.

> 9. Andrew Young, like Mr. de la Mare, has been at work for many decades, without touching the fringes of

> literary fashion. He has therefore received less attention from the critics than from the reading public. He carries no contemporary philosophy of life, and invents none of his own. He is a Christian of that kind who is content to relate faith to his love of the creatures of this world ; the birds, beasts, flowers, clots of earth, trees, hills and streams, and an occasional human. Those manifests, moving or rooted, are his evidence of a paternal surveillance, and he is never tired of presenting them, intimately and individually, as demonstrators of a wisdom larger than the event in which he detects them.—*NS*

This passage lacks precision and sharpness because the writer has given scant attention to little points of vocabulary, punctuation and idiom.

(*a*) The comma after *decades* should be omitted. But ' touching the fringes of literary fashion ' is a confusion of the Biblical ' touching the hem of ' and ' being only on the fringe of '. The second of these is intended, with the necessary adjustment to the sentence: ' and has been (or *is*) only on . . .'

(*b*) The *therefore* of the second sentence is a trifle hard on the critics.

(*c*) ' carry weight ' but ' follow a philosophy '.

(*d*) The word *faith* is vague. Does the writer mean faith in the general sense, or the Christian faith? Probably the latter; and if so, should the word be qualified by *his*?

(*e*) The semi-colon after *world* should be a colon.

(*f*) Why not ' clod of earth ' instead of *clot*—leaving *clot* for blood, and for the figurative sense (' The man is a mere clot ')? The use of *human* for *man* or ' human being ' is not (yet) recognised in good English.

(*g*) A number of points arise in the last sentence:

  (i) Should *manifests* be *manifestations*, or is some rather obscure metaphor, derived from shipping, intended?

  (ii) The plural subject (*manifests*) with a singular complement (*evidence*) is awkward.[1]

  (iii) *paternal surveillance:* this Latinism may possibly be justified here; but it seems oddly out of place.

[1] See *Good English*, p. 18.

(iv) The last phrase ' as demonstrators . . .' has an air
of profundity, but defies analysis. How is a clot
(or clod) of earth detected in an event?

10. This absorption of brave heresies into the main stream
of knowledge and opinion, this perpetual conversion of
original genius into the commonplace, a rhythmic
process so familiar to the old, so incredible to the un-
grateful young, has certainly overtaken Jane Harrison's
work. Her fearless historical imagination was able to
seize upon the innovations of archaeology and anthropology and make them stir the over-disciplined studies
of classical mythology and religion to the very bottom.
If the works of her friend James Frazer, from whom
she drew so much of her early inspiration, have remained
longer in current use, it may be because her ideas have
been far more completely accepted than his, and have
therefore been assimilated, whereas *The Golden Bough*
endures a vast store of raw materials—*NS*

(a) In the second phrase ' original invention ' or some
such term would be better than ' original genius ', where
the ambiguity of *genius* rather blurs the antithesis. But
exactly what has *overtaken* Jane Harrison's work? Not
surely this absorption and this conversion, but a certain
neglect arising from them.

(b) ' Stir up, we beseech Thee ' is the beginning of a
famous collect; but not ' *stir* to the very bottom '. There
is here, probably, some muddled confusion of ' stir up ',
' plumb to the very bottom ' and ' drink to the dregs '.
However that may be, ' innovations of archaeology and
anthropology ' make rather queer spoons.

(c) ' whereas *The Golden Bough* endures a vast store of
raw materials ': (i) As the *whereas* implies a contrast
between Jane Harrison's work and Frazer's *Golden Bough*,
a qualifying *his* is not merely desirable but necessary
here; (ii) To me this clause is unintelligible; I leave the
reader to puzzle it out.

11. The debate will never cease as to the propriety of
publishing the private letters of public people. Matthew
Arnold was deeply shocked by the love-letters of John
Keats to Fanny Brawne. It made him realize the
difference between a man who had been to Rugby

School and a man who had not. He thanked God, or
he would have thanked Him could he have believed
there was a God, that he was a Rugby man and therefore
saved from the danger of being mawkish toward a young
woman, as he thought Keats was toward Fanny.

Does the artist in letters have a special duty to the
general public, that he should be willing for everything
he (or she) writes to be put into book form ; even his
laundry lists, and his unguarded outpourings of personal
anguish to some adored person? I do not know the
answer. Each individual case may best be judged on
its particular circumstances. Maybe time has some say
in the matter.—*JL*

A good (or bad) example of that kind of journalistic
prose which betrays an insensitiveness to words and
idioms. The following points are especially to be noted:

(*a*) *as to*:[1] Certainly ' debate as to ' is not sanctioned by
usage. There is here a woolly confusion of

   (i) ' The question of the propriety of publishing . . . is
     still open '

  (ii) ' The question whether it is proper to publish . . .
     is still open '

 (iii) ' The debate concerning the propriety of publishing
     . . . will never cease '.

(*b*) ' mawkish *about* ', not *towards*.

(*c*) The writer even raises a sex problem: ' he should
be willing for everything he (or she) writes '. If, through
the parenthetic alternative he makes the sex distinction
at the end, he must make it also at the beginning.

(*d*) ' judged on its *merits* ', not ' on its *circumstances* ';
' according to its circumstances ' would be permissible.

(*e*) The Americanism *maybe* (English *perhaps*) is out of
place in this context.

12. A familiar journalistic gambit is to divide people into
two classes—those who like tripe and those who don't,
or those who do and those who don't enjoy making
snowballs in May. My own favourite example is between
those who secure their ties with a paper fastener, and
those who don't. (It was years after I left Cambridge
before I discovered that this was not a universal practice,

[1] See *Good English*, p. 158.

just as it was only quite recently that I learnt that some people put on their overcoats one arm after another instead of both together as I naturally do.) Another division of mankind brought to my notice is between those who hold the handle of their attaché cases firmly and confidently with all their finger-tips tucked out of sight, and those who keep a forefinger cautiously extended down the side of the lid.—*NS*

A paragraph of loose carelessness in thought and expression:

(*a*) The writer twice uses *between* in an indefensible construction. ' My favourite example is between— ' is obviously meaningless; the sentence must be recast: ' My own favourite *pair* is those[1] who . . .'. In the last sentence *between* should be *into*, or the sentence may be recast according to the pattern of the other one, just noted. The comma after *sight* is unnecessary.

(*b*) ' that this was not a universal practice ': What is *this*? With or without paper fastener? Presumably with; but the construction leaves the matter in doubt.

(*c*) ' just as . . .': The only logical continuation would be ' . . . it was years after I left the Air Force ' or some such phrase; ' just as ' is an equals sign, and both sides of the equation must be balanced. Substitute *and*.

13. Scott is impossible to partition. He shows a perpetual intercommunication of nascent dignities and nascent faults ; and, in subsequent writings, much that was nascent in Scott has become departmentalized. The weakness of Mr. Roberts's case of Scott v. Trollope is that they are brought together on terms of industriousness, and contrasted on Trollope's terms, as if that was all there was in it. It is the contrast between a great explorer and another kind of traveller. It shows how unsafe it is to make predictions, says Mr. Roberts ; nevertheless, it may here be predicted that, as to that contrast, it is Scott who will remain.—*TLS*

A baffling passage of verbose obscurity. I have read it several times and am no wiser. So once more I leave

[1] Note that here there is no disagreement of subject and complement in number; the complement is a defined pair which may be represented by the symbols — a and $+ a$.

the interpretation to the reader. I merely jot down a few points that occurred to me:

Scott, I suppose, means ' Scott's work ', and *partition* ' divide into *e.g.* categories of style or theme '. The faults and the dignities are being born (*nascent*) and are communicating with each other all the time; but afterwards most of them become *departmentalized*, whatever that may mean.

In the second sentence ' *they* are brought together '. Who? What? Is ' brought together ' antithetical to *contrasted*? If so, how exactly are the terms contrasted, and how is the contrast related to an explorer and another kind of traveller? Who is the explorer, and who the traveller? Scott? Trollope? Why does Mr Roberts say it is unsafe to make predictions? What does the last clause mean (' as to that contrast, it is Scott who will remain ')? See *as to* (p. 162).

14. But the play is primarily the people and what is it that has gone wrong here? Why is it that we hardly ever smile at them? Why is it that we never *care*? The questions and their answers are linked. The constant component in all the different feelings that Chekhov's characters evoke in us should be compassion. Our laughter at them is indulgent, our tears for them of pity, our judgment over them suspended. They stumble through their human antics so seriously and yet so absurdly, and the seriousness and the absurdity are one and the same thing. But the producer here seems to have missed this point; he seems almost to have allotted the characters into groups—the serious and the funny; the three sisters in the first category, they are serious to the point of solemnity; the schoolmaster and the officers are funny; the visiting Colonel, Vershinin, somewhere in between. But of course we should be smiling at the over-seriousness of all the sisters just as there are times when we should be touched by the schoolmaster. Too many of the characters here are single- when they should be double-faced. This is in fact not tragedy but tragi-comedy, a kind of comedy that mixes smiles and sighs. Missing here is just this double dimension.—*NS*

A passage abounding in small errors and ambiguities:

(a) There must be some kind of stop, either a comma or a semi-colon, after *people*, to divide the statement from the question.

(b) ' The questions and their answers are linked '. This is ambiguous. It might mean that the questions are linked with their (hypothetical) answers; but as that is true of all questions and answers it was hardly worth stating. More probably it means that the three questions posed in the previous sentences (and therefore, by implication, their answers) have something in common.

(c) component *of*, not *in*; the writer, however, probably means ' element in '.

(d) ' Our laughter . . . suspended ': If the pattern of the sentence is to be symmetrical, as it should be, the adjective phrase ' of pity ' should be replaced by the simple adjective *pitiful*; ' our judgment *of* ', not *over*.

(e) ' allotted the characters into groups ': Mixed idiom:— ' *allot* a character *to* a group ', ' *divide* characters *into* groups '.

(f) ' they are serious . . .': Why this odd and quite unnecessary subject in apposition?

(g) ' just as . . .': An ' equals ' sign, as in sentence 12, p. 162. The sentence should therefore begin, ' But of course there are times when . . .' Or, the first clause being retained, a simple *and* should be substituted for ' just as '.

(h) ' Missing here . . . dimension ': This inversion is as odd and irresponsible as the apposition already noted. And by what scientific theory is the mixing of smiles and sighs a ' double dimension '?

15. The secret language emerging from Cavafy's idiomatic amalgam is sober, lapidary and infinitely subtle, a mysteriously musical algebra that penetrates deep layers of wisdom and sensibility with an unerring and tragic impact unattainable by more luxuriant techniques. Strange and sultry fumes rise from these smouldering equations: the ecstasies, the fevers and remorse of heterodox passions, the whiff of decay from overblown Hellenistic kingdoms from which all but one remaining petal—the sense of the elegant, the aesthetically appropriate gesture—has moulted.—*O*

I must again resort to the comprehension test:

   (i) Define ' idiomatic amalgam ', ' secret lapidary language '.

  (ii) How subtle is infinitely subtle?

 (iii) Would it be true to say that musical algebra differs from ordinary algebra in that it has penetrating power? If so, compare its penetrating power with that of more luxuriant techniques. Estimate roughly the force of its impact.

 (iv) From what smouldering equations do the strange and sultry fumes arise?

  (v) An overblown Hellenistic kingdom is—a flower, a bird, a domain? Underline the appropriate word.

16. The web of European civilization seems to have been slung between the ideas of Christianity and those of a half-secret rival, centring perhaps (if you made a system) round honour; one that stresses pride rather than humility, self-realization rather than self-denial, caste rather than either the communion of saints or the individual soul; while the words I want to look at here, whether in their hearty or their patronizing versions, come somewhat between the two, for they were used both to soften the assertion of class and to build a defence against Puritanism.—WILLIAM EMPSON: *The Structure of Complex Words*

A notable example of muddled thought and expression:

(*a*) For the opening metaphor see p. 111.

(*b*) Why the parenthesis? If you made a system of what? Presumably of the half-secret rival; and if so, why not say so?—' a half-secret rival system '.

(*c*) For ' centre round ' see p. 79.

(*d*) No comma is necessary after *rival*, and the semi-colon after *honour* should be either a colon or a dash. This point is discussed on p. 137.

(*e*) ' while the words . . .': This is apparently the antithetical *while* (=*but*); but there is, in fact, no antithesis. The web is slung between the two points, and the words come somewhat between them, whatever that may mean. At any rate, the web and the words seem to be roughly in the same place.

(*f*) ' whether in . . . or *in* ': See p. 40.

(g) ' for they . . .': This explanatory clause is obscure. The act of softening the assertion of class puts the words on the Christian side, but that of building a defence against Puritanism puts them on the side of the rival system only if Puritanism is considered synonymous with Christianity. And how does this illustrate that the words are ' somewhat between ' the two systems?

17. A certain claim to a workmanlike completeness is necessary if a dictionary is to seem more than a toy. Short dictionaries could, I think, be improved, and I will try in this chapter to say how, but most of the symbols used in this book would be out of place. In a dictionary claiming completeness I hope that all my symbols, or something corresponding to them, would be useful; but the undertaking would of course be an enormous one, and the N.E.D. collection of material is not likely to need improving except in minor detail. The idea of a still bigger dictionary than the N.E.D. is obviously impracticable if not ludicrous. But a revised edition of it is presumably envisaged for the eventual future, and it ought not to seem presumptuous for any member of the public to discuss how it should be recast. My general proposal is that the interactions of the senses of a word should be included, and if this is to seem reasonable I need to show that such a plan could be carried out without making the dictionary much longer. The obvious way to do this is to show that in its present form it is unnecessarily long, and I shall make here a few complaints about it to illustrate that point; but I ought first to say clearly, what I hope is already obvious, that such work on individual words as I have been able to do has been almost entirely dependent on using the majestic object as it stands.
—WILLIAM EMPSON: *The Structure of Complex Words*

(a) First sentence: It is the workmanlike completeness that is necessary, not the claim to it.

(b) ' Short dictionaries . . . minor detail ': There are some loose *ands* and *buts* in this passage. In the first sentence the *and* is better omitted and the clause made frankly parenthetic—that is, enclosed between dashes or brackets. The other two clauses are not properly or clearly antithetical. The writer means ' could be improved by the use of symbols, but (or better, *though*) the symbols used . . .'. In the second sentence *undertaking* is so vague and general that the *but*, which implies some further reference to the symbols, has no true force. The *and* introduces a clause that seems to have no relevance at all in this context.

(*c*) The idea of a bigger dictionary is not impracticable or ludicrous. Indeed, it has suggested itself to Mr Empson. But the making of such a dictionary may be. There should be a comma after *impracticable*.

(*d*) What is the *eventual* future? Is it farther off than the ordinary future?

(*e*) ' My general proposal ' becomes later ' such a plan '. But in this context the two are not properly equated.

(*f*) ' The obvious way to do this ': To do what? The reference back from an active verb to a passive (' could be carried out ') is always a loose and faulty construction.

(*g*) The OED has been called many things, but never before a ' majestic object '. This is a piece of elegant variation that would have delighted Fowler.

18. He does not write too much (though the fourth chapter dealing with them is drier than it need have been) about the aridities of literary intrigue and warfare. Perhaps, though, he writes too little of the real substance of the poems, the interests and the habits of imagination and personality they reveal, the poet at once of Palladian order and the tree released from topiary, of man as " the glory, jest and riddle of the world " and of the sane, keen recognition of the risible and ridiculous. I should have liked more of Pope in his verbal grotto —the sparkling grotto of words, rhythms, periods and subtleties.—*O*

This is taken from a review of a critical study of Pope. In the first sentence the pronoun (*them*) inside the parenthesis very awkwardly precedes the noun it relates to (*aridities*). The remedy is to put the parenthesis at the end of the sentence, preferably taking out the brackets and marking it with a comma after *warfare*. Owing to the writer's careless and arbitrary treatment of *of* it is difficult to follow the construction of the next sentence. There should certainly be an *of* before ' the interests ' and before ' the poet '. But what does ' of the poet at once of Palladian order and the tree released from topiary ' mean? Possibly ' at once ' should be taken out, since there is no convenient balance here, and *of* should be inserted before ' the tree ' to make another item of the enumeration.

No doubt ' his verbal grotto ' is a reference to Pope's famous grotto in Twickenham; but it would be obscure to those who had not chanced to read the detailed description of this grotto with its various sorts of stones, flints, crystals and the like.[1] In any case, ' should have liked more of Pope in his verbal grotto ' is syntactically unintelligible.

19. We want for them, as you want for your children, conditions and opportunities that will give them the best chance in life: well qualified teachers; classes small enough to permit us and our pupils to do justice to ourselves and to them; a proper school place for every child; school buildings which are at least decent in terms of modern amenities, and a sufficiency of tools with which to do our job.—*Schoolmaster*

This sentence manages to keep out of trouble down to the word *teachers*, except that a hyphen is lacking in *well-qualified*. After that, the writer first forgets his beginning, and then slips into wordy and woolly pomposities. Having begun, not in general terms ' We want ', but with the specific expression ' We want for them ', the writer cannot refer to ' our pupils ' and ' every child ' as if they are outside the whole category represented by *them*. He should write ' permit us and them to do justice '. Even then, ' and to them ' at the end of the phrase is meaningless. To whom? There is no answer. For the next phrase I can suggest nothing better than ' proper school places ', which has some kind of meaning and is vague enough to appeal to any reasonable educationist. Certainly we cannot add ' for them all ' since the original ' for them ' is still potent. We then come upon buildings ' decent in terms of modern amenities '. This means nothing more than ' with decent modern amenities '. The phrase ' in terms of ' defies analysis. Except in mathematical language (' Express y in terms of x ') it is nearly always meaningless

[1] Given in Edith Sitwell's *Alexander Pope*, p. 147 (Penguin edition).

and therefore unnecessary. The last sentence is a piece of schoolmasterly pedantry for ' and enough tools to do our job with '.

20. Both Lucretius and Jeans are philosophizing in terms of infinitesimal units of matter or energy, or what not —so insignificant that it is painfully headachy, except for scientific adepts, to bring the mind to bear on them at all, but which exist more tangibly than difficult generalizations because they answer troublesome questions ' beautifully ' (Jeans' word).—ROBERT GRAVES: *The Common Asphodel*

Again the phrase ' in terms of ' has no recognisable meaning. Are Lucretius and Jeans using these units as mathematicians use x and π? If so, how do these units or terms answer troublesome questions? And how do they exist *tangibly*—that is, susceptible to touch? Little wonder that the writer also perpetrates a remarkable piece of but-whichery. A purist would object to the colloquialisms ' and what not ' and *headachy* in the midst of so much pseudo-philosophical jargon, and to the loose parenthesis at the end. *Jeans's* is better than *Jeans'*.

CHAPTER X

A MIXED BAG

MOTH: They have been at a great feast of languages, and stolen the scraps.—*Love's Labour's Lost*

1. *An Agenda*

Sir, I have observed a movement lately, both in the Press and on the air, in favour of the phrase ' an agenda '. Surely this is an errata, or should I say a corrigenda? It certainly strikes me as a strange phenomena, but perhaps there is a data somewhere which justifies the use of the phrase, and which I have overlooked. Perhaps it should be possible to have a referenda on this question,

Yours etc.,

D. F. FERGUSON

—Letter in *The Times*

Though the dictionaries are non-committal on this point it is safe to say that *agenda* is frequently, indeed usually, singular in modern English. Arguments of this kind are based on a false conception of language. They seem to regard the borrowed word as static, not liable to the changes of the language that assimilated it. But that is not so, even when the word, like *agenda*, keeps its original form. The following sentence accords with normal usage:

Both the Americans and the Russians seem to want an absolutely rigid agenda.—*NS*

If we omit the indefinite article (' want absolutely rigid agenda ') we sacrifice living English to dead Latin. To the Englishman *agenda* does not mean ' things to be done '; it means ' a list of things to be done '. So he makes it singular. He would even, if there were any occasion for it, make a new ordinary English plural—*agendas*. Even Fowler implies that *agenda* is always plural; he says: " If a singular is required it is now *agendum*, the former singular *agend* being obsolete ".

Mr Ferguson's satire would have been more usefully directed against the illiterate use of *juvenilia* as a singular in the following sentence:

I can select passages, however, to show how this young

poet had matured after a precocious juvenilia, to become
an artist comparable to the composer Scriabin.—*JL*

2. *-ics and -ic*

In Hollywood, they have pressed on with the tactic
which might be described as Operation Whitewash, or
redressing the redskin.—*O*

The shift of Taste was complete, though its ethic was
rather confused.—*JL*

Mr. Steegman, in his examination of nineteenth century
aesthetic which he calls, with an uncharacteristic touch
of jocosity, *Consort of Taste*, enlarges the statement with
a justice that hardly ever lets the scales tilt.—*TLS*

The question of the grammatical number of words in
-ics is discussed in *Good English*. These three sentences
raise another problem. The writer of the first, obviously
assuming that *tactics* is a real plural, and himself preferring
a singular, resorts to the ' unpluralised ' form *tactic*; that
is, he considers a *tactic* to be one of a number of *tactics*.
But *tactic* (as singular of *tactics*) is not yet recognised in
English, though it quite often slips into (especially journalistic) writing. The reader, however, is counselled for
the time being, at any rate, to stick to *tactics* and treat it
syntactically as a plural.

The second writer forgets a legitimate and useful distinction. There is a ' singular ', *ethic*, which means the whole
philosophical system or formulation of morals, as in the
phrase common among theologians ' the Christian *ethic* '.
Ethics (plural) is a commoner word; it simply means the
morals, or system of morality, associated with a person, a
sect, or an abstract quality, like *Taste* in the sentence
quoted. The writer should have said ' its *ethics* '. So we
speak of ' a man's *ethics* ', ' the *ethics* of the modern novel ',
and (distinguished from ' the Christian *ethic* ') ' the *ethics* of
Christianity '.

There seems to be no real reason for the third writer's
use of *aesthetic*. The normal word is *aesthetics* (' usu. pl.
as collect. sing.'—SOED), and there is no reason in this context to lop off its characteristic *s*. Probably the writer was
thinking of *ethic* in the use noted above; but (to speak mathe-
matically) *aesthetic* is not to *aesthetics* as *ethic* is to *ethics*.

Two *-ics/ic* words are, by the way, more obviously distinguished: *physics*, the study of the whole natural world, and *physic*, taken, after meals, three times a day.

3. *Official English*

Here is a paragraph from a schedule issued by the Office of Wages Boards and Councils, which was quoted recently by a correspondent in the *Daily Telegraph*:

> If a contract between a worker and his employer provides for the payment of less remuneration than the statutory minimum remuneration clear of all deductions it is to have effect as if for that less remuneration there were substituted the statutory minimum remuneration clear of all deductions and if any such contract provides for the payment of holiday remuneration at times or subject to conditions other than those specified in that order it is to have effect as if for those times or conditions there were substituted the times or conditions specified in the Order.

Now this is a perfectly good specimen of legal or quasi-legal English. In its own idiom it is quite clear and comprehensible, and is appropriate to a formal document intended for the instruction of an employer or, for example, the Secretary of a Trades Union. But according to the correspondent it had to be kept posted up where it could be conveniently read by the workers. In that position and with that function it becomes bad English, since no layman, reading it casually as he would read any other displayed notice, could understand it except with the utmost difficulty. English is often good or bad according to its content and purpose. Set up to be read by all and sundry the notice should run something like this:

> In future you will be paid the standard (or *statutory*) minimum wage clear of deductions; and your holiday pay also will be fixed according to the conditions laid down by the Government.

4. *Bernard Shaw on ' Let you and I '*

" You and me " is so often spoken incorrectly that it produces an effect of vulgarity even when it is correct. " You and I " is so often spoken correctly that it sounds right even when it is in the accusative. The Dauphin thinks so. You think so. I think so. None of us

would dream of saying " Let I mind my own business "
but only by a violent effort to be pedantically grammatical can we make ourselves say " Let you and me
mind our own business." Yet we always say " Let us "
and not " Let we."

There was no ' slip ' in the business. The Dauphin
says just what he would have said if he had spoken
English though he would certainly not have said " Que
vous et je " instead of " Que vous et moi."

This is a quotation from a letter from Bernard Shaw
on the ' Let you and I ' problem. It appeared in an
article contributed to the *New Statesman* by Mr Allan M.
Laing, who had written to Shaw pointing out that the
Dauphin (in *Saint Joan*) was made to say " Let you and I ".
Shaw's argument is unsound. It is not true that ' you and
me ' is often spoken incorrectly. Nobody would say ' you and
me ' when the phrase is obviously subject; and it only rarely
occurs as a complement (' It's you and me '). But it is true
to say that ' you and I ' has become a kind of colloquial cliché
which defies the rules of case. In speech it is pretty well established, but the literary language holds out against it.[1]

5.   *Brief Interlude on the Language of Sport*

When Gray wrote in the *Ode on a Distant Prospect of
Eton College*

To chase the rolling circle's speed
And urge the flying ball

he was unconsciously providing a model for all future
sports reporters. The old clichés, ' wield the willow '
' boot the leather ', and the like, have almost been laughed
out of court now. For what a recent sports commentator
called " the almost comically hackneyed terms of low level
reporting " have been substituted new and, on the whole,
more pungent idioms and a crisper turn of phrase. It is
the high-level reporting, influenced on the one hand by
Cardus and on the other by the almost incredible
fatuities of the broadcast commentary (especially on
cricket), that nowadays is both amazing and amusing.
In the main, it is concerned with cricket and golf, though
sometimes the superior football correspondent indulges
in a few ' phoney ' linguistic whims. Here, for example,

[1] See *Good English*, p. 38.

is a sentence from the *Observer*, where the sentimentalised background irrelevancies of broadcasting idiom suddenly develop into a very old and sorely tried cliché:

> On a somewhat sleepy afternoon, with a mist-ringed sun shining over the riverside trees, Portsmouth beat Fulham at Craven Cottage yesterday by the odd goal in five.

But it is the cricket correspondent who excels. The reader may like to translate the italicised phrases in the following sentences into ordinary idiom or the normal technical language of the game:

> Johnson and Morris played out the few minutes to lunch *without much agitation of bat*.—O

> Five runs later Mansell, offering no stroke at all, watched the ball hit his pads and the umpire *raise his finger*.—MG

> Statham got one that popped up sharply and again Cheetham *in the gully had employment*.—O

> Parkhouse's bat made *pleasant if passive* movements. —MG

And here, from the *Manchester Guardian*, is the precious and the portentous. It must be admitted that the use of *fretful*, though archaic in standard English (" like quills upon the fretful porpentine "), has a certain aptness here. All the same, it has also a certain ' over-literary ' and artificial air:

> If the pitch did at periods take some spin it was only sufficiently fretful to explain how utterly ill-equipped even some of the more competent contemporary batsmen are to play a turning ball with comfort.

The peculiar influence of cricket on the prose style of those who write about it is remarkable. I have already mentioned Cardus. Here is a paragraph to show how even a writer like Edmund Blunden can falter when he is under the fascination of bat and ball:

> I was going into the Oval ground, and as I went I was raising my head to spy over the hats of the front rows of spectators; and I saw the most terrifying fast ball wing down that I had seen. It did nothing; it was a full toss. But the authorship even to my eye was unique. I had seen, if I saw nothing more by that

hand, the best fast bowler of the day. . . . At Manchester, when the Australian innings was hardening inexorably, Woodfull's partner played the ball well down past Hammond in the slips—a safe run. Hammond moved, gathered, turned and flung and Woodfull, spying danger and making a vast attempt to get home, was out. Nobody in that learned cricket crowd seemed less bewildered than I or very possibly than the batsman. Hammond appeared to have cancelled the duration of time. These are but commas in the careers of the players mentioned, but they linger written on a spectator's brain. Greatness can be identified, like the touch of a painter, in a detail. Prescience is worth seeing in a sceptical world.

(from *Cricket Country*)

It is full of fustian words and phrases and ' fuzzy ' English—' the Oval *ground* ', ' *wing* down ', ' had seen ' (for ' had ever seen '), *authorship*, ' by that hand ', ' hardening inexorably ', ' a *vast* attempt ', ' learned cricket crowd ', ' cancelled the duration of time '. What is the meaning of the comma metaphor, and what has prescience to do, or not do, with scepticism?

Some of the phrases in that passage might well come from a report on golf; for your golfing correspondent is a great purveyor of odd adjectives, and adverbs and metaphors, the undertones and overtones of a language that seems to belong especially to club and dormy houses. A few examples follow, most of them from *The Times* and the *Daily Telegraph*:

After luncheon it was *odiously* cold with a strong, bitter northerly wind.

Bennett played a second shot just as *wicked* as his morning one had been *virtuous*.

. . . and had holed a most *unkindly*[1] long putt for one of the 3's.

Bennett holed a good putt almost *to shut the door* at the 17th and then gave it a resounding bang with a pitch to within a few feet of the home hole.

A. D. Evans and F. van Donck started *fantastically* against H. J. Roberts and A. Poulton, and were five up.

[1] See p. 88.

They took the match to the eighteenth before they
bowed their heads to the tune of two holes.

6. *Pun and Word-play*

Now and then in higher journalism pun and word-play,
so tedious in Shakespeare and other Elizabethan writers
and so excessively beloved by Lamb and Hood, show
ominous signs of coming back. Here are four examples,
all from the *Observer*. The first is comparatively innocuous:

> What we get in *The Gay Invalid* is not so much a version
> of the French as a diversion in English.

But the descent to the merely slick and facetious is an
easy one:

> Peter Cotes managed with great tact—shared by his
> cast—to save Marguerite Buller's dialogue from embar-
> rassing us too much by its Marie Corelli lushness: a
> putting-it-on that can only put us off.
> Cole Porter must be dwindling to a cinder if he can
> pass this. But " In My Fashion " has the real glow of
> his remarkable talents. There he is in proper form.
> Such great-souled fellows [policemen] have a grand
> retirement waiting them on the golf course.

" Not on thy soul, but on thy sole, harsh Jew "—this
last pun is at least as old as Shakespeare. It occurs in a
short article in which the author all the way through
not only plays with words but also indulges in the new
trick of playing with quotations. The older writers, like
Hazlitt and Lamb, would mark time, as it were, and
introduce their quotation (not always accurate) with a
flourish. There was no doubt about it. It was immediately recognisable, even if the reader did not know its
source. But the fashion today is to introduce the quotation
obliquely, to twist it to fit the context, to give it a kind
of *ad hoc* figurative meaning, even to pun upon it. Here
is an example from the article I have already mentioned:

> Let those who are putting a paunch as well as a punch
> in it glue themselves to the clay and get Mother Earth
> well stuck beneath the arches.

Elsewhere, the writer does not hesitate to play upon a fixed
stereotyped idiom:

Obese sportsmen cannot over-swing and so become objects of horror to the eye, as well as murderers of their game, if they are well-grounded and unquestionably down at heel.

The writer's main argument is that when playing golf we should wear heavy boots and stand rooted to the soil. He begins his sentence with a pun and ends with a twisted quotation (" Underneath the Arches ", by the way, is the title of the article). And he cannot leave it there. His final sentence is:

Hail, then, to the Fallen Arch, which, on the eighteenth green, is indeed the Arc de Triomphe.

I give a few further examples. The reader is invited to spot the quotations, and relate each (if possible) to its context. There is no suggestion here that this literary device is to be condemned. Its rather dubious association with the pun has already been hinted at; and it has in extra measure the disadvantage of all quotation, that it tends to argue a certain superiority on the part of the writer. At its best it can be witty and effective, as in sentence (*d*) below; but when, as in sentence (*b*) the writer overdoes it, or, as in passage (*e*), plays havoc with his quotation, it becomes a tedious and irritating trick. My own comments on the examples given are on p. 185.

(*a*) But the shades of the prison house close with a too prolonged procrastination around the adolescents, and Miss Chapman, holding a good hand, shows it too soon and too often. The much less, and how much more it would be!—*O*

(*b*) What, for example, will *The Martins' Nest* contain? Plainly a family of Martins, with the ' semi-basement in East Putney ' as their procreant cradle. The ' credits ' allow for ' sink and plumbing,' ' gas-meter,' ' beer ' and ' nylons.' The cast includes a Detective-Sergeant. Will it be murder in the maisonette? Or suicide in the cellarage, deeper than did ever plumber sound? Or a bride in the bath? Joan Morgan's tale (at the Westminster Theatre) emerges near to tragedy. Shades of the mental home and prison-house begin to close upon the growing boys. . . But if Providence watches over the fall of a sparrow, why not over Putney-haunting martlets?—*O*

(c) Now that the National Jubilation is in full blast, every community in the land has come out in cross-garters.—*S*

(d) A policeman's wife is not a happy one, that is if she keeps queer company.—*O*

(e) It was said that she possessed a man's mind; that may well be true; but she also possessed a very feminine temperament.—*O*

(f) Yet he serves Hayley well; the hospitable Hermit's Good deserves, however ephemerally, to be disinterred from his grave: for whatever Evil has lived after him is, after all, in the comic vein.—*NS*

(g) At first he was suspect for his unwarranted optimism, for stubbornly maintaining that the year's at the spring when Hardy and Housman had convinced poetry readers that it was at its most suicidal sere — *O*

(h) So throughout two volumes this Roman statesman is harried with all the slings and arrows which scholarship can devise and hatred employ. *NS*

(i) In the Church Hall was staged an exhibition of relics a few flakes of the snows of yester-year.—*S*

7. *Who and Whom*

Sir,—The winning entry in your competition last week was a supposed extract from *The Times* that contained a grammatical mistake—" to whomsoever may suffer." I shall be interested to learn whether the judge thought this mistake characteristic or merely did not notice it.

Yours faithfully,
RAYMOND MORTIMER

Sir,—I remember the shock that I received when I saw in *The Times* a year or two ago, and not in the correspondence columns, the same grammatical mistake as that contained in the winning entry for your competition. The competitor must, I feel sure, have purposely introduced the solecism, and the judge, no doubt having been previously shocked, quite rightly awarded him the prize after careful consideration of the more typical substance of the passage.

The distressing misuse of ‘ who ’ and ‘ whom ’ has, by the way, enormously increased in the last twenty-five years.—Yours faithfully,

GRAHAM HOGGARTH
—*Spectator*

In our dealings with *who* and *whom* we are rather like St Paul in his dealings with good and evil: the *whom* that we should write that we write not, and the *who* that we should not, that we write. Even Mr Churchill has his doubts:

> By whom is he employed? Who is he under?—*Their Finest Hour*

In the phrase quoted *whomsoever* is not object of *to* but subject of its own clause; it should therefore be *whosoever*. But the truth is that *whom* and its compounds (*whomever*, *whomsoever*) have an uneasy existence in English. There are signs that the inflection is gradually disappearing through misuse and disuse. Impressive evidence of this development in modern usage has been supplied to me by a German correspondent, Studienrat Eitzen of Hamburg, to whose courtesy and erudition I am indebted not only for this but for other commentaries:

> *Who* would they find for him?—ALDOUS HUXLEY: *Green Tunnels*
>
> *Who* do you think I should offer them to?—WILFRED PARTINGTON, *Thomas J. Wise in the Original Cloth*
>
> " It does not matter *who* you marry."
> " *Whom*, not *who*."
> " Oh, speak English! "
>
> —BERNARD SHAW: *Village Wooing*
>
> One of the many duties of an assistant stage manager is to notice *who* steals from *who*.—JOSEPH MACLEOD: *Curtain Call*
>
> " *Who* did you want them for? "
> " *Whom*," corrected Miss Whittaker.
> " *Who*! " thundered Tubby.
>
> —P. G. WODEHOUSE: *Summer Moonshine*
>
> . . . a person *who* perhaps we are not particularly proud of.—THE BISHOP OF LONDON.
>
> In America an ' intellectual ' has been defined as ' one who wears horn spectacles and says " whom " ', while, in such a centre of culture as Boston, even the owls are reputed to emit the cry, " To-whit, to-whom."
>
> —ERNEST WEEKLEY, *The Spectator*, December 10, 1948

If what the second correspondent calls the " distressing misuse of *who* and *whom* " gives us in the end a single indeclinable *who* for subject and object, so much the better. The language will be simplified, and at least one mistake will be made impossible.

8. *Mr Addison*

In an amusing letter communicated to the *Sunday Times* by Mr Charles Morgan masquerading as Tom Tremble, a student of Mr Joseph Addison, several examples are given of 'discouraging' English in a Ministry of Education circular. "Even", says Tom Tremble, "in the brief extracts from it given by the Press ' in the field of ' appears six times and ' in view of ' or ' with a view to ' five. The document gives us other reasons to believe that Mr Addison may have lived in vain ". Two of Tom Tremble's examples, with his suggested amendments in brackets, are given:

> In the field of primary and secondary schools she (the Minister) regards it as important that proper standards of teaching should be maintained. (*It is important to maintain high standards of teaching in primary and secondary schools.*)

> The Minister considers that this increase in expenditure on administration cannot be wholly justified on the basis of factors outside the control of authorities. (*. . . that this increase in administrative expenditure is partly within the authorities' control.*)

Such woolly English, which is all too common in circulars of the Ministry of Education, deserves trouncing. It ought to be said, however, that Mr Joseph Addison is not necessarily a safe guide to *modern* English usage.

9. *Top-spin*

P. G. Wodehouse's Psmith, masquerading as a modern poet who had perpetrated the line "Across the pale parabola of joy ", and being asked what it meant, replied indulgently, " Well, perhaps I did put a little top-spin on that one ". Most modern poets since the days of the earlier Eliot have been top-spinners; indeed, not to be—to write ' poetic ' poetry in ordinary English—was to commit artistic suicide. The cult of the difficult has had a surprisingly long run, perhaps because what is hard for the reader is easier for the writer, who after all can and does resort to a private syntax and a private imagery which in the nature of things are outside the canons of ordinary criticism. *The Waste Land*—though itself nowadays (I believe) a little outmoded —is symptomatic of the modern fashion. In the waste land there are no landmarks; your poet is the only one who knows the way.

In prose, the great influence of James Joyce has made fashionable a 'stream of consciousness' style, a kind of prose which avoids, in the main, the 'periodic' sentence of interrelated subordinate clauses but flows on with the aid of simple connectives, like water running out of a tap:

> He could not get out the answer for the sum but it did not matter. White roses and red roses: those were beautiful colours to think of. And the cards for first place and third place were beautiful colours too: pink and cream and lavender. Lavender and cream and pink roses were beautiful to think of. Perhaps a wild rose might be like those colours and he remembered the song about the wild rose blossoms on the little green place.—*Portrait of the Artist as a Young Man*

From this it is only a step to the telegraphese of *Ulysses*, the total abandonment of punctuation (see p. 149), and finally the running together of words and syllables in *Finnegans Wake*. Whether the Joycean eccentricities of language will have a permanent effect on normal syntax and idiom remains to be seen. At present they have not gone beyond the realm of fiction. The prose of criticism, for example, normally follows conventional modern usage.

With the novelist of today, syntactical tradition is suspect. No doubt the 'tough' American style of the Hemingway type (represented, for example, in Joyce Cary) has a great influence. The significant moment is not to be interpreted, mirrored, or described in the ordinary framework of subject and predicate, the conventional grouping of phrases, the normal grammatical pattern. Old rhythms must be broken down, lest emotion and sentiment rear their head. Taut, spare, economical, masculine, intellectual, nervous—these are the watchwords. 'Style' in the old traditional sense is taboo. A sentence should show its bones.

There is a curious manifestation of this in certain writers who deliberately use a syntax that is, as it were, a trifle ' off-centre '. Elizabeth Bowen is one of them. I give a few examples from her novel *The Heat of the Day*:

(i) The use of the inflected (apostrophe *s*) possessive for other than personal nouns:

' Nothing but the fire's flutter and the clock's ticking '; ' another post's bomb '; ' the lamp's dazzling shade '; ' on the restaurant's wall '; ' the senses' harmony'; ' these hundreds of books' indifference.'

(ii) The use of repetitive stammer, common also in much modern verse:

They need not come coming round after her.

An hour ago, perhaps, what had been being said had become not necessary.

Who was it who was here whom I didn't know?

(iii) The use of exaggerated inversion:
— decapitated, he said he shouldn't wonder if many of them were.

(iv) A deliberate variation in normal word order and phrase grouping. In the last two sentences there is again the repetitive stammer:

The restaurant at which they met most often was this morning, he was sorry to tell her, closed.

She was thinking, was this to be, after all, all?

In the street below, not so much a step as the semi-stumble of someone after long standing shifting his position could be, for the first time by her, heard.

It is difficult to see the end of all this. Usage changes slowly, but it does change. Fowler, for example, is already a little out-of-date. But the question, after all, remains ' What is usage? ' Are the poets, and especially the novelists, of today modifying or defying convention by hurrying on a new convention? Or is their work independent of the normal pattern of English syntax and idiom as it is so far developed? Is ' Literature ' (with a capital L), in fact, creating for itself more than ever before a private idiom of its own, unrelated to the common idiom? These are difficult questions. We can only wait and see.

ANSWERS TO QUESTIONS IN THE TEXT

P. 22.

The bracketing, with the *of* inside the brackets, suggests that the antecedents (*muddles, inspiration*) are to be taken separately; but that makes impossible the correct agreement of the verb. I should bring the *of* outside the brackets—'examples of (the muddles as well as the inspiration)'—so that the antecedent is of the *a + b* pattern, and therefore plural.

P. 24.

    (*a*) Better 'What *stands* out . . . *is* not'; that is, *what* is a singular pronoun.

    (*b*) No change necessary, though *what* could conceivably be singular here.

P. 57.

'terms between most relations': for 'terms upon which most relations live'. The writer has sought to avoid 'relationship *of* or *between* relations' and has resorted to the loose construction with *terms*.

P. 80.

    (i) Probably *clues*. But the half-dead metaphor should be dropped. For *viewpoints* substitute *interpretations*.

    (ii) Yes. But 'leads to a variety of points of view' is still metaphorically muddled. See (i) above.

    (iii) No: *another* standpoint, but not a *wider* one. Substitute 'with a wider conception/understanding we may see our fuel difficulties as . . .'.

    (iv) Both 'angle' figures defy mathematical analysis, but both are idiomatically sound.

P. 82.

In none of these sentences is the antithetical *if* really justified.

    (*a*) Recast: 'The spectacle . . . seems . . . , but that is only half the story'.

    (*b*) The *if* of this sentence may not be antithetical but really conditional. If so, the sentence may stand.

    (*c*) '. . . in his relations with Cowper, both as friend and biographer, he achieved some little measure of it'. The antithesis is between *blundered* and *achieved*.

    (*d*) Here the *if* could stand if the order of the clauses were reversed; that is, the sentence would rise to a climax: 'If the accounts are interesting . . . the chapters are absorbing'.

(e) See p. 114.

P 108.

(a) If you are on the horns of a dilemma at all, you are, willy-nilly, on both horns. You cannot pick and choose. The writer of this sentence has no understanding of the dilemma image; and his wrong use of it has rendered his sentence unintelligible.

(b) You cannot at one and the same time be *on* the horns and *between* them. Where exactly this writer intends you to be is difficult to determine.

P. 159.

. . . that in the end it is useless to be discriminate with aloof detachment, and that it is her duty to be emotionally involved in everything.

P. 178.

(a) Shades of the prison-house begin to close
   Upon the growing boy.
       —WORDSWORTH: *Ode on Intimations of Immortality*
   The little more, and how much it is!
   And the little less, and what worlds away!
       —BROWNING: *By the Fireside*
The phrase 'with a too prolonged procrastination' is a piece of heavy facetiousness. On the whole, the paradoxical reversal of the Browning quotation is legitimate and apt.

(b) A clever but ostentatious display, with an ingenious pun (iv) thrown in:
   (i)   No jutty, frieze,
      Buttress, nor coign of vantage, but this bird
      Hath made his pendent bed and procreant cradle.
                              —*Macbeth* i. 6.
   (ii) *Murder on the Second Floor*—title of play
   (iii) You hear this fellow in the cellarage.—*Hamlet* i. 5.
   (iv) Deeper than did ever plummet sound.—*Tempest* v. 1.
   (v) Shades of the prison-house. See (a) above.
   (vi) the fall of a sparrow.—Matthew x. 29.
   (vii) the temple-haunting martlet.—*Macbeth* i. 6.

(c) and cross-gartered, a fashion she detests.—*Twelfth Night* ii. 5.
Used of Malvolio in his appearance before Olivia. Here apparently figurative for 'gaily', 'festively'.

    (*d*) A policeman's lot is not a happy one.—GILBERT: *Pirates of Penzance*.

    (*e*) I have a man's mind, but a woman's might.—Saying attributed to Queen Elizabeth.

The antithesis is spoilt here by the repetition of the verb and the use of the adjective *feminine*.

    (*f*) The evil that men do lives after them,
        The good is oft interred with their bones.
                    —*Julius Caesar* iii. 2.

    (*g*) The year's at the Spring.—BROWNING: *Pippa Passes*

The apt contrast is lost in the phrase ' at its most suicidal sere.' Why not ' at the Winter '?

    (*h*) The slings and arrows of outrageous fortune.—*Hamlet* iii. 1.

    (*i*) Où sont les neiges d'antan?—FRANÇOIS VILLON.

THIRTY QUESTIONS

A NUMBER of questions is here propounded to the reader on various points of usage. My own answers and comments, in which from time to time I have taken the opportunity of discussing questions and problems that have not been dealt with in the text, are to be found on pp. 204 ff. It need scarcely be said that the aim of this examination (which need frighten nobody) is not to make pedants, but to render those who have an interest in language alert to its dangers and aware of its possibilities. The reader is advised to make his own decision before seeking mine; and to remember that provided he puts away prejudice and uses his intelligence to the full he may with an easy conscience enjoy the luxury of disagreeing.

1. Comment on the grammatical number of the verbs italicised in the following sentences. Which of the verbs would you justify? Which not? In which of the sentences would you be tempted to sacrifice pure grammar to convenience?

(a) . . . and neither Parliament nor the electorate *have* any part in these decisions.—*NS*

(b) · . . none the less harmful because neither he nor Lord Hankey *are* aware of the sleight of hand which they are perpetrating on the unwary reader.—*NS*

(c) Of course, neither he nor his colleagues *have* ever urged that on any matter or substance the Government should stand up to the Americans.—*NS*

Subsidiary question:
Is *perpetrating* the right word in sentence (b)? If not, why not? What word would you substitute for it?

2. Using the three following sentences and the first sentence of this section as a text, write a note on grammatical *attraction* and the collective noun as subject:

(a) But unfortunately a proportion of the map references in the text are inaccurate.—*O*

(b) A number of correspondents have written asking me whether it will not be possible " to co-ordinate the activities " of the various bodies now working to avert war.—*NS*

(c) Only a tiny minority of pacifists denies the need for a reasonable armament programme for legitimate purposes of Western defence.—*NS*

3. In the following sentences verb and subject disagree in number. What led the writer astray? State as briefly as you can a general rule governing this construction, for his guidance and your own:

(a) There are a wealth of stories in this novel, all curious, all good, and seldom have a collection of eccentrics been welded into a book whose outstanding attitude is a boisterous acceptance of normalcy.—*O*

(b) . . . for there are a lengthy table of dates and bibliography.—*TES*

4. Common usage would require *is* for *are* in the following sentence. Why?

Conformity to British world policy, belief in the sagacity of the British Government and its expert advisers are wide and deep.—*S*

Subsidiary question:
Should there be a comma after *advisers*?

5. In each of the following sentences the writer begins with a singular pronoun or pronoun-adjective (*neither, everyone*), forgets it, and follows on with a related plural (*were, selves*). Explain briefly why. Correct the sentences, if you think they need correction.

(a) Neither catch was easy but were of the kind which Lancashire usually hold.—*MG*

(b) . . . which anyhow gives everyone a chance to play their own selves without bothering about acting.—*NS*

(c) Everybody will now return to their normal functions, feeling that life is horribly quotidian.—*S*

6. Show that in each of the following sentences verb and subject disagree in number:

(a) Another memorable scene is that where the child Ellen, with a little white boy who has befriended her against the will of his puritan Scottish mother, conspire together to water regularly a little vegetable garden by moonlight. —*JL*

(b) The originality, and for the reader the amusement, lies in the reaction of these two cosmopolitan children to the school and the school to them.—*JL*

(c) *Catherine Brooke* is one of those novels that is less interesting in its own right than as an archetypal example.—*NS*

(d) Mr Louis Golding's *Five Silver Daughters*, whose birth and upbringing were recorded in a novel which I reviewed here years ago, have since become a world-wide currency, of sterling value.—*JL*

(e) There is no alternative but to do what the newspapers and every other periodical has done or will, we believe, be compelled to do very soon.—*NS*

Show that this disagreement affects the whole meaning of sentences (a) and (d). Would you justify the verb in sentence (b)? Comment on the agreement in the following sentence:

(f) She produces character after character who not only moves but breathes in print.—*JL*

Supplementary Question:

Would you justify the use of the word *alternative* in sentence (e)?

7. Recast each of the following sentences by establishing a correct relationship between the verbal phrase and the main sentence. Indicate in some way the words qualified or modified by the phrases.

(a) Looking back over the years, it seems certain that this race began to be won when the tortoise entered it.—*T*

(b) After listening to so much of that broadcast back-chat they call discussion it was a pleasure to hear a bout of civilised conversation on the Third Programme.—*O*

(c) Noting the spread of the cult and paying all due respect to the good offices of glasses, hope may be breathed that they never become, for the well-dressed woman, compulsory.—*T*

8.

(a) But of course the play stands or falls by Harry, and there is never the slightest danger of *it doing* the latter.—*S*

(b) He began by being a mathematician but discovered, as I remember *him telling* me . . . .—*NS*

(c) The result is a reconciliation, and the prospect of *the married lovers being* given a fair start . . .—*JL*

(d) Why should he not appreciate amateur, junior and schoolboy football *being assessed* as seriously as the professional game?

What is grammatically wrong with the phrases italicised? Which of them would you justify? Why? Correct the others.

Subsidiary Question:

Comment on the use of ' the latter ' in sentence (a).

9. (i) Show by the use of mathematical signs and symbols that each of the following sentences contains a double negative:

(a) He is an observer who has read many books and reflected much upon them; but his true interest is not in literature nor the literary.—*JL*

(b) But if respect for the confines of the hearth teaches actors not to shout nor gabble Shakespeare, nor to speak him in a special Shakespeare voice, I am all for the homespun way of doing it.—*O*

(c) M. Clair does not often go beyond the obvious mechanical tricks, nor develop the style he created for himself some twenty years ago.—*O*

(d) There is certainly a heresy of the Left, and the only way in which it can be tested is for men as sincere and devoted as Mr. Leslie Paul to treat their own lives as laboratory experiments, and to say: " Socialism does not either describe my nature nor satisfy it."—*S*

(e) Play without either Hulme or Bastin on the wing, yes; but play without neither of them there, and entrust the two wings to young reserves in a cup-tie, never.

Add, for sentence (d), a comment on false correlatives.

(ii) Assuming that there is a double negative in the following sentences, recast them so that they express the intended meaning of the writers:

(a) This is a show you should not fail to miss.

(b) Quite plainly, in my view as a lawyer upon the evidence in this case, I cannot find it very difficult to see how you can fail to find that this woman is not guilty of manslaughter.

(c) No one could go to the villages of Greece and see the complete destitution and loneliness of the people there

without failing to realise how urgent it was for something
to be done—through the Church—Sir Andrew declared.
—*Evening Dispatch*

10. Recast the following sentences so that the correlatives
in each of them are correctly placed:

(a) . . . to undergraduates in university honour schools of
English who aim at a safe Second, and have no ambition
to surprise their examiners with a fine excess either of
perception or enthusiasm.—*NS*

(b) These lectures do not contain philosophy in the sense
in which that term would be understood either by the
logical analyst or his pamphleteering critics.—*NS*

(c) Can some North Country readers help by either confirming this version or by supplying an alternative
one?—*JL*

(d) His many oddities fail to make either an interesting
work of art by themselves or to suit the half-hearted
perversities and whole-hogging opulence of the Straussian
score—or for that matter to match the mastery of that
score. —*O*

(e) Their case is different, however, partly because their
value to the nation depends almost as much on their
research as their teaching.—*TES*

(f) The result of the competition for the new Coventry
cathedral, announced last week, illustrates the extreme
difficulty of designing a building which will both express
a religious attitude and will yet seem to belong to the
modern world.—*O*

(g) It is set in the time of the First Crusade at the end of
the eleventh century, and Mr. Lington is very good
indeed both in his evocation of the period and of the
East generally.—*JL*

(h) The theme was " the growth of democratic Government
in Britain ," but handled in such a way as to trace not
only the history of democratic government, how it has
grown, but also to show what it has grown into, and this
not by lectures alone but by inspection of the thing in
action.—*TES*

(i) But Shakespeare had not only a gift for metaphor
but for comparisons of all kinds, discovered in a range
of experience which seemed universal in its interest.—*JL*

(*j*) It has one feature which not only absolves it from all charge to the contrary, but which puts it head and shoulders above all its prototypes. — ANTHONY BERKELEY: *The P. C. Case*

(*k*) His people are neither caricatures nor are they types who show one side of themselves only.—*O*

Supplementary Questions:

  (i) Comment on the double *or* in correlation with *either* in sentence (*d*). Comment also on the punctuation of this sentence.

  (ii) Show that sentence (*e*) as it stands is ambiguous.

  (iii) What (if anything) does the participle phrase at the end of sentence (*i*) mean?

  (iv) Is the word *prototypes* correctly used in sentence (*j*)?

11. Comment on the position of *only* in the following sentences:

(*a*) Nor will the publication only interest those beginning school broadcasts.—*TES*

(*b*) It is not only familiarity that makes these things move us so deeply any more than it is only familiarity that makes certain things in Shakespeare move us deeply. —*JL*

Supplementary Question:

  Can you suggest a way of avoiding the repetition of ' move us deeply ' in sentence (*b*)?

12. Explain why *or* should be *and* in each of the following sentences:

(*a*) *You* and *ye* are used indifferently in the Nom., both in addressing one or several persons.—H. C. WYLD: *History of Modern Colloquial English*

(*b*) This addition to the Home University Library is equally useful for serious amateurs or for students who want to order their more detailed but scattered knowledge. —*NS*

Comment on the use of the correlatives in sentence (*a*), and make the necessary correction.

13. Comment on the use of *between* in the following sentences:

(*a*) . . . or the revealing difference in quality between the Duce's and the Führer's laugh.—*O*

(b) It was in organisation and negotiation, in bargaining from a position of carefully prepared strength, in the power of appeal to the social conscience of ordinary people and in the genuine concurrence of interest, properly understood, between managements, workers and public that he put his faith.—*S*

(c) A proportion of the map references in the text are inaccurate because the grid system has been changed in the interval between the book being written and published without a corresponding alteration in the text.—*O*

(d) The Gardens' centre piece—the Grand Vista—is an inspired combination in frivolous design between Osbert Lancaster and John Piper.—*NS*

(e) The possible treatments of a single fact well illustrated by a comparison between the use of the same detail by Flaubert, Dickens, and Shakespeare.—*TES*

(f) A friend, visiting the South Bank Exhibition last week-end, found a refreshment kiosk serving a queue of people with tea in soiled plastic beakers, which were cleaned between the various pairs of lips which drank from them only by a hasty wipe round the rim with a filthy cloth.—*NS*

(g) *To Begin Tomorrow* is a French book, apparently a first novel, that shows an unusual synthesis between the sensitive and the sympathetic.—*O*

14. In each of the following sentences it is necessary either to alter or to take away *one* word if usage is to be satisfied. Make the alterations and deletions, and add any necessary comments:

(a) All of the guests who come to the house have some grudge against life.—*JL*

(b) He replied: " When you and I were young we sweated the agricultural worker like we did the miner."—C. R. ATTLEE, as reported in the *Daily Telegraph*

(c) . . . and it is very hard to recall that Burgess Meredith, who directs as well as playing an apparently half-witted knife-grinder, was once the bright, clear shining star of the beautiful " Winterset ".—*O*

(d) Out comes the horrid truth—the poet has done nothing whatsoever in these four years except to scribble some masterpiece of his own devising (and which we have to take on trust).—*O*

T—G

(e) " The Prince of Darkness " whom Mr. Law, unlike Edgar in *Lear*, considers to be " no gentleman ", has had a pretty free hand in human affairs from the time that Darwin's theory of evolution undermined the religion and morality of Victorian England.—*NS*

(f) The taste for these is now also upon the wane.—*O*

(g) Nothing can appear on his pages without it has been sifted through the sieve of his moral canon.—LORD DAVID CECIL: *Early Victorian Novelists*

(h) The ivory, apes and peacocks are borrowed from the Book of Kings but from a different chapter than the one dealing with Hiram.—ROBERT GRAVES: *The Common Asphodel*

(i) But any cavils one may make against this work are on minor points of detail: the work as a whole is immensely welcome.—*S*

(j) *A Long Day's Dying* is a first novel by a young American writer who is preoccupied by the literary *intelligentsia.* —*TLS*

(k) Freud and Marx have been the two important influences over Mr. Auden's verse.—*TLS*

15. Criticise or justify the use of ' *the* question of ' in the following sentences. Explain the difficulty, and give two possible correct constructions, with examples.

(a) Even so there would be the question of how these scenes are to fuse with the farce of the others.—*NS*

(b) But even had these additions been made Burke would still dominate the picture, and the question of what he left for posterity to say would remain unanswered.—*DT*

(c) It really is not a question of whether one believes or disbelieves in the particular theology.—*O*

16. Make any necessary corrections in the following sentences. They do not necessarily all require correction, but all might be improved.

(a) Food at the pre-war Paris Exhibition was so delicious that the prestige of France as a place to live and visit went up all over the world.—*NS*

(b) In fact, their gaiety and freshness, their unaffected enthusiasm and their enthusiastic affection, contrast sharply with any similar collection compiled, say, in the hedonistic twenties or thirties.—*DT*

(c) Provided all this will not encourage carelessness, I welcome and approve of it.—*NS*

(d) His single moment of humanity is when, confronted in the witness box by the man whose trouble he is partly responsible for, he hesitates for a second or two before pulling himself together and plonking down his deliberate lie.—*NS*

(e) Of the two writers reviewed here, Miss Bradbrook's was probably the more difficult task.—*NS*

(f) . . . and they seem to be just as good (or at any rate no worse) in the Silly Season than they are, say, during the autumn or the spring.—*JL*

(g) The parents must agree, or disagree, to this before the child enters the secondary stage of his education.—*TES*

(h) The last Hemingway novel, *Across the River and into the Trees*, had the worst reception from the critics of any book by a leading author published in England or America since the war.—*JL*

(i) Perhaps the greatest of contemporary French poets, his story has a magical freedom.—*O*

(j) Why women were shy of glasses may be because they loomed so large on elderly male noses.—*T*

(k) Though superficially it may be vastly more readable than the poet's, the psychiatrists', or the mystic's novel, the journalist's shares a common defect with them all.—*NS*

17. In each of the following sentences a word that implies a plural is related to a singular. Explain this. Would you argue that the constructions in these sentences are according to usage?

(a) In any case a comparison of indices can give no more than the roughest guide, since in no two countries is the method of compiling the index exactly alike.—*DT*

(b) Every book is different, a story unto itself.—*JL*

(c) Every member of the society of Fellows is differentiated, and sharply so.—*JL*

(d) Long ago, even in the early eighteenth century, critics discovered that Shakespeare's language was somehow different.—*JL*

(e) To tell us that the English and French attitude to sex is not the same is both irrelevant and platitudinous.—*O*

18. In each of the following sentences two idioms or idiomatic constructions are mixed. Indicate for each sentence the two idioms or constructions concerned:

(a) I am sure that my pleasure in vocal shades and niceties has been whetted by long sessions beside the radio.—*JL*

(b) The Big Four have this at least in common, that none of them want to shoulder the odium of appearing, in the eyes of an expectant and anxious world, to be blocking, in advance, a Foreign Ministers' conference. —*NS*

(c) The earlier speech which Mr. Churchill delivered to his vast audience was cast in a sombre vein throughout.— *Evening Standard.*

(d) Only under the heading 'code of conduct' do I take any issue with Mr. Brend.—*S*

(e) The merit of Mr. Annan's study is that along with a solid analysis of Leslie Stephen's contribution to literary criticism he analyses acutely the limitation of the Agnostic position to which Stephen sacrificed so much. —*TLS*

(f) Far and away better than any other literary miscellany that one can think of.—*L*

(g) A contention often adduced by American writers is that while European civilisation is superior to that of the United States, it would corrupt an American finally to succumb to it.—*O*

(h) He himself defined it that his kind of play could not have been written had it not been for Shaw, though in claiming the same for Mr. Rattigan and Mr. Priestley he was, I think, in error.—*NS*

(i) By 1865 he had abandoned all vestige of belief in dogmatic Christianity.—*JL*

(j) It is the scene and the spirit of an epoch that count, and they count up to a great deal.—*O*

19. Comment on the use of the words italicised in the following sentences and phrases:

(a) For the third time Hogg came into the circle of Shelley's life, though now *posthumously*, and each time it was as a lover.—*JL*

(b) That there is something odd in that relationship is true, but Shaw should be allowed to make a joke without *research* being undertaken for its psychological interpretation.—*TLS*

(c) One of the most agonising dramas of the world's history has been *gentled* here into pain under anaesthesia.—*O*

(d) As he unfolds his story we realise that he has found in Hayley an endearingly comic character and one whose habit of carrying an umbrella on horseback with dire effects on his steed and himself *enhances* his resemblance to the White Knight.—*MG*

(e) Several others followed suit, and from a dozen cherry trees in the *forefront* of the orchard, out of the mist, this wistful gaiety filled the air.—*S*

(f) Admitting our ignorance, we are left with the *discomforting* suspicion that something may be seriously wrong with our attachment to the Russian writers we do admire.—*NS*

(g) The Turks have condemned and *hung* an innocent man for political reasons—a Christian native whom some regard as a crank but who had a strange influence on some of the local population.—*NS*

(h) Into its tapestry are woven the implications and by products of a town's development, *patterned* in the life of a family which, through its inter-marriages, has all these problems within itself.—*S*

(i) Nevertheless the *draftsmanship* is more nervous and confident than in the earlier poems.—*NS*

(j) I was fortunate in discovering that the horse was partial to a mixture of old ale and *draft* Bass.—*NS*

(k) The sweep of time—no, the creep of time, just behind us, so that we look quickly round—charms us with its fearful *realism*.—*NS*

(l) What he had come to see is that Marxism is a system which treats human personality as an insignificant factor in a theory of *historic* development.—*S*

(m) Competitors were faced with two main problems: to present a defence of a particular newspaper in its own particular style, and to *editorialise* in a manner which was convincing.—*S*

(n) It looked all over bar the shouting, which grew in intensity as the moments ticked by and despair slowly gave way to a *pinpoint* of hope.—*T*

(o) The notion is that each decade of the last fifty years shall be *pin-pointed* in a summary of its characteristics of belief and taste.—*O* (*p*) With these figures she begins to lose control of her immediate environment, and to wander back and forth between now and the past, and she goes on into the *respective* fields of imagination congenial to those periods of her life.—*JL*

(*q*) The performance is not *unscripted*, I am glad to say— for good extempore speaking on the wireless seems *practically* unattainable.—*RT*

(*r*) It is *questionable* if he ever wrote a sentence capable of giving pleasure in itself, and so *rebarbative* is his use of words, his grammar, his syntax, that a sustained reading of *An American Tragedy* is as lacerating to the *sensibility* as the *continuous* grinding of electric drills.—*NS*

(*s*) Neither *streamlining* of the conference agenda nor the *steam-rolling* of rank-and-file resolutions by methods not unknown to Transport House could prevent a vote for and against the official case.

(*t*) The story is *flawed* by a touch of rather precious feeling now and then.—*S*

(*u*) Professor Atkins's book will be of *enormous* use to any student of literature and to anyone interested in the history of ideas.—*S*

(*v*) What was probably of greater significance was the *enormous* increase in the reasonably cultured reading public.—*S*

20. In each of the following sentences the writer's meaning is recognisable but his expression of it is illogical. Explain this, and rewrite the sentences so that they are logically sound:

(*a*) Ever since 1940, if not before, it has been customary in the English-speaking world to regard the French as ' feeble '.—*NS*

(*b*) I have concealed so far from the reader, unless, of course, he knows it already, that Sir Leslie Stephen was the father of Virginia Woolf and of Vanessa Bell. —*JL*

(*c*) *Born Yesterday* (Odeon) is one of those smart Hollywood comedies, based on a sharp American stage play, that will certainly be dead tomorrow, but give a good deal of pleasure during their brief existence.—*O*

(*d*) It is a long time since I remember seeing so many *happy* people in a cinema as there appeared to be at the Plaza, when the lights went up after *The Galloping Major*.—*O*

(e) A mission is not simply the work of the missioners. They are, so to speak, the spearhead in the great effort, but we must be behind them preparing the way for them, following up the work after they are gone.

21. Comment on the use of colons and semi-colons in the following sentences, and repunctuate where necessary:

(a) I can recommend an excellent pamphlet *Cleaner Food and How to Get It*, by Morley Parry and Ronald Wentworth; published by the Institute of Public Administration at 1s.—*NS*

(b) The actor, off-stage, derides his nightly part: it is ' phoney ', sentimental; then he finds himself playing it in reality, and was that theatrical conclusion so false after all?—*O*

(c) Living his private life publicly (I mean without reserve), arresting public life tactlessly with the private instance; ingenuously, unguardodly, compulsively mixing the two together, Mr. Spender took the Fool's part in the distracted comi-tragedy of duty which was played out in that decade.—*NS*

22. —and on the commas in the following sentences:

(a) The Cotswolds were one of the last strongholds of the witch-cult and saw, late last century, the last trial for witchcraft in England.—*JL*

(b) It is easy to read, in that the information one seeks can be readily found, and, in so far as we have tested it, it is accurate and up to date.—*NS*

(c) This is the London Journal which Boswell wrote in 1762 and 1763 when, twenty-three years old, he came to London to get a commission in the Guards and, failing in that, met the man who was to be his god, his subject and his insurance of fame.—*NS*

(d) Unfortunately for those who liked to see, if not to wear, them, they have too much style for this utility age. The lady who, with the aid of her lorgnette, could stare the shopkeeper into disgorging something from under the counter would be, in an idiom of which she might disapprove, a very tough baby indeed.—*T*

Subsidiary Question:

In sentence (b) should there be hyphens in *up to date*?

23. In each of the following four sentences the end ' forgets the beginning '. Explain this, and rewrite the sentences:

(a) Morris, in playing the ball between Compton and Evans, cracked his bat for the second time, much as a piano, not played on, loses heart and tone.

(b) Elsewhere she spoke more kindly of him: of his gift of amusing his children by drawing animals and telling stories; and though he was old-fashioned in his views about the vice of luxury and the sin of idleness, and even if he forbade his daughters to smoke cigarettes, he gave them intellectual freedom.—*JL*

(c) Because he was brought up on the French eighteenth-century writers and has the classical manner which does not yield its full meaning and richness, nor show its close intellectual texture, at the first glance, Pushkin has been thought not sufficiently exotic, morbid and Russian by the French reader; just as English readers of *Onegin* have been both prepared for it and spoiled by *Don Juan.*—*NS*

(d) No longer does the Shakespearian schoolmaster demand aggressively that the bard and all his sonorities should be banished from the garish boards and kept for the inner ear as a musician pores over his full score by the fireside.—*TLS*

Subsidiary Question:

Comment on (i) *nor*, (ii) *spoiled*, (iii) the use of commas in sentence (c).

24. The following sentence is taken from a leader in *The Times* deploring certain alleged misconstructions in English. What misconstructions are illustrated? Correct the sentence.

If these sort of things go on, whom will say if in time the England language shall not be nothing but a string of nouns, like some savage dialects are.

25. In a Ministry of Labour pamphlet the following sentence appeared:

Separate departments in the same premises are treated as separate premises for this purpose where separate branches of work which are commonly carried on as separate businesses in separate premises are carried on in separate departments on the same premises.

Is there any way of simplifying what seems at first sight an oddly complicated statement, and of avoiding the repetition of *separate*? Try your hand at rewriting the sentence, keeping the full and exact meaning intended.

26. Comment on the metaphors and other figures of speech in the following sentences:

(a) He accepts as a fact the contemporary dethronement of Hellenism from its supreme pedestal.—*TLS*

(b) Hassett and Morris were pinned to the crease and prodded away like lonely householders who rake under the beds for non-existent burglars.

(c) The sweep of time, right up to our own back-doors, is the conception of history which grips the contemporary imagination.—*NS*

(d) The present translation, though a shade Gallic here and there, is admirable; it crisply transmutes the hard, clear, nonchalant prose of Stendahl with its faint smell of gunpowder—the duellist's pistol has just gone off.—*NS*

(e) Emotional honey no doubt attracts, and will always attract, more people than Pope's nervous honey of the head and senses contained in a steel honeycomb.—*O*

(f) There is no end to the passages that might be quoted, cameos of carved syllables, in which every tint and flaw of the object described is used by the artist toward the creation of her pattern and atmosphere.—*JL*

(g) For this packed verse needs reflecting upon, to be digested out of its richness, double, triple significances being savoured for the nourishment of the reader's mind and spirit.—*JL*

(h) He is trying to make words approximate to the thought, the feeling, and to move on into silence, like a meteor flashing down the night sky.—*JL*

(i) Douglas comes magnificently out of that test, for his mind was fertile in phrases that come over the reader's heart like a hand-touch, a caress.—*JL*

27. How far are you justified in actually translating a foreign phrase that has established itself in English? Use the following sentence as the text for your note:

But the secret of the best-seller even more than of, say, the success of esteem, is in the treatment of the subject.—*S*

28. Comment upon and if possible paraphrase each of the following passages:

(a) Instead, it is painted in pastel shades, somewhat removed from actuality, in the manner of Mauriac, sharing that master's faculty for intensity of passion veiled in a faintly crepuscular concourse of events.—*JL*

(b) I like the concise idea on which that poem is built; an idea based on religious faith and historical knowledge, two cornerstones for the edifice of a civilized mind.

These architectural necessities enhance the structure even of a tiny lyric, giving it strength, and a fulcrum upon which to swing a free articulation. In the same way a beetle's wing is built and balanced, by an Artificer who has spent a million years on the microscopic task. I would also instance the dexterity of the maker of a jewelled wrist-watch. Somewhere between the ancient craftsmanship of God, and the patient application of the Swiss watchsmith, lies the skill of the poet, using wisdom for the jewels and history or tradition for the balance.—*JL*

(c) SIR,—Grateful as all right-thinking persons must be for the Yale edition of Boswell's *London Journal*, it will not, I trust, seem grudging to express the hope that, in the case of the numerous future volumes of Boswelliana that we are promised, some little trouble may be taken to remove from the English editions that small amount of preliminary matter and foot-of-the-page commentary which, however proper it may be in the United States edition, merely constitutes itself an irritation to English and Scottish readers of the present work.—Letter in *TLS*

29. Comment upon the words and phrases italicised in the following sentences:

(a) The obvious comparison is with " The Good Companions ", and it must be said that *by comparison with that book*, whether one admires it or not, " Festival at Farbridge " falls very short.—*NS*

(b) Is he Lucifer brought down by Pride, Macbeth destroyed by vaulting ambition, or *is he* Lear demented for his destruction?—*O*

(c) The quality on the whole today is not so high that it can be weakened without serious consequences. *On the other hand*, the quantity can only be reduced by shortening compulsory school age.—*TES*

(d) The difficulty, as the committee see it, is that of finding an active serious audience for good talks and *to make* the broadcasts a stimulus to discussion and reading. —*TES*

(e) And, in its pragmatic way, this realism succeeds, up to a point. The novelists who *practice* it have exposed abuses, awakened the conscience, made awareness of evils plainer and *have* created an atmosphere in which injustice cannot easily be tolerated.—*NS*

(*f*) . . . when the 2nd New Zealand Division, although short of much vital equipment, lost in Greece, put up a stubborn resistance to Hitler's parachutists, who *were literally poured into the island.*—*O*

30. Write a letter in answer to each of the following:

(*a*) SIR,—In his interesting review of *The BBC Hymn Book* in your issue of October 26th Canon Adam Fox, a former Professor of Poetry in the University of Oxford, after saying that " to produce a new hymn book . . . must surely be worse than venial sin," adds this sentence: " but the BBC have a perfect *alibi*." To see a Canon of Westminster using ' alibi ' in this way is really very shocking. He knows that the word means ' elsewhere ', and yet he uses it in the sense, presumably, of excuse . . . It would be interesting to hear whether Canon Adam Fox has a perfect *alibi*.

> Yours faithfully,
> TEMPLAR
> —*Spectator.*

(*b*) SIR,—Peterborough mentions a recent White Paper on defence of the Suez Canal area and describes a Foreign Office reference to the ' progressive civilianisation of the base ' as another deplorable example of ' official ' English.

What is wrong with ' civilianisation '? Does ' de-militarisation ' explain better the meaning and purpose?

The astonishing ingenuity of the English language to form new words *à l'improviste* is to its credit and proves its vitality and flexibility.

After all, English is not classical Latin, ancient Greek or Aramaic.

> Yours truly,
> A.E.
> —*Daily Telegraph.*

THIRTY ANSWERS

1. (*a*) Alternative (singular) subject; ∴ verb should be *has*. Since both parts of the subject (*Parliament, electorate*) may be considered collective, however, and therefore plural, the plural verb may stand.

   (*b*) Alternative (singular) subject; '*is* aware', '*he is* perpetrating'.

   (*c*) Alternative subject, mixed number. Grammatically this construction is not permissible since the verb cannot agree with both subjects at one and the same time ('neither he . . . *have* ever'). In practice, we wink at attraction, as in this sentence; the verb (*have*) agrees with the nearest subject (*colleagues*).[1]

   Subsidiary Question:

   No; *perpetrate* a crime, blunder, anything outrageous (COD). Substitute *practising*.

2. When the subject is of the pattern collective noun + *of* + plural noun (partitive genitive)[2] the verb is usually plural by attraction unless the collective is itself considered clearly singular rather than plural, like *minority* in sentence (*c*). The first sentence of the section *Thirty Questions* is a deliberate piece of stilted English; modern usage would prefer a plural verb (*are*).

3. Normally the introductory adverb *there* falsely attracts the verb into the singular;[3] but in these sentences a plural noun following the verb has exerted a stronger attraction. The real subject in each sentence (*table, wealth, collection*) is singular, not collective; the verb should therefore be singular (*is*). When the subject follows the verb it is important to check its number and person.

4. The subject in this sentence is not double, but 'parallel' (see p. 22). The verb, therefore, agrees with each part of the subject in turn; and as each part is singular the verb should be singular (*is*).

   Subsidiary Question:

   Yes.

5. The indefinite pronouns *everyone, everybody* are grammatically singular. But they have a plural significance

[1] See *Good English*, p. 24. [2] See *Good English*, p. 17.
[3] See *Good English*, p. 23.

204

which almost, if not quite, justifies plural relationships. If they are treated as singulars the question of the gender of a related pronoun arises (*his* or *her*). The safest and best way is to resort to the undoubted plural *all*, or to a plural noun: ' gives all the actors a chance ', ' all of us return to *our* normal functions '.

In the first sentence the phrase ' neither catch ' implies two catches, but is itself singular. The writer merely forgot the subject of his second predicate, which should be *both*: ' neither catch was . . . but both catches were . . .'. As the sentence stands, the second half means exactly the opposite of what the writer intended.

6.	SUBJECT	VERB
(a)	the child Ellen (singular)	conspire (plural)
(b)	the originality and the amusement (plural—double subject)	lies (singular)
(c)	that (plural—relative pronoun) with plural antecedent, *novels*)	is (singular)
(d)	*Five Silver Daughters* (title of book—singular)	have become (plural)
(e)	the newspapers and every periodical (plural—double subject)	has done (singular)

In sentence (a) there is a confusion of two constructions:
' The child Ellen *conspires* with a little white boy '
  and

' The child Ellen and a . . . boy *conspire together* '.
The singular verb in sentence (b) is justified, as the two subjects *originality* and *amusement* can be thought of separately.

In sentence (d) the writer has tried to make the phrase *Five Silver Daughters* at once the title of a book (by italicising it) and a normal enumeration to be taken at its face value. The result is nonsense, which is emphasised by the vague and muddled metaphor at the end. There is nothing to be done; the sentence is past help. In sentence (f) the subjects may be considered parallel, and so the singular verb would be justified. Normally, subjects of the type ' character after character ' are considered idiomatically singular (see p. 15);

but when they act as an antecedent to a relative pronoun they are rather plural than singular; *move* and *breathe* would be more idiomatic.

> *Subsidiary Question:*
> See p. 65.

7. (a) ' Looking back over the years, WE feel certain. . . .'
  (b) ' After listening . . . I FOUND it a pleasure . . .'
  (c) ' Noting the spread and paying due respect, WE may breathe the hope. . .'

8. In each of the sentences the verb part in -*ing* is a gerund—that is a noun; and the pronouns or nouns qualifying it should be possessive. But with nouns this possessive becomes difficult. In sentence (a) substitute ' *its* doing ' and in sentence (b) ' *his* telling '. But ' married *lovers*' being ' (c) and ' *football*'s being' (d), though correct, are stilted. Since the construction as it stands is suspect, it is wiser to find an alternative: (c) ' and the prospect that married lovers will be given '; (d) ' appreciate the fact that amateur etc. football is assessed '.

> *Supplementary Question:*
> It is a good rule to avoid the use of ' the latter ' except in contexts where it can be formally linked with its correlative ' the former ', relating precisely to two nouns previously used. On its own ' the latter ' is apt to be vague and indeterminative. Normally, repeat the original word in an appropriate form: here, ' slightest danger of its falling '.

9. (i) (a) is *not* (in literature *nor* the literary)
         —(a — b)
     (b) *not* (to shout *nor* to babble *nor* to speak)
         —(a — b — c)
     (c) does *not* (often go *nor* develop)
         —(a — b)
     (d) does *not* (describe *nor* satisfy)
         —(a — b)

In this sentence the mistake is aggravated by the use of the positive *either* with the negative correlative *nor*.

     (e) *without neither*
         (— a)(— b)

   (ii) (a) This is a show you should not miss.
            or
        This is a show you should not fail to patronise.

(b) I find it difficult to see how you can find this woman guilty.

(c) . . . without realising how urgent . . .

10. (a) ' *either* of perception *or* of enthusiasm ' ⎫
    ' of *either* perception *or* enthusiasm ' ⎭

(b) ' *either* by the logical analyst *or* by his
          pamphleteering critics ' ⎫
    ' by *either* the logical analyst *or* his
          pamphleteering critics ' ⎭

(c) ' *either* by confirming *or* by supplying ' ⎫
    ' by *either* confirming *or* supplying ' ⎭

(d) ' fail *either* to make *or* to suit *or* to match '

(e) ' as *much* on their research *as* on their teaching '

(f) ' *both* express a religious attitude *and* seem to belong '

(g) ' in his evocation *both* of the period *and* of the East generally '

(h) ' as *not only* to trace *but also* to show '

(i) ' had a gift *not only* for metaphor *but* for comparison of all kinds '

(j) ' which *not only* absolves it *but* puts it '
    (Note in the original the repetition of *which*.)

(k) ' are *neither* caricatures *nor* types '

The expressions immediately following the correlatives are identical in pattern—*e.g.* an infinitive (*d*), a preposition + noun phrase (*g*), a verb tense (*j*), a simple noun (*k*).

Supplementary Question:

(i) The *either* is better omitted. See p. 40. The punctuation is justified since the last phrase is parenthetic.

(ii) There are two possibilities:
' almost as much on their research as (on) their teaching '
    and
' almost as much on their research as their teaching (does) '.

(iii) The phrase presumably qualifies *gift*. How this gift was ' discovered ' in a range of experience is not at all clear. Perhaps ' the result of an experience which . . .' is fairly near the intended meaning.

(iv) No; *prototype* (Gk. *protos*, first) means an original in relation to a copy or a later specimen. Here it is used in the sense of ' fellows ', ' similar types '.

11. (a) ' interest only those '; there is no reason why *only* should not be in its proper place here.

(b) In this sentence *only* is not out of position; but in order to avoid ' not only ', which seems to anticipate ' but also ', *only* is better turned into an adjective (*alone*) and placed after the noun: ' It is not familiarity alone that . . . any more than it is familiarity alone that . . .'.

Supplementary Question:

Yes; leave out the first ' move us deeply ' and (preferably) put a comma after *things* and *Shakespeare*.

12. The words *both* and *equally* imply a pair or a double, not an alternative: $a + b$, not *a* or *b*; so the plus sign (*and*) is required for *or*.

The various constructions with *equal(ly)* (verb, adjective, and adverb) are worth noting:

> *a* is equal to *b*
> *a* equals *b*
> *a* and *b* are equal
> equally for *a* and *b*
> *a* and *b* are equally (+ adjective, e.g. *guilty*)
> *a* is (noun, adjective) equally with *b*.

Note that in ' *a* is equally as guilty as *b* ' *equally* is superfluous

In sentence (*a*) the correlatives should be *both . . . and*, not *both . . . or*. They are not correctly placed in the sentence. Amend: ' *both* in addressing one *and* in addressing several persons ' or ' in addressing *both* one *and* several persons '. Even then there is a problem of number, since by ellipsis (p. 51ff) *one* is made to qualify the plural *persons*. It is better to use the ellipsis elsewhere: ' *both* in addressing one person *and* in addressing several '.

13. (a) Apparently *between* governs a singular (*laugh*). But ellipsis has been at work; we understand *laugh* after *Duce's*.

(b) Between *a*, *b*, and *c*. In spite of the derivation of *between* (*tw-* is of the same root as *two*) this construction is (rather doubtfully) admitted in modern usage. See p. 68. But whether ' concurrence between ' is sound is another matter. To be on the safe side amend ' and in the genuine concurrence of the interests ', since *concurrence*, ' running together ', implies a plural.

(c) The gerund possessive occurs here, and complicates the construction with *between*. But amendment is easy: ' between the writing and the publication of the book '.

(d) Better ' combination *of a* and *b* '; ' collaboration *between* '.

(e) Who or what are being compared? Flaubert's use, Dickens's use, and Shakespeare's use. The idiom is ' comparison *of* ', not *between*; and the neatest way to avoid all the difficulties is to amend: ' comparison of Flaubert, Dickens, and Shakespeare in their use of . . .'.

(f) Apparently the glasses were cleaned while they were actually between the lips of the drinkers; but surely this did not occur, even at the South Bank Exhibition. The writer meant, we may suppose, ' were cleaned after each drinker '.

(g) Synthesis (=' combination ', ' putting together ') *of a* and *b*, not *between*.

14. (a) Delete *of*. In modern usage *all* and *both* usually stand in apposition to a noun, without the intermediate *of*: ' all the guests ', ' both the boys '.

(b) For *like* say *as*. The use of *like* as a conjunction is an Americanism that is gaining ground in modern usage.

(c) ' as well as *plays* '; the compound conjunction *as well as* is a mere plus sign here (= *and*), joining two similar verb forms.

(d) Delete *to* before *scribble*. For the ' and which ' in this sentence see p. 55.

(e) ' from the time *when* '; *when* = a phrasal relative, ' at which ', ' during which '.

(f) ' *on* the wane '

(g) For *without* substitute *unless*. In modern usage *unless* has taken over all the conjunctive functions which it once shared with *without* and *except*.

(h) ' *another* chapter *than* '

(i) ' cavils *at* or *about* ', not *against*.

(j) ' preoccupied *with* '

(k) ' influences *on* '

15. Constructions with *question* are so difficult and tricky that it is advisable to stick to the following working rules:

(i) Whenever ' the question ' or ' a question ' is followed by a clause which is itself an indirect question (beginning, e.g. with *whether, how, who*), the word *question* and the clause are directly in apposition— that is, there is no intermediate *as to* or *of*.

    (ii) But if the above construction is inconvenient or
inappropriate, use the formula ' question *of* or *as
to* + noun.' Thus—

> The question whether we are entitled to compensa-
> tion will also arise.
> but

> The question of compensation will also arise.

In sentences (*a*) and (*b*) take out the *of*. Sentence (*c*) is
better recast: ' is not a question of one's belief or disbelief
in . . .'.

16. (*a*) ' as a place to live *in* ' is better.
    (*b*) ' contrast with those of any similar collection '. In
a contrast or comparison there must be a common
basis; gaiety and enthusiasm cannot be contrasted
or compared with an anthology.
    (*c*) This sentence is passable; but there is a danger of
false bracketing, ' (welcome and approve) of ', where
of would wrongly follow *welcome*. To be on the safe
side, say ' approve of and welcome '.
    (*d*) The verb *to be* has so little ' active ' meaning that *is*
and *was* are better not followed by an adverb clause
of time. In other words, avoid ' is when ' and ' was
when '. Substitute *occurs*.
    (*e*) This is a confusion of—

> 'Of the two tasks, Miss Bradbrook's was probably
> the more difficult '
>   *and*
> 'Of the two writers reviewed here, Miss Brad-
> brook had the more difficult task '.

One or other is possible, but not a mixture of both.
    (*f*), (*g*) In both sentences there is a false economy. Sentence
(*f*) requires recasting, thus: ' they seem in the Silly
Season to be just as good as or at any rate no worse
than they are '. The brackets are unnecessary.
Sentence (*g*) should run: ' The parents must agree
to, or disagree with, this . . .'.
    (*h*) Here is an old problem. Logically, the writer
means: ' The novel had the worst reception of all
the receptions of books by famous authors etc.'.
The question is whether the drastic ellipsis is justified.
Since it is common (' the biggest circulation of any
morning newspaper ') and is not really ambiguous,
there is something to be said for it on the score of
brevity; and only logic argues against it. But

logic has a strong case, especially as the change to a perfectly sound comparative construction is easy: ' had a worse reception from the critics than any other book by a leading author published in England or America since the war '. Here there is ellipsis of the verb in the *than* clause: ' than any other book . . . has had . . .'. Note ' any *other* book '. The single book mentioned must be separated from the *others;* it cannot be one of them. So in the following sentence *other* should precede *poet:*

> But he has attempted something more, perhaps, than any poet of his generation.—*NS*

(*i*) A misrelated phrase (*cf.* participle phrase, p. 58). Recast: ' Perhaps the greatest of contemporary French poets, HE is the subject of a story that has magical freedom.'

(*j*) Elliptical for ' the reason why '; so the construction is ' the reason is *because* '.[1]

(*k*) Tautology. If the defect is common, it goes without saying that they share it. Recast: ' shares a defect with ' or ' has a defect that is common to them all '.

17. In these sentences *alike, different, differentiated* and *same* imply a relationship with a plural. Sentence (*a*) may easily be recast—' are the *methods* exactly alike '. It may be argued that in sentences (*b*), (*c*), and (*d*) the use of *different* and *differentiated* is elliptical: every book is different from other books; every member is differentiated from every other member. In sentence (*d*) *different* has a colloquial ' absolute ' meaning, as in ' That's different ' or ' He is somehow different '. The ellipsis in sentence (*e*) is associated with and complicated by a problem of agreement. It is impossible to ' understand ' a double subject, ' the English attitude and the French attitude ', while the verb (*is*) is so uncompromisingly singular. Recast: ' that the English and the French are not the same in their attitude to sex '. See p. 49.

18. (*a*) ' pleasure *in* vocal shades has been increased ' *or* ' appetite *for* . . . has been whetted '

(*b*) ' shoulder the burden, responsibility ' *or* ' incur the odium '

(*c*) ' in sombre vein ' (without the indefinite article) *or* ' cast in a sombre mould '

(*d*) ' join issue with ' *or* ' take sides against '

[1] For this solecism see *Good English*, p. 161.

(e) ' that along with a solid analysis of Leslie Stephen's contribution ... it contains an acute analysis of ...' *or* ' that in addition to analysing Leslie Stephen's contribution ... he analyses acutely ...'

(f) ' Much better than any other ...' *or* ' Far and away the best of the literary miscellanies ...'

(g) ' A contention often made ...' *or* ' A fact (conclusion) often deduced ...'

(h) ' declared that his kind of play ...' *or* ' defined his kind of play as one that ...'

(i) ' abandoned all belief ...' *or* ' retained no vestige (= sign, mark; *lit.* ' footprint ') of belief ...'

(j) ' count for much ' *or* ' mount up to a great deal '.

19. (a) The adverb *posthumously* modifies *came*, and therefore refers to Hogg. But it was not Hogg's ghost that came ' into the circle of Shelley's life '.

(b) The writer means ' a *search* for '; ' research into ' is far too strong an expression in this context.

(c) Noun-verb as in sentences (h) and (q). See p. 45. But what ' gentled into pain ' means is a puzzle, even if the pain is ' under anaesthesia '.

(d) For *increases*. See p. 96.

(e) *Forefront* is an emphatic ' doublet ' that has certain limited uses—' the forefront of the battle ', ' He is always in the forefront '. Here, though not incorrect, it is unidiomatic. Substitute *front* or ' front part '.

(f) *Uncomfortable* is a better word here, or *discomfiting*.

(g) In modern usage *hanged* is used of men, especially referring to judicial execution.[1]

(h) *patterned*: noun-verb. See sentence (c).

(i), (j) The following are worth remembering:

Banker's *draft*; *draft* (= detachment) of soldiers; *draft* of a bill or speech.

game of *draughts*; *draught* of air; *draught* beer; *draught* horse; ship's *draught*; *draughtsman* (= man who works in a drawing office); *draftsman* (= one who drafts a bill, letter etc.).

The verb is usually spelt *draft*. In these two sentences the spelling is not according to usage. See also p. 122.

(k) Substitute *reality*; *realism* in modern usage means the quality of ' realness ' in something (e.g. fiction) which is not real. The adjective corresponding to

---

[1] See *Good English*, p. 31.

reality is *real*, that corresponding to *realism* is
realistic. We use both noun and adjective (*realism,
realistic*) of, for example, a novel, a play, a piece of
acting.

(*l*) There are in English several pairs of adjectives
with the termination *-ic, -ical*. Usually, there is
not much to choose between them; but in the ordinary
progress of language one of a pair tends gradually
to oust the other. Thus we now prefer *dynamic* to
dynamical and *hysterical* to *hysteric*.
But in a few pairs there is real differentiation:

politic = wise, prudent (a *politic* approach, decision)	*political* = connected with politics (*political* parties)
economic = relating to economics (an *economic* crisis)	*economical* = relating to economy, ' saving ' (an *economical* holiday)
historic = noted in history (a *historic* battle)	*historical* = belonging to, treating of, history (a *historical* novel, a *historical* personage)

For *historic* in this sentence substitute *historical*.

(*m*) See Introductory Chapter, p. 11.

(*n*), (*o*) Pinpoint (or better, *pin-point*) was originally a
metaphorical word for something very small (as,
rather unusually, in this sentence). Then during
the late war it was used of a small target; hence
the verb ' pin-point '—that is, aim at a strictly
limited, defined area. After the war, the word got
a footing in the ordinary language with a metaphorical
extension of the Service meaning. Purists argue
against it; but there is no real reason to exclude it
from a context like that of sentence (*o*).

(*p*) This sentence is so vague that *respective*, which is
a word of special and definite reference[1] has no real
force.

(*q*) *unscripted*: noun-verb—see sentence (*c*). The word
practically in the sense of *virtually*, *almost* is now
accepted English. COD records it with those
meanings without comment or condemnation. Sir
Alan Herbert rather foolishly questions and half-

[1] See *Good English*, p. 188.

heartedly condemns the usage, and is surprisingly
followed by Partridge (*Usage and Abusage*).   Fowler
uses it himself in the text of *Modern English Usage*:
" Words accepted as practically˙ English ".

(*r*) (i) *Questionable* means ' open to question or suspicion '
—questionable motives, dealings, business. Substitute ' It is a question whether he . . .'.   See p. 63.

(ii) *rebarbative*: A word dated 1892 in SOED and
marked ' rare '.   It means ' crabbed ' ' bristly ', from
French *barbe*, ' beard '.

(iii) *sensibility*: The following are worth remembering:

sensible (i) having one's senses (= conscious, as
distinct from unconscious or insensible)

(ii) having or displaying sense (a sensible
girl, decision)

(iii) perceptible   )
(iv) (archaic) sensitive[1])

But the noun *sensibility* is much commoner than,
and scarcely distinguishable from, *sensitiveness*,
sensitivity.   Since the difference is so small as to
baffle most of us, it is wise to use *sensibility* boldly
in any context where the adjectives *sensitive, susceptible* and *alert* (emotionally and intellectually) would
be appropriate.   The writers of the following sentences were a little afraid of it— hence the apologetic
inverted commas in the first and the insurance cover
of *sensitivity* in the second:

. . . written with that "sensibility" which is the preroga-
tive of a very fine intelligence.—*O*

Jane Franklin, née Griffin, was a walking contradiction
in terms; she united the sensibility and sensitivity of a
Sterne to the toughness of a Wellington.—*DT*

continuous: For *continual*.   The distinction between
continuous and *continual* is difficult: but
continuous is better limited to contexts
in which the idea of strict and complete
continuity of time or space is present—
that is, when there is no suggestion or
possibility of intermittence.[2]

(*s*) Noun-verbs derived from modern metaphors.   See
sentence (*c*).   They are now establishing themselves
as what may be called telescoped idioms.

(*t*) Noun-verb.   See sentence (*c*), and *faulted*, p. 46.

[1] See *Good English*, p. 187.　　　　[2] See *Good English*, p. 192.

(*u*), (*v*) The use of *enormous* in both these sentences is an example of colloquial hyperbole.[1]

20. (*a*) The tense (*has been*) is not appropriate to both the adverbial phrases that modify it: ' since 1940 it *has been*', but ' before 1940 it *was*'. However, recasting is so difficult that a natural ellipsis may be pleaded in justification.

(*b*) The conditional (*unless . . .*) clause is illogical, since the writer has concealed the fact, whether or not the reader already knew it. It is safer to take this clause right out of the sentence and set it by itself as an afterthought: ' Perhaps he knew it already '.

(*c*) This is a matter of construction rather than of logic. Apparently the participle phrase (' based on ') qualifies the particular film, *Born Yesterday*, whereas the relative clause (' that will certainly . . .') qualifies *comedies*. If all the films are based upon sharp American plays, the participle phrase should make it clear.

(*d*) Not a bit of it. The writer remembers something at any rate while he is actually writing. He means either ' It is a long time since I saw ' or ' I do not remember seeing . . .'. In his sentence two actions *remembering* and *seeing* are confused in time.

(*e*) Where are we? Behind or before?

21. (*a*) No semi-colon needed after *Wentworth*, since the following (participle) phrase is adjectival, qualifying *pamphlet*. Substitute a comma.

(*b*) The punctuation of this sentence is as loose and irresponsible as its construction. Here is a suggested reconstruction, in which the final direct question is made indirect:

The actor, off-stage, derides his nightly part—it is ' phoney', sentimental. Then he finds himself playing it in reality, and begins to wonder whether that theatrical conclusion was so false after all.

(*c*) The writer carefully builds up his sentence with three successive participle phrases qualifying his subject (*Mr Spender*), but spoils the effect by cutting off the last of these phrases from the other two with a semi-colon:

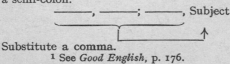

Substitute a comma.

[1] See *Good English*, p. 176.

22. (*a*) Strongholds of the witch-cult and saw?
    Comma required after *witch-cult*.

(*b*) Preferably delete the comma after *read* and the comma after *and*; but a case could be made out for both of them.

(*c*) The conjunctions *when* and *and* are left 'hanging' (see p. 141). Insert comma after *1763* and after *Guards;* a comma after *subject* is advisable (see p. 143). That puts *when* and *and* between commas, but as the sentence stands it cannot be helped.

(*d*) Delete comma after *see, wear, who, lorgnette*. Preferably, make the phrase 'in an idiom . . .' definitely parenthetic and put it between dashes.

Subsidiary Question:
No.

23. (*a*) There is no real equation here. No doubt the writer meant 'Morris cracked his bat, which lost its driving power much as a piano . . .'. The beginning and the end are not properly related because he omitted the middle.

(*b*) The writer promises us a whole series of his kind thoughts, introducing them formally with a colon. But in fact he gives us only one, and forgets the rest.

(*c*) Again, the equation breaks down. The 'equals' sign ('just as') implies properly equated terms. It is difficult to recast the sentence because the writer is vaguely allusive. But the general pattern should be:

Pushkin has been thought not sufficiently *a, b,* and *c* by the French reader just as in *Onegin* he has been thought not sufficiently *x, y,* and *z* by the English reader who has memories of *Don Juan.*

(*d*) Passive must follow passive: 'the bard and all his sonorities should be banished . . . as the full score is studied by the musician by the fireside'.

Subsidiary Question:
(i) *nor*: double negative
(ii) *spoiled*: for *spoilt*. See *Good English,* p. 36.
(iii) Delete comma after *texture* and add comma after *morbid.*

24. Here the solecisms illustrated are so obvious and even blatant that the sentence loses all its point. They are:

(i) 'these sort of things': A construction sanctified by long usage, in which, by attraction of *things*, 'sort

of things ' becomes a plural collective. But it is easy
to satisfy grammar by eliminating the attraction:
' this sort of thing '.

(ii) *Whom* for *who* (subject).

(iii) *England* should be *English*.

(iv) ' shall not be nothing '. Double negative; *shall* for
will.[1]

(v) Use of *like* for *as*. See p. 209.

25. No, there is no safe way of simplifying this sentence
if the full and exact meaning intended is to be kept. It is
tempting to cut it down to this: ' For this purpose separate
departments in the same premises count as separate premises '.
But this does not cover all the official and possibly legal
implications of the original. Modern enthusiasts for ' plain
English ' too often recklessly condemn a sentence of this
kind, and assume that a simplified version is possible.

26. (a) *Dethronement* from a pedestal is an odd process.
The sentence should end at *Hellenism*.

(b) A far-fetched simile; if the householder is *raking*,
who or what is he *prodding?*

(c) By the phrase ' the sweep of time ' is meant a vast span
of time (centuries, ages). Here the writer suggests
this meaning, but also incongruously associates *sweep*
with a broom and the back-door.

(d) The gunpowder figure and elusive parenthesis about
the duellist's pistol have no real relevance in this
sentence, and blur the meaning. They should be
elaborated in a sentence of their own. It is difficult
to see what *transmutes* means here—surely not
' changes '.

(e) This is a good (or bad) example of that kind of
metaphor which is inextricably mixed up with
literal thought and expression, and in the end becomes
ludicrous. All the writer means to say is that people
prefer emotional to intellectual writing; but having
thought of honey as an image of the emotional, he
has to pursue his metaphor to the end. So ' emotional
honey ' (which is bad enough) becomes ' nervous
honey of the head and senses ' incredibly and absurdly
stored in a steel honeycomb.

(f) It would be interesting to see a cameo made out of
carved syllables and breathe an atmosphere of tints
and flaws. There is a faulty construction also:
' use *for* or *in* ', not *toward*.

[1] See *Good English*, p. 27.

(g) The ' packed verse ' needs (i) reflecting upon (ii) to be digested out of its richness, whatever that queer process may be, and all the time its double, triple significances (whatever they may be) are being savoured for nourishment. It is tempting to imagine that ' packed verse ' suggested to the writer ' packed lunch '.

(h) A simile completely without point. How does a meteor, or a poet for that matter, ' move on into silence '? It is difficult to find any intelligible meaning in the sentence.

(i) Here ' come over the reader's heart ' is the main difficulty. In what sense can a hand-touch or a caress come over anything? And how does a hand-touch differ from a caress?

27. Strictly, you are not justified in translating a borrowed word or phrase, for the simple reason that it is borrowed only because an English equivalent does not exist. It sometimes happens that a translation does half establish itself. Thus *pen-name* is often used as the English equivalent of the French *nom-de-plume*; but *nom-de-plume*,[1] somewhat paradoxically, is standard, and *pen-name* is phoney, English. Sometimes the translation is unsatisfactory or inadequate; thus 'blind alley ' for *cul-de-sac* fails because in English *alley* has a special limited meaning. But the English ' between ourselves ' or ' between you and me ' are now so natural and idiomatic that the French *entre nous* could be dispensed with altogether. Certainly the translation in this sentence of the French *succès d'estime* into ' success of esteem ' is unnecessary and meaningless. There is, in fact, no English equivalent for the French *succès d'estime;* ' polite reception ' is as near as we can get, and that is not very near. Not only the anglicisation but also the construction is wrong in this sentence; a play or a book *has*, not *is*, a *succès d'estime*.

28. (a) This is merely an example of reviewers' writing in which phrases and words like ' pastel shades ', *veiled*, *crepuscular*, with their vague suggestion of something indefinable in art, are made to do duty for plain sense. He means that it (the book) has a faint air of unreality, like a novel of Mauriac's.[2]

---

[1] The real French is *nom-de-guerre*; *nom-de-plume* is itself a kind of anglicised French.

[2] This double possessive is an interesting and useful idiom in English.

(b) (i) For *enhanced* see p. 96.

(ii) The imagery is oddly mixed. These 'architectural necessities' (elegant variation for *cornerstones* suddenly become a fulcrum on which a 'free articulation' is hung. A beetle's wing is built 'in the same way '—that is, apparently, on a fulcrum made out of cornerstones. Then, however, a new image appears—the jewels and balance of a watch-maker. But although the skill of the poet is halfway between the Artificer's and the watchsmith's, only the balance image remains at the end; the cornerstones and the fulcrum are forgotten.

(c) This sentence is perfectly constructed and controlled except that ' the case of ' is quite unnecessary;[1] but it is an example of epistolary pomposity. It might be recast somewhat in this way:

Sir,—All right-thinking people will be grateful for the Yale edition of Boswell's *London Journal*. I should, however, like to make one suggestion about the promised future volumes of Boswelliana—that in English editions preliminary matter and footnotes appropriate only to the American editions be omitted. They are merely an irritation to English and Scotch readers.

29. (a) Unnecessary. There is a confusion of construction here. Recast: ' The obvious comparison is with *The Good Companions*, and it must be said that, whether one admires that book or not, *Festival at Farbridge* falls very short of it '.

(b) Unnecessary. There was no need to repeat this, The construction is: ' Is he Lucifer, Macbeth, or Lear? '

(c) Omit. There is no antithesis here.

(d) Continue the original construction: ' that of finding and of making '.

(e) Omit. The auxiliary (*have*) has already been expressed once. For *practice* read *practise*.

(f) Not *literally* poured, surely.

30. (a)

8 Eastern Road
Southtown
Wessex.

12 November 1951

Dear Sir,

      I was glad to read Templar's good-humoured letter concerning the use of *alibi* in the

---

[1] See *Good English*, p. 143.

sense of *excuse*. Quite recently I heard *alibi* so used
by Mr Christopher Mayhew in the Argument programme on the wireless. He said twice, in slightly
different ways, that the Government had, or would
have, no alibi for this, that, or the other. Now
alibi, a borrowing from the Latin, has a limited and
defined use in legal language, and has been made
popular by the detective novel. But there is no
reason why it should take to itself the function and
meaning of *excuse*, especially as it has never been
naturalised. However, since this abusage, as Eric
Partridge would call it, is becoming common, Canon
Fox might paradoxically claim an alibi on the score
of usage.

Yours faithfully,
JOHN SMITH

The Editor
The *Spectator*
99 Gower Street
W.C.1.

(b)

8 Eastern Road
Southtown
Wessex.
9 January 1952

DEAR SIR,
        I am in complete agreement with your
correspondent A. E. in his defence of the word
civilianisation. In its context, " the civilianisation
of the base ", the word is intended to imply something
more than *demilitarisation*. It is positive, while
demilitarisation is negative; and its meaning is
immediately apparent. Nor is its construction
seriously open to question. The use of *civilian* as
an adjective (' civilian dress ') has long been established; and there is no reason to condemn the
formation of an abstract noun from the *civilian* base,
whether noun or adjective. A similar objection is
sometimes made to the formation of new verbs in
-ise (or *-ize*) from nouns. " Atticus " of the *Sunday
Times* recently, " at the request of a protesting
reader ", condemned the " philological atrocity "
unitized in the phrase " with particular reference to
turbo-alternators unitized with reheater boilers ".
There is in fact nothing to condemn; *unitized* is not
a philological atrocity but a regular and useful

formation, standing for the somewhat cumbersome phrase ' making a unit with '. To argue against it and similar formations by inventing, as Sir Alan Herbert did in a subsequent letter, irregular words like *laterize* and *betterize*, where *-ize* is added not to a noun but to an adjective, is to ignore the genius of the language. Witch-hunting among verbal inventions has become a popular pastime. It can be as wrongheaded and objectionable as witch-hunting in any other realm.

Yours faithfully,

JOHN SMITH.

The Editor
The *Daily Telegraph*
Fleet Street
E.C.4.

INDEX

No reference is made to the authors of illustrative sentences.